Proceedings of the
Comparative Literature Symposium, Vol. VII

January 23, 24, and 25, 1974

JOSEPH CONRAD:
Theory and World Fiction

Editors
Wolodymyr T. Zyla
Wendell M. Aycock

Editorial Board
Kenneth W. Davis
Carl Hammer, Jr.
Patricia M. Hopkins

INTERDEPARTMENTAL COMMITTEE ON COMPARATIVE LITERATURE
TEXAS TECH UNIVERSITY
LUBBOCK, TEXAS, 1974

Proceedings of the Comparative Literature Symposium may be obtained on an exchange basis from, or purchased through, the Exchange Librarian, Texas Tech University, Box 4079, Lubbock, Texas 79409.

The Texas Tech Press
Lubbock, Texas
U.S.A.

Table of Contents

Preface 5

Joseph Conrad: A Commemoration

"The Precious Yesterday": Commemorative Remarks for the
Joseph Conrad Symposium 13
David Leon Higdon

Symposium Lectures

Conrad's Picaresque Narrator: Marlow's Journey from
"Youth" through *Chance* 17
Alan Warren Friedman

Joseph Conrad: Polish Cosmopolitan 41
Adam Gillon

Conrad, Graham Greene, and Film 71
Bruce Harkness

James Wait as Pivot: Narrative Structure in *The Nigger
of the "Narcissus"* 89
Marion C. Michael

Conrad and the Idea of Honor 103
Zdzisław Najder

The Imprint of Polish on Conrad's Prose 117
I. P. Pulc

The Essential Conrad 141
Norman Sherry

Flaubert and the Structure of *The Secret Agent*: A Study
in Spatial Form 151
Jeffrey R. Smitten

Conrad's Legacy: The Concern with Authenticity
in Modern Fiction 167
Ivo Vidan

Luncheon Presentation

Conrad as Editor: The Preparation of *The Shorter Tales* 189
Donald W. Rude

Notes on the Authors 197

Preface

The growth of scholarship that centers upon the work of Joseph Conrad reflects the interest that he has aroused in present-day readers, who, in increasing numbers, recognize the importance of his achievement. Because he does speak to the modern reader, one can safely say that he has accomplished the aim that he referred to in the Preface to *The Nigger of the "Narcissus"*: "My task which I am trying to achieve is, by the power of the written word to make you hear, to make you feel—it is, before all, to make you *see*. That—and no more, and it is everything. If I succeed, you shall find there according to your deserts: encouragement, consolation, fear, charm—all you demand—and, perhaps, also that glimpse of truth for which you have forgotten to ask."

The Seventh Annual Comparative Literature Symposium, together with the Ninth Annual Symposium of the Department of English, which were presented on January 23-25, 1974, undertook the theme "Joseph Conrad: Theory and World Fiction," in order to examine selected aspects of Conrad's fiction and to compare his work with that of other authors. This was the first of the major symposia in 1974 devoted to the commemoration of the life and works of Joseph Conrad on the fiftieth anniversary of his death (1924). The speakers at the symposium have contributed their essays to make up this volume.

The commemorative address for this symposium was presented by David Leon Higdon, General Editor of *Conradiana*, Texas Tech University. The address included a call to demonstrate "the respect and natural love created by long acquaintance with the works and the personality of Joseph Conrad" in order to give Conrad his "real life," that which continues to grow through his fiction. In the first lecture of the symposium, "The Essential Conrad," Norman Sherry, University of Lancaster, England, pointed out the moral assumptions in terms of social ideals in Conrad's typical figures who appear in various environments that demand special virtues.

Zdzisław Najder, Warsaw, Poland, in his presentation, "Conrad and the Idea of Honor," said that, "true to his heritage," Conrad "explored not only the triumphs of honor, but its dangers and pitfalls. Frequently misunderstood by writers and critics, Conrad as a moralist left a powerful legacy for other writers and for his readers."

Alan W. Friedman, The University of Texas at Austin, presented "Conrad's Picaresque Narrator: Marlow's Journey from 'Youth' through *Chance*." He stressed "Marlow's charming self-deprecation, humane and open questioning, sensitive if fruitless intruding of himself into the lives of others" even if this is "at our peril."

Adam Gillon, State University of New York at New Paltz, in his paper, "Joseph Conrad: Polish Cosmopolitan," maintained that Conrad's literary heritage was an important factor which contributed to his cosmopolitanism as well as to the reception of his work in different parts of the world. "But," Gillon continued, "Conrad is not a citizen of the world in the political sense of the term 'Cosmopolitan.' " Jeffrey R. Smitten, Texas Tech University, in his presentation, "Flaubert and the Structure of *The Secret Agent*: A Study in Spatial Form," indicated that "fragmentation of the narrative sequence and juxtaposition of those fragments, and unification of the juxtaposed fragments in the reader's mind through his perception of the analogy and contrast among them" are the two general techniques applicable to *The Secret Agent* which point to *Madame Bovary* "as a paradigm of the novelistic form they describe."

Ivo Vidan, University of Zagreb, Yugoslavia, gave a lecture on "Conrad's Legacy: The Concern with Authenticity in Modern Fiction," in which he stressed that "novelistic tradition established by Conrad is apparent in the manner in which an awareness of vocation makes men define themselves through their various assumed codes of ethics." Therefore "the authenticity of the Conradian personality is tested in terms of its adequacy to its fundamental choice, in a manner unique to Conrad but foreshadowed in the Puritan inheritance of Henry James and the Protestant conscience of George Eliot's heroines." Irmina P. Pulc, Northampton, Massachusetts, in her presentation, "The Imprint of Polish on Conrad's Prose," said that "traces of Polish can be most easily discerned in Conrad's diction, for throughout his writing career Conrad weaves Polish sayings, idioms and metaphors into the fabric of his language." She maintained that "it is the Polish warp of his sentence, interlaced with its English weft, that gives Conradian prose its special character."

Marion C. Michael, Texas Tech University, in his paper, "James Wait as Pivot: Narrative Structure in *The Nigger of the 'Narcissus,'* " argued that, in order to understand what is happening in Conrad's *The Nigger of the "Narcissus*," one must certainly come to grips with Conrad's structuring of the novel in terms of "Wait's psychology"; and, especially, one must center on Conrad's use of two distinct narrative voices by which Conrad "authenticates his narrative on two levels of meaning existing simultaneously." In the last lecture of the symposium, "Conrad, Graham Greene, and Film," Bruce Harkness, Kent State University, maintained that "Greene learned from Conrad the technique of the narrator and the technique of the time shift. But in a paradoxical sense Graham Greene rejects the outer society which, for all his pessimism, Joseph Conrad ultimately accepted."

The luncheon speaker, Donald W. Rude, General Editor of *Conradiana*, Texas Tech University, in his "Conrad as Editor: The Preparation of *The Shorter Tales*," examined Conrad's unpublished letters concerning *The Shorter Tales* and discussed Conrad's participation in the publication of this volume.

The symposium lectures were followed by panel discussions and comments from the audience. The observations made by the panelists and members of the audience were indicative of their genuine interest in Conrad's works and in the papers that were presented. The symposium panel discussion members were Alan W. Friedman, Adam Gillon, Bruce Harkness, Zdzisław Najder, Irmina P. Pulc, Norman Sherry, Ivo Vidan, guest speakers; Edmund A. Bojarski, Abilene, Texas, Andrew Busza, University of British Columbia, and A. Maynor Hardee, University of South Carolina, guest panelists; and James G. Allen, Alfred Cismaru, James W. Culp, Ann A. Daghistany, Kenneth W. Davis, Vivian Davis, Floyd E. Eddleman, Everett A. Gillis, David Leon Higdon, Patricia M. Hopkins, J. James Johnson, Marion C. Michael, Jeffrey R. Smitten, Warren S. Walker, faculty members at Texas Tech University; and Wayne Cook, Kenneth Hammes, Jr., Catherine Morales, and Dennis Organ, graduate students at Texas Tech University. In all its sessions the symposium was attended by approximately 1,850 persons, including faculty members, graduate students, and undergraduates from Texas Tech University and from twenty-eight other universities and colleges.

In addition to the lectures, the symposium program included theatrical and musical performances and two exhibits. *The Secret Agent* by Joseph Conrad, directed by Jan Slusher, was presented by the reading theater of the Department of Speech and Theater Arts, Texas Tech University. The musical program consisted of Ballade in F Minor, Op. 52 by Frederic Chopin, performed by Norma Holmes Auchter; four oriental songs on poems from the Tang Dynasty (unpublished works) by Johann Yang, performed by Charles Post, tenor, and Trudi Post, pianist; and Romance, Op. 22 and Scherzo-Tarantelle, Op. 16 by Henri Wieniawski, performed by Virginia Kellogg, violinist, and Norma Holmes Auchter, pianist, faculty members of the Department of Music, Texas Tech University. The Uni-

8

versity Bookstore featured a display of visiting lecturers' works, and
The Museum of Texas Tech University presented "A Look at Conrad's World: Manuscripts, First Editions, and Photographs." The
latter exhibit contained material provided by Warren Roberts, Director, Humanities Research Center of the University of Texas at
Austin; Edmund A. Bojarski, Abilene; Marion C. Michael; University Library; and The Museum of Texas Tech University. During the
symposium lectures, there was on display a large portrait of Joseph
Conrad created by Paul R. Milosevich, Department of Art, Texas
Tech University. There were also two television programs devoted to
the symposium theme and presented on Texas Tech Television Station (KTXT-TV), in which the participants were Zdzisław Najder,
Norman Sherry, and Ivo Vidan, guest speakers; and Wendell M.
Aycock, Kenneth W. Davis, Floyd E. Eddleman, David Leon Hig-
don, Marion C. Michael, and Donald W. Rude, faculty members at
Texas Tech University.

This volume of the Proceedings is divided into three parts: the
Commemoration, the Symposium Lectures, and the Luncheon Presentation. The lectures appear in alphabetical order. The cover for this
work is based on the artistic design of the symposium poster, created
by Jerry D. Kelly. Kelly also designed the sketches of the speakers that
are here included. This volume contains a portrait of Conrad by Paul
R. Milosevich and photographs of the symposium activities. An exchange publication, the Proceedings are placed in 662 libraries
throughout the world in order to stimulate the growth of comparative
literature studies.

In conclusion we should like to express our deep appreciation and
gratitude to the distinguished guest speakers, speakers from the University, guest panelists, and panelists from Texas Tech, who made this
symposium possible. Thanks are due to all guests from other universities and colleges and guests from the Polish community who attended this symposium. We thank the Departments of Art, Music,
Speech and Theater Arts, and The Museum of Texas Tech University,
the University Library, and the University Bookstore for their helpful
cooperation. We are indebted to the Lubbock Chamber of Commerce
for their help in registration. Thanks are due to Editors of *Conradiana*
for the preparation of a reception honoring our guest speakers and
guest panelists. Thanks are furthermore due to all colleagues at Texas
Tech University who helped in this symposium by working on various
committees. Our sincerest thanks go to those who served as chairmen
of various symposium meetings: Norwood H. Andrews, Jr., Glenn
E. Barnett, Mary Louise Brewer, Kenneth W. Davis, Lawrence L.

Graves, Carl Hammer, Jr., William R. Johnson, J. Knox Jones, Jr., Marion C. Michael, and Donald W. Rude. We wish to express our appreciation to Craig C. Black, Director, The Museum of Texas Tech University and to Ray C. Janeway, Dean of Library Services at Texas Tech University, for their help and assistance. We are especially grateful to Grover E. Murray, President of Texas Tech University, and J. Knox Jones, Jr., Dean of the Graduate School, for their generous support of the comparative literature symposium project.

The Editors

Joseph Conrad: A Commemoration

"The Precious Yesterday": Commemorative Remarks for the Joseph Conrad Symposium

David Leon Higdon

Tonight we begin the first of four major symposia devoted to the life and works of Joseph Conrad. This symposium will be followed by one at the University of Miami (7-9 February), the International Conference on Conrad to be held at the University of Kent, Canterbury, England (14-19 July), and a final meeting late in August at the University of California, San Diego. But these are more than symposia: they are commemorations of Joseph Conrad fifty years after his death. Scholarly time is told in centuries and half-centuries. Anniversaries of an author's birth or death provide appropriate moments for scholars to look back over the fifty years to see what has been done and how well it has been done. More importantly, this moment of consolidation and assessment then turns to the future as scholars look ahead to what must be done over and what remains to be done for the first time.

However, commemorations are more than papers, publications, ceremonial openings, and new friendships. They should be—in the truest sense of the word's etymology—a calling to remembrance. Not surprisingly, the most appropriate and the most eloquent words I could find for such an occasion were written by Joseph Conrad, himself commemorating a fellow writer, Alphonse Daudet. He wrote: "It is sweet to talk decorously of the dead who are part of our past, our indisputable possession. One must admit regretfully that to-day is but a scramble, that to-morrow may never come; it is only the precious yesterday that cannot be taken away from us. A gift from the dead, great and little, it makes life supportable, it almost makes one believe in a benevolent scheme of creation. And some kind of belief is

13

very necessary. But the real knowledge of matters infinitely more profound than any conceivable scheme of creation is with the dead alone. That is why our talk about them should be as decorous as their silence. Their generosity and their discretion deserve nothing less at our hands; and they, who belong already to the unchangeable, would probably disdain to claim more than this from . . . mankind . . . . "[1] Each of us has his own private memories of how Joseph Conrad became his own "indisputable possession" and how Conrad's art took the "scramble" of our today with its restless inner selves, our isolation, our alienation, our displacement in the world, and with utmost generosity made it "supportable."

However, we too have a gift to give. In *Under Western Eyes*, Conrad twice paraphrased his favorite lines from Novalis, those he had used as an epigraph to *Lord Jim*. Early in the novel, the narrator remarks "A man's real life is that accorded to him in the thoughts of other men by reason of respect or natural love."[2] And near the end of the novel, he repeats the idea: "The dead can live only with the exact intensity and quality of the life imparted to them by the living."[3] The responsibility for the intensity, quality, and reality of another's life simultaneously demands and frightens. How have we responded to this demand? Have we granted intensity and quality with the same generosity of the silent; have we spoken and written decorously of the gift from the dead? Our presence here tonight demonstrates the respect and natural love created by long acquaintance with the works and the personality of Joseph Conrad. Without doubt, we have given Conrad a "real life." In this, one necessary correction of the biographies must be recorded. Both Georges Jean-Aubry and Jocelyn Baines note that Joseph Conrad was born December 8, 1857 and died August 3, 1924. We know, however, that Conrad's "real life"—the life granted him by his audience—began April 29, 1895 when 1650 copies of his first novel, *Almayer's Folly*, appeared in bookstores in England and America, and we know that this "real life" continues strong today. Tonight, then, begins more than a symposium, more than a commemoration: it begins a celebration of the continuing vitality of Joseph Conrad.

NOTES

[1]"Alphonse Daudet," *Notes on Life and Letters*, Kent Edition (New York: Doubleday, Page, 1926), p. 20.

[2]*Under Western Eyes*, Kent Edition (New York: Doubleday, Page, 1926), p. 14.

[3]*Under Western Eyes*, p. 304.

Symposium Lectures

Conrad's Picaresque Narrator: Marlow's Journey from "Youth" through *Chance*

Alan Warren Friedman

ABSTRACT

A distinctive feature of twentieth-century fiction is its self-conscious pluralism, especially in the form of the multivolume novel in which the whole becomes more than the sum of its parts. Read as a unit, Conrad's Marlovian fictions—"Youth," *Heart of Darkness*, *Lord Jim*, and *Chance*—differ markedly from what they are in isolation, for Marlow, the intrusive "interpreting consciousness," becomes the moving center of a larger episodic fiction—both framing the tales he narrates and framed by an anonymous narrator, and also aging from tale to tale. The four fictions offer different characters with the force and validity of protagonists in their own right, yet together the four shape stages in Marlow's personal, moral, and esthetic journeying from youth to maturity (or senility). But there is also a disturbing consistency beneath Marlow's evolving, a profound inadequacy that his immediate human appeal seeks to mask: racism, sexism, moral myopia, an utter inability to reconcile words and deeds. He makes numerous grand pronouncements with complete assurance, yet subsequently contradicts every one—and usually without realizing it. As man and narrator, Marlow's charming self-deprecation, humane and open questioning, sensitive if fruitless intruding of himself into the lives of others seem compelling; but we trust him, like all self-professed moral guides, at our own peril. Marlow ultimately causes us to doubt and to test our instincts, for he embodies the multiple claims our deepest experiences make upon us, not the answers but the quest that life's central questions imply. (AWF)

One of the notable phenomena of twentieth-century fiction is the extent to which it has become extended. Forster gave the term "novel" one meaning when he defined it as a prose work in fiction of a certain extent. But many novels have moved beyond "certain" to become "indefinite." For since the novel has become psychological and open, the novelist who would terminate the stream of his fiction finds that it has no necessary ending, that it goes on multiplying perspectives and possibilities—often into several or many volumes.

This is not to say that twentieth-century novels are simply longer than their predecessors—for certainly Samuel Richardson, Fielding, and Trollope, for instance, had few qualms about excessive verbiage. The later novelists, in fact, tend to write shorter novels, but once having written them they frequently find the job less than complete— and so write them again from a somewhat different angle or vision, and sometimes again and again. The result is a genre that might be called the modern multivalent novel.

In a sense, the very extension of a novel into several volumes is an ineffaceable act of self-consciousness, and therefore an assertion of multiple perspectives. The multivolume novel—almost invariably self-conscious and pluralistic because simultaneously both a series of discrete parts and a unity—necessarily creates and defines a context, a pattern, for itself. The separate volumes must stand on their own, and yet their interrelated existences require of us a compara-tist's eye and judgment. The whole becomes the sum not only of the parts but also of something more: the interconnectedness between and through the parts that sweeps us back as well as forward as we move through the several volumes. For the temporally linear act of reading, like Proust's madeleine cake, creates responses that ripple outward both with and against the conventional current of time—and never more so than in the multivolume novel with its self-contained dramas that are yet acts within a larger play. On the grandest scale one might, with Balzac, call that play the human comedy and write a hundred of its countless acts.

Read as a unit, Conrad's Marlovian fictions—"Youth," *Heart of Darkness, Lord Jim*, and *Chance*[1]—differ markedly from what they are in isolation. In the four works taken together, Marlow himself be-comes the moving center of an episodic, larger fiction in which char-acters and incidents spin off and revolve about him, as in one of the inner circles Lord Jim seems to emit characters like Brierly and the German captain, Brown and the French lieutenant—all aspects of the whirling, prismatic protagonist of one experiential focus. Conrad's seemingly depersonalized narrator emerges over the course of several works first as character and then as protagonist. In the beginning of *Heart of Darkness*, Marlow says, " 'I don't want to bother you much with what happened to me personally,' " which provokes the narrator to comment that Marlow showed "in this remark the weakness of many tellers of tales who seem so often unaware of what their audi-ence would best like to hear" (*HD*, p. 179). Yet Marlow immediately indicates that his purpose in recounting his Congo experience is to have his listeners " 'understand the effect of it on me' "— Marlow's tales are self-revelatory above all.

Conrad constructs the Marlovian tales on two main series of relationships and two dynamic sequences. First, Marlow interacts both with the sympathetic yet dubious protagonists of his narratives, and with the narrators who frame him; second, temporal revelations portray not only the young Marlow, Kurtz, Jim, and Flora, but also Marlow's own picaresque journeying from one narrative stage to the next. The stories within the stories express an independent reality and validity like that which Chaucer creates within *The Canterbury Tales* —and as great a symbiotic interdependence with the framing context. The narrated tales are beguiling in their own terms, for each dramatizes an extraordinary sequence of adventures and misadventures in which an energetic questor reaches, with varying degrees of success, towards identity and control. The four narrated sequences lose in chronological ordering but gain in significance by being filtered through what James calls the "interpreting consciousness," Marlow's plus at least one other. Yet the four also exist—and perhaps most fundamentally, certainly most organically—as temporal stages in the development of Marlow himself. For through Marlow, Conrad achieves at once the intimacy and distance he sought in the shifting perspectives of *The Nigger of the "Narcissus."* It is our task, then, to consider how this oddly constructed tetralogy—growing much longer and more cumbersome each step of the way—negotiates the personal, moral, and esthetic evolution of its central spokesman.

"Youth" and *Heart of Darkness* are both narrated by an anonymous ex-seaman, one of five characters (along with the director of companies, the lawyer, the accountant, and Marlow) who recall and verbalize a similar past. "Between us there was, as I have already said somewhere [in "Youth"], the bond of the sea. Besides holding our hearts together through long periods of separation, it had the effect of making us tolerant of each other's yarns—and even convictions" (*HD*, p. 175). But "Youth" is straightforward, for in it Marlow has no moral lesson to learn or teach. The tonal difference between "Youth" and *Heart of Darkness* parallels the deepening passage from *Tom Sawyer* to *Huckleberry Finn*, but the three later Marlovian works erect structural and narrative complexities far more fundamental than tonal shifts. Kurtz in *Heart of Darkness*, Jim in *Lord Jim*, and Flora and Powell in *Chance* take us away from Marlow to a large extent; they appear to us with the force and validity of protagonists in their own right. We may even be annoyed at times by the incessant verbalizing of that infuriating word spinner who seems congenitally incapable of telling his tale, and who keeps intruding himself between us and it. Wayne Booth, however, suggests that teller and tale, like Yeats's dancer and dance, are indistinguishable: "Is 'Heart of Darkness' the story of Kurtz or the story of Marlow's experience of Kurtz? Was Marlow invented as a rhetorical device for heightening the meaning of Kurtz's moral collapse, or was Kurtz invented in order to provide Marlow with the core of his experience of the Congo? Again a seamless web, and we tell ourselves that the old-fashioned question, 'Who is the protagonist?' is a meaningless one. The convincing texture of the whole, the impression of life as experienced by an observer, is in itself surely what the true artist seeks."[2] And yet the question has meaning if we take the four Marlow narratives as a whole, as Conrad, by his interwining of them, encourages us to do.

Lord Jim, the greatest of the four Marlovian tales, is unique in including an *extra* narrative layer, a multifarious,[3] seemingly objective, commentator. He portrays the titular character: "He was an inch, *perhaps* two, under six feet, powerfully built" (*LJ*, p. 1; italics mine). Then he parlays that "perhaps" into a full-scale attack on the very validity of this type of narration: "They wanted facts. Facts! They demanded facts from him, as if facts would explain anything!" (*LJ*, p. 23). And then he merges into an auditor-narrator analogous to the one in "Youth," *Heart of Darkness*, and *Chance*:

> And later on, many times, in distant parts of the world, Marlow showed himself willing to remember Jim . . . .
> Perhaps it would be after dinner, on a verandah draped in motionless foliage . . . . (*LJ*, p. 27)

The main difference between the multifarious and personal voices lies in the breadth of "many times" and the vagueness of that last "Perhaps"; but from this point until the return to multifarious narration at the end of Chapter XXXV, the narrative perspective of *Lord Jim* is identical to that of the other three tales: a companion of Marlow's narrates Marlow's narrative.

Why does Conrad employ a multifarious frame narrator for *Lord Jim*? The question admits of no easy and direct answer, but may best be approached by considering why Conrad abandons the strategy for the bulk of the novel. In a manner perhaps derived from the depiction of Henry Fleming in *The Red Badge of Courage* (a novel Conrad knew, admired, and consciously sought to surpass[4]), Conrad's multifarious narrator takes us inside Jim's youthfully foolish ego: "At such times his thoughts would be full of valorous deeds: he loved these dreams and the success of his imaginary achievements . . . . They had a gorgeous virility, the charm of vagueness, they passed before him with a heroic tread . . . . There was nothing he could not face. He was so pleased with the idea that he smiled, keeping perfunctorily his eyes ahead . . . " (*LJ*, p. 16). The narrator's mocking attitude speaks through the hollow rhetoric of "valorous deeds," "the success of his imaginary achievements," "gorgeous virility, the charm of vagueness," and "heroic tread"; this attitude is also apparent in the climactic self-deception of "there was nothing he could not face," and in the devastating betrayal of trust implicit (and retrospectively *explicit*) in "keeping *perfunctorily* his eyes ahead." As elsewhere, the narrator here verges on turning into the sarcastic presiding genius of *The Secret Agent*. The intense derision directed at Jim—increasingly obvious with each rereading—requires counterbalancing if Jim is to be afforded any sort of sympathetic response: thus, Conrad conceals from his reader what everyone else knows (that the *Patna* failed to sink), abandons the frame narrator, and offers Marlow as intercessor between Jim and the reader.

A further distinction between the narrators of *The Secret Agent* and *Lord Jim* is that the latter never really plays what John Fowles in *The Magus* calls "the god game"—dry, ironically detached, and near-solipsistic narration and manipulation. Rather, when Marlow passionately declares to Jewel that Jim is not good enough (because no one is good enough), it seems clear that he speaks also for the novel's uncertain multifarious narrator who, in the novel's first line, announces Jim's height as *perhaps* five feet ten inches and then rails out against facts just before the anonymous listener and Marlow take over the narration. Such a narrator is far removed from that of *The Secret Agent*, who accepts as valid the irony of facts and the triviality of all human endeavor.

Lord Jim's frame narrator, however, after denouncing facts in a manner wholly sympathetic with Jim's perspective, then depicts Jim's attitude toward the Inquiry as follows: " . . . he had come round to the view that only a meticulous precision of statement would bring out the true horror behind the appalling face of things. . . . He wanted to go on talking for truth's sake, perhaps for his own sake also; and while his utterance was deliberate, his mind positively flew round and round the serried circle of facts that had surged up all about him to cut him off from the rest of his kind. . . . He was made to answer another question so much to the point and so useless, then waited again" (*LJ*, pp. 24-26). Such an approach to facts precisely parallels the attitude and technique of the book as a whole and Marlow in particular, and has as a central purpose our continuing deception.

Here is the technique at its most blatant, though we do not realize it on first reading. Marlow is speaking about the Inquiry: "There was no incertitude as to facts—as to the one material fact, I mean. . . . Its object was not the fundamental why, but the superficial how, of this affair. . . . 'the questions put to him necessarily led him away from what to me . . . would have been the only truth worth knowing. You can't expect the constituted authorities to inquire into the state of a man's soul—or is it only of his liver?' " (*LJ*, pp. 47-48). The problem here is that we who are ignorant of factual reality are also made to believe that "there was no incertitude as to facts," and so we are unprejudiced by their actuality—or, rather, we are prejudiced by what we are deceived into assuming they are. We share Marlow's outrage at official insensitivity because we think we share his superior moral insight. Only later do we discover that we have done so because we have been duped. Yet such is the nature of moral commitment that it becomes virtually impossible for us to deny our initial identification, to distance ourselves from the moral trap that Marlow (perhaps unintentionally) and certainly Conrad have laid for us. Perhaps the only way out is to recognize, as R. W. B. Lewis has said of Faulkner, that the difficulty of such narratives "lies in the order of their telling. . . . What *happens* in a Faulkner story is the most important thing in it, except perhaps the moral excitement that produces the happening. But we are let in on the event secretively, gradually, almost grudgingly, from different viewpoints and at different times."[5]

But *Lord Jim's* frame narrator, with his uncertainty and his attack on facts from a perspective we first accept as "omniscient," creates an aura of excessive reliability around Marlow's tale. It is the frame narrator preceding the introduction of Marlow who empathizes with Jim's platonic equation of esthetics and morality in responding to the German captain on board the *Patna*: "The odious and fleshy figure . . . fixed itself in his [Jim's] memory forever as the incarnation of everything vile and base that lurks in the world we love . . . " (*LJ*, p. 17). Without this context, this subtle and seductive use of the plural personal pronoun by the multifarious narrator, Marlow's similar perspective would be immediately suspect—the defensiveness of a partisan—and would thereby fail to elicit our sympathetic involvement with Jim, an involvement basic to the vertiginous ambivalence at which the novel aims. The multifarious narrator both gives license to Marlow's unreliability and lulls our suspicions concerning what Conrad is having him foist off on us. In this sense, *Lord Jim* is simply an elaboration of *Heart of Darkness*, for Marlow's concealing from us the real reason for Jim's flight (thus causing us to assume a less damning one) reworks in daringly expanded form the trick of keeping Kurtz from us until we, like Marlow, make the mistake of choosing him.

As character and narrator Marlow typically experiences and expresses what seem at first commonplace approach/avoidance attitudes —towards lies (smacking of mortality though sometimes necessary), towards work (he dislikes it, but likes "what is in the work, the chance to find yourself. Your own reality," *HD*, p. 203), towards exoticism ("the fascination of the abomination," *HD*, p. 177), towards youth and the sea (the time and place of fleeting glory), towards women (human beings "very much like myself," yet devoid of "masculine decency," *C*, pp. 53, 63). The accreted effect of such dualism, however, is ambivalence carried to the point of confusion, and Marlow, his masks of sarcasm and human sympathy simultaneously in place, becomes a curious Janus-faced guide whom we trust at our peril.

Thus, much of the tension in *Heart of Darkness* and *Lord Jim* arises from Marlow's failure to resolve major contradictions. The "one of us" theme in *Lord Jim*, for example, is as central to *Heart of Darkness*, though in the earlier work it goes by the name of "idea." Marlow complacently begins his Congo tale by dubiously asserting the moral superiority of English colonists to Roman conquerors. He adds: " 'The conquest of the earth, which mostly means the taking it away from those who have a different complexion or slightly flatter noses than ourselves, is not a pretty thing. . . . What redeems it is the idea only. An idea at the back of it; not a sentimental pretence but an idea; and an unselfish belief in the idea—something you can set up, and bow down before, and offer a sacrifice to . . .' " (*HD*, p. 179; Conrad's ellipsis). Marlow reiterates this notion halfway through *Lord Jim* when he speaks of being deeply impressed by earlier adventurers and traders: " 'It seems impossible to believe that mere greed could hold men to such a steadfastness of purpose. . . . To us, their less tried successors, they appear magnified, not as agents of trade but as instruments of a recorded destiny, pushing out into the unknown in obedience to an inward voice. . . . They were wonderful . . .' " (*LJ*, pp. 195-96). Certainly this is historically a popular view (witness "manifest destiny"), yet Marlow also *repudiates* this position in *Lord Jim*, as he had in the earlier tale. Despite Marlow's pronouncements, *Heart of Darkness* depicts not only "the utter savagery" of the uncivilized, but the far more frightening darkness at the heart of men of ideas. Thus Marlow, heading for the crisis, begins to think of the howling natives as other than human—and then worse, *as* human: "one of us."

In *Lord Jim*, Gentleman Brown is also treated as "one of us" (e.g., pp. 337, 344). Marlow maintains that his accomplices " ' were merely vulgar and greedy brutes, but *he* seemed moved by some complex intention' " (*LJ*, p. 306). In Brown's murder of Dain Waris, Marlow adds, " 'there is a superiority as of a man who carries right—the abstract thing—within the envelope of his common desires. It was not a vulgar and treacherous massacre; it was a lesson, a retribution—a demonstration of some obscure and awful attribute of our nature which, I am afraid, is not so very far under the surface as we like to think' " (*LJ*, p. 352). Similarly, Marlow insists that "while Jim was one of *us*," Dain Waris was "one of *them*" (*LJ*, p. 314). And when Marlow comes to choose a soul-mate to receive word of Jim's death, that "privileged man," like Gentleman Brown, embodies Marlow's racial biases carried to their extreme. "You said," Marlow writes, "that 'giving your life up to them' (*them* meaning all of mankind with skins brown, yellow, or black in colour) 'was like selling your soul to a brute.' You contended that 'that kind of thing' was only endurable and enduring when based on a firm conviction in the truth of ideas racially our own, in whose name are established the order, the morality of an ethical progress. . . . In other words, you maintained that we must fight in the ranks or our lives don't count" (*LJ*, p. 294). Marlow's comment is an ambiguous "Possibly!" because a clear-cut response would deny the validity of either his racial views or else of what he sees as Jim's magnificent triumph of fate. Marlow characteristically wants it both ways.

The same concern for us and them surfaces as early as "Youth," where Marlow identifies with humanity (rejecting Carlyle who was not a man but "either more—or less," *Y*, p. 146), with Caucasians (fearing the fascination of the abomination, " ' the lands of brown nations, where a stealthy Nemesis lies in wait, pursues, overtakes so many of the conquering race, who are proud of their wisdom, of their knowledge, of their strength,' " *Y*, p. 170), with Englishmen (exalting the *Judea*'s ragged crew: " 'it was something in them, something inborn and subtle and everlasting. I don't say positively that the crew of a French or German merchantman wouldn't have done it, but I doubt whether it would have been done in the same way. There was a completeness in it, something solid like a principle, and masterful like an instinct—a disclosure of something secret—of that hidden something, that gift of good or evil that makes racial difference, that shapes the fate of nations,' " *Y*, p. 161).

On first encountering the Congo, Marlow discovers an absurd world antithetical to the natural or grotesquely mocking it: a boat "shelling the bush" causing nothing to happen; a "dead" railway truck "lying there on its back . . . [like] the carcass of some animal"; "objectless blasting"; emaciated slaves wearing masks of "deathlike in-difference," unhappy savages who "were called criminals" (*HD*, pp. 186-88). With typical sarcasm, Marlow speaks of being greeted by the despicable manager as "a part of the great cause of these high and just proceedings" (*HD*, p. 189). In a somewhat similar tone he later alludes to the human heads on Kurtz's posts: " 'I am not disclosing any trade secrets. In fact, the manager said afterwards that Mr. Kurtz's methods had ruined the district. I have no opinion on that point, but I want you clearly to understand that there was nothing exactly profitable in these heads being there. They only showed that Mr. Kurtz lacked restraint in the gratification of his various lusts, that there was something wanting in him—some small matter which, when the pressing need arose, could not be found under his magnifi-cent eloquence' " (*HD*, p. 234). Curiously and characteristically, Marlow suggests that Kurtz's actions are somehow less reprehensible because they are motivated not by greed but by undefinable desires.

Immediately there follows Marlow's climactic summary of Kurtz—"he was hollow at the core"—a chilling conclusion to his quest: " 'I was curious to see whether this man who had come out equipped with moral ideas of some sort, would climb to the top after all and how he would set about his work when there' " (*HD*, p. 205). Thus Marlow's thesis concerning the redemptive nature of ideas (above all, "the white man's burden") and his implication that the Congo represents unfortunately uncongenial soil for their implantation, are wholly misleading: Kurtz's "moral ideas" are hollow and he brings with him the evil he encounters. Like *Lord Jim*, *Heart of Darkness* becomes a very different work on second and subsequent readings because we become sensitive to the hollowness of Marlow's own posi-tion. There is a subtle horror in his thesis, perspective, choice, action, and justification, all of which he offers in his narrative with little or no examination. Similarly, he takes no note of his own telling imagery, like Kurtz's "ivory face" (*HD*, p. 247) and the Intended's "forehead, smooth and white" (*HD*, p. 254), a wonderfully sardonic pairing of form following function that he tosses out but fails to confront. Thus, Marlow's pose of Buddha-like inscrutability seems in the end to de-ceive no one so much as himself.

Marlow first uses the term "one of us" early in *Lord Jim*. He is fascinated by the dichotomy in Jim of his "sham and reality." Jim's appearance is compelling ("clean-limbed, clean-faced, firm on his feet, as promising a boy as the sun ever shone on . . ."), and Marlow is furious: " 'I was as angry as though I had detected him trying to get something out of me by false pretences. He had no business to look so sound.' " Not for the last time, Marlow finds Jim's casualness odious: " 'I waited to see him overwhelmed, confounded, pierced through and through, squirming like an impaled beetle—and I was half afraid to see it too. . . . ' " And then comes Marlow's identification and generalization, the basis for fear greater than that encountered in the heart of savage darkness.

> "From weakness that may lie hidden, watched or unwatched, prayed against or manfully scorned, repressed or maybe ignored more than half a lifetime, not one of us is safe. . . . he was one of us. He stood there for all the parentage of his kind, for men and women by no means clever or amusing, but whose very existence is based upon honest faith, and upon the instinct of courage . . . backed by a faith invulnerable to the strength of facts, to the contagion of example, to the solicitation of ideas. Hang ideas! They are tramps, vagabonds, knocking at the backdoor of your mind, each taking a little of your substance, each carrying away some crumb of that belief in a few simple notions you must cling to if you want to live decently and would like to die easy!" (*LJ*, pp. 33-36)

Having experienced the *in*decency of Kurtz's life and the difficulty of his death, Marlow now condemns the moral supremacy of ideas, the thesis of *Heart of Darkness*. Now older and more weary, he rejects them here as he had exalted them there. In *Lord Jim* he espouses something more substantial, the reality and validity of appearance and imagination—and they fail and betray him as well.[6]

The theme of "one of us," of "idea," intertwines as well with that of imagination and duty. Conrad's simple "good" men—Singleton in *Nigger of the "Narcissus,"* Captain MacWhirr in "Typhoon," *Lord Jim*'s French lieutenant—function well because their intellectual and moral makeup precludes their seriously entertaining alternative courses of action; in *Chance*, Captain Anthony is essentially and ultimately of this same order. The successes of such characters are wholly admirable (and precisely what Jim is circuitously seeking), yet they themselves are inadequate because they are seemingly mechanical, lacking in divergent impulses, not "one of us"—the very characteristics that insure their successes. The extreme of this type are the presumably non-introspective helmsmen in *Heart of Darkness* and *Lord Jim*. Marlow says of Kurtz, " 'I can't forget him, though I am not prepared to affirm the fellow was exactly worth the life we lost in getting to him. I missed my late helmsman awfully. . . . Perhaps you will think it passing strange this regret for a savage who was no more account than a grain of sand in a black Sahara. Well, don't you see, he had done something, he had steered; for months I had him at my back —a help—an instrument' " (*HD*, pp. 226-27). Marlow opts for the nightmare Kurtz represents over that of the rapaciously bourgeois manager—" 'Ah! but it was something to have at least a choice of nightmares' " (*HD*, p. 239)—without ever noting the possible un-nightmarish choice that the helmsman's example offers. He compares Kurtz unfavorably to his helmsman (as he later does Jim to those of the *Patna*), but his racial scorn is strongly evidenced. The helmsman's surprising devotion to duty and his failure to act like a bestial savage —like the cannibal crew's extraordinary restraint, their failure to "have a good tuck in for once" (*HD*, p. 216) as white men would presumably have done in their position—merits the respect due a faithful pet or a useful tool. Kurtz, a true savage in word and deed ("hollow at the core"), receives from Marlow, like Jim and Gentleman Brown, the homage due to "one of us."

Throughout his narratives but especially in *Lord Jim*, Marlow's deceptive unreliability undercuts the values on which he and we presume to stand, while seeming at first to reinforce them. Intentionally or not, Marlow works to arouse our sympathy for Jim while denouncing him. He speaks of being pitiless, but immediately adds, " 'You must remember he believed, *as any other man would have done in his place*, that the ship would go down at any moment . . .' " (*LJ*, p. 73; italics mine). Marlow exploits the advantage he has of us. At this point, near the start of his narrative, *we* still believe that the *Patna* did sink, and that Marlow is therefore holding Jim up to extraordinary moral criteria. Yet he then reverses himself and damns with faint praise where he had praised with faint damnation: " 'He was not afraid of death perhaps, but . . . he was afraid of the emergency. . . . His confounded imagination had evoked for him all the horrors . . . of a disaster at sea he had ever heard of. He might have been resigned to die but I suspect he wanted to die without added terrors, quietly, in a sort of peaceful trance' " (*LJ*, p. 75). As usual, Marlow's prophetic impulse is correct in a sense, in a way we would not have anticipated: Jim *does* "die . . . quietly, in a sort of peaceful trance," but orchestrating it fully himself, on centerstage, with all eyes fixed upon him.

Halfway through *Lord Jim*, Marlow gives us what he calls "the last word" on Jim's Patusan success while characteristically denying the possibility of anyone's doing so: " '. . . the last word is not said,—probably shall never be said. . . . I have given up expecting those last words, whose ring, if they could only be pronounced, would shake both heaven and earth. . . . My last words about Jim shall be few. I affirm he had achieved greatness; but the thing would be dwarfed in the telling, or rather in the hearing. Frankly, it is not my words that I mistrust but your minds. I could be eloquent were I not afraid you fellows had starved your imaginations to feed your bodies' "

(*LJ*, p. 194). As elsewhere, Marlow gives himself away in every line: in forgetting the lesson of *Heart of Darkness* (that "those last words" may indeed be pronounced, and that they change nothing), in forgetting the lesson of "Youth" (that for him too "the romance of illusions" has long since yielded to "Pass the bottle!"), and especially in his typical thrusting of conclusions at us before the evidence. We are surely meant to question the ultimate authority of such a grand pronouncement occurring, as it does, halfway through the novel and before his narrative proper concerning Patusan. Had we come to experience Patusan uncontaminated by Marlow's prejudicial contextualizing, we would be in a position to distance ourselves from his conclusion and would likely do so. In addition, Marlow's attack on his listeners' lack of imagination has the force and validity of a *non sequitur* since only two pages before he had asserted that, unlike Jim, "I have no imagination."

Marlow's own *final* conclusion about Jim's achievement is very different from this early one. He first speaks with bemused wonderment of Jim's being " 'satisfied . . . nearly. This is going further than most of us dare. I—who have the right to think myself good enough—dare not. Neither does any of you here, I suppose? . . . But he is one of us, and he could say he was satisfied . . . nearly. Just fancy this! Nearly satisfied' " (*LJ*, p. 281). But then after detailing Jim's death in richly lyrical terms, he says, " 'Is he satisfied—quite, now, I wonder? We ought to know. He is one of us—and have I not stood up once, like an evoked ghost, to answer for his eternal constancy? Was I so very wrong after all? . . . Who knows?' " (*LJ*, pp. 362-63). Further, as Marlow reminds us, our experience of Jim is very different from his: " 'He existed for me, and after all it is only through me that he exists for you. I've led him out by the hand; I have paraded him before you' " (*LJ*, p. 194).[7] For us, Jim is a work of art and Marlow the artist with words; and, as the narrator of *Under Western Eyes* tells us, "Words . . . are the great foes of reality."[8] No wonder, then, that we perceive Jim initially as Marlow would have us, and yet that Jim defies the static definition the artist would impose upon him. It thereby becomes incumbent upon us not only to perceive the product as process, but also to call into profoundest questioning the voice of the artist—not *qua* artist, but as purveyor of reductive pronouncements concerning what his art has wrought.

As he almost invariably does, Marlow again anticipates us, for he strikes exactly this note when, on taking leave of Jim for the last time, he speaks of re-entering the world of moral complexity and uncertainty: " 'I had turned away from the picture and was going back to the

world where events move, men change, light flickers, life flows in a
clear stream, no matter whether over mud or over stones. . . . But as
to what I was leaving behind, I cannot imagine any alteration. . . .
They exist as if under an enchanter's wand. But the figure round which
all these are grouped—that one lives, and I am not certain of him. No
magician's wand can immobilize him under my eyes. He is one of us' "
(*LJ*, pp. 286-87). This may be the clearest indication yet of what
"one of us" means: those born to inhabit the world of moral challenge
and inadequacy, those doomed to imagination, freedom, and flux—as
if this were not, as Marlow himself indicates elsewhere, the common
fate of all mankind.

Marlow's response to Jim alternates from extreme to extreme
throughout his narrative. He maintains that Jim had no business looking so sound (*LJ*, pp. 33-34) since there was a "subtle unsound-
ness" about him (*LJ*, p. 77), that there could be no "convincing
shadow of an excuse" for his action (*LJ*, p. 43), for its "real significance [lay] in its being a breach of faith with the community of mankind" (*LJ*, p. 135). Jim had, Marlow tells us, "jumped into an ever-
lasting deep hole. He had tumbled from a height he could never scale
again" (*LJ*, p. 96). No wonder that Marlow's attitude is pitiless (*LJ*,
p. 68), that he directs a "deep-rooted irony" at Jim. At a climactic
moment, he declares himself "unexpectedly to be thoroughly sick of
him" (*LJ*, p. 204). And yet, to counterbalance, he immediately adds,
"Youth *is* insolent; it is its right—its necessity; it has got to assert itself, and all assertion in this world of doubts is a defiance, is an in-
solence" (*LJ*, p. 204). Further, Marlow simultaneously asserts a
wholly opposed analysis, one that defines Jim as the victim of "a
fiendish and appalling joke" (*LJ*, pp. 104-105), and who, on the
Patna, "believed, as any other man would have done in his place, that
the ship would go down at any moment . . ." (*LJ*, p. 73). He had
helplessly faced and "had survived the assault of the dark powers"
(*LJ*, p. 213), and then at the end "was overwhelmed by the inexplicable; he was overwhelmed by his own personality—the gift of that
destiny which he had done his best to master" (*LJ*, p. 296). Marlow
agrees with Jim that "You've been tried" (*LJ*, p. 107), that he is a
gentleman (*LJ*, p. 112); he is pleased that the French lieutenant takes
"the lenient view" (*LJ*, p. 127); he asserts Jim's greatness and devotion in the face of Jewel's bitter love and sense of betrayal.[9]

Ultimately and typically, Marlow seeks to resolve polar contradictions, to synthesize antitheses. Jim, he says, "appealed to all sides"
(*LJ*, p. 80); at times Jim seems not univocal but unclear to Marlow
and perhaps "not clear to himself either" (*LJ*, p. 152); it was hard to

know "whether his line of conduct amounted to shirking his ghost or to facing him out" (*LJ*, p. 169); and finally Marlow sees Jim as great and pitiful "in the loneliness of his soul" (*LJ*, p. 343)—as, that is, a tragic hero who necessarily synthesizes and embodies *all* the contrarieties with which Marlow attempts, without success, to fix Jim in place like one of Stein's butterflies.

Perhaps the most glaring inconsistency in Marlow's entire narrative concerns Brierly's offer of money if Jim will flee. Marlow first tells us: "Of course I declined to meddle. . . . I became positive in my mind that the inquiry was a severe punishment to that Jim, and that his facing it . . . was a redeeming feature in his abominable case. . . . Brierly went off in a huff" (*LJ*, p. 58). Later, Marlow recasts the events in a wholly different light. " 'He was guilty—as I had told myself repeatedly, guilty and done for; nevertheless, I wished to spare him the mere detail of a formal execution. . . . I don't defend my morality. There was no morality in the impulse which induced me to lay before him Brierly's plan of evasion . . .' " (*LJ*, p. 131). And Marlow's bitter anger at Jim's failure to run—" 'Better men than you have found it expedient to run, at times' " (*LJ*, p. 133)—comes to sound very much like Brierly. As elsewhere, Marlow successfully manipulates us both ways: his "Of course I declined to meddle" arouses our "braving it out" instinct; his laying before Jim "Brierly's plan of evasion" appeals to our sense of arrogant defiance—and only the most alert reader catches the blatant contradiction. Marlow plays upon the sensibilities of his listeners and readers with the sure touch of a skilled surgeon and the gall of a buccaneer.

Marlow's own untrustworthiness may be seen as finally focusing on Stein, whom he calls "one of the most trustworthy men I had ever known" (*LJ*, p. 174). Stein begins his self-revelation by suggesting that man is the product of an "artist [who] was a little mad" (*LJ*, p. 179), and then unconsciously offers himself as exemplum. He tells of calmly killing three men and finding "the clean earth smiling at me,"[10] and then of rapturously capturing a unique butterfly. "When I got up I shook like a leaf with excitement, and when I opened these beautiful wings and made sure what a rare and so extraordinary perfect specimen I had, my head went round and my legs became so weak with emotion that I had to sit on the ground. . . . 'On that day I had nothing to desire; I had greatly annoyed my principal enemy; I was young, strong; I had friendship; I had the love . . . of woman, a child I had to make my heart very full—and even what I once dreamed in my sleep had come into my hand, too!' " (*LJ*, pp. 181-82). The clue to Stein, and to the Marlow who finds him trust-

worthy, lies in the disproportion not only of emotion but also of language: "annoyed" as a euphemism for three killings. In the tradition
of life-denying artists of nature, Stein now lacks all that his values
implicitly negated: youth, friend, wife, child, and soon strength. Stein
himself is what he tags his butterfly, "a remarkable specimen," but
hardly what Marlow proclaims him: a reliable, Virgil-like guide
through *Lord Jim*'s moral inferno. His deflation at the end, the revela-
tion of hollowness we have previously associated with Kurtz, is in
fact implicit in this moment of our first encounter with him.

Before depicting that deflation, Marlow offers us a description of
Jim's death that is as lyrically ambiguous as anything Conrad ever
wrote. He speaks of Jim's " 'last flicker of superb egoism,' " of his
final " 'proud and unflinching glance,' " of,

> "the alluring shape of such an extraordinary success! For it may very well
> be that in the short moment of his last proud and unflinching glance, he
> had beheld the face of that opportunity which, like an Eastern bride, had
> come veiled to his side.
>
> "But we can see him, an obscure conqueror of fame, tearing himself out
> of the arms of a jealous love at the sign, at the call of his exalted egoism.
> He goes away from a living woman to celebrate his pitiless wedding with a
> shadowy ideal of conduct." (*LJ*, p. 362)

Marlow's romanticizing of Jim's death offers rich, metaphoric coun-
terpointing to his early assertion of Jim's greatness. What seems to
happen is that Jim's ritual suicide, unlike his youthful dreams and
Patusan success, offers no moral guidance for Westerners ("us"), no
exemplum for Marlow to puff and pass on. So he finds both Jim and
the significance of his actions obscured by impenetrable shadows at
the last.

Marlow then concludes *Lord Jim* with a series of unsettling questions concerning Jim and his death, and an even more unsettling picture of those who remain behind. "Is he satisfied—quite, now, I
wonder? We ought to know. He is one of us—and have I not stood up
once, like an evoked ghost, to answer for his eternal constancy? Was
I so very wrong after all? . . . Who knows? He is gone, inscrutable at
heart, and the poor girl is leading a sort of soundless, inert life in
Stein's house. Stein has aged greatly of late. He feels it himself, and
says often that he is 'preparing to leave all this; preparing to leave . . . '
while he waves his hand sadly at his butterflies" (*LJ*, p. 363). Marlow
seeks a final note of mystery, poetry, and sadness; yet what really is
inscrutable here is not Jim—who is clearly defined by his own sense of
worth and a repeatedly amazed awareness of his failure to realize it, a
common enough form of schizophrenia—but Marlow and his perva-
sive despair over Jim's lack of single-facetedness. Marlow's refrain,

"one of us," *should* suffice to define Jim as white and English, duty-bound, a successful embodiment of Western notions of fidelity and progress. Marlow revealingly says: " 'He was like a figure set up on a pedestal, to represent in his persistent youth the power, and perhaps the virtues, of races that never grow old, that have emerged from the gloom. I don't know why he should always have appeared to me symbolic. Perhaps this is the real cause of my interest in his fate' " (*LJ*, p. 229). But despite appearances Jim fails to play the part he and Marlow assign him: " 'I would have trusted the deck to that youngster on the strength of a single glance, and gone to sleep with both eyes— and, by Jove! it wouldn't have been safe. There are depths of horror in that thought' " (*LJ*, pp. 36-38). Such a truth (and Marlow's need to learn it) invalidates his central assumption concerning racial superiority and the equation of appearance and reality, just as both *Heart of Darkness* and *Lord Jim* repudiate his faith in the nobility of evil done in the service of professed ideals.

Marlow's depictions, therefore, are *necessarily* of "inconclusive experiences" (*HD*, p. 179), for they neither support his initial theses nor cause him to confront and revise them after refutation by events. Marlow's virtues as man and narrator are also his vices: charming self-deprecation, humane and open questioning, refusal to make definitive pronouncements where warranted (or else an asserting of contradictory ones), sensitive if fruitless intruding of himself into the lives of others. And they represent a compelling self-depiction of one who is surely "one of us." Yet Marlow's hesitations and irreconcilabilities reflect an unreliability seriously at odds with the surface dependability of his narrative stance.

The one work of Conrad's that Wayne Booth cites in his "Gallery of Unreliable Narrators" at the end of *The Rhetoric of Fiction* is *Heart of Darkness* (presumably for Marlow's narration rather than that of the anonymous frame commentator); yet *Lord Jim* warrants inclusion at least equally as much, for in both of these, Marlow becomes profoundly, dynamically, and grotesquely unreliable—"grotesque" in the sense that Sherwood Anderson's writer uses that term at the beginning of *Winesburg, Ohio*: "It was his notion that the moment one of the people took one of the truths to himself, called it his truth, and tried to live his life by it, he became a grotesque and the truth he embraced became a falsehood."[11] As we have seen, Marlow seizes grotesquely on the morality of ideas (any ideas) in *Heart of Darkness*, and on the congruence of appearance and substance in *Lord Jim*; and yet his dartingly vital imagination causes them to remain problematical, a matter demanding continual struggle, always in motion.

Chance, however, is radically different, for such dynamics offer sharp contrast to the bland superiority of tone Marlow assumes toward Flora, Anthony, Powell, and the others in his last narrative. T. S. Eliot has noted that we are alive to the extent that we do good or evil; Marlow's intellectual and moral detachment in *Chance* has about it a stench of death and decay, what he calls mediocrity. He says, in *Chance*, " 'It's certainly unwise to admit any sort of responsibility for our actions, whose consequences we are never able to foresee. . . . the incapacity to achieve anything distinctly good or evil is inherent in our earthly condition. Mediocrity is our mark,' " (*C*, p. 23). There was a time, he notes, when he saw the world with different eyes: " 'When one's young human nature shocks one' " (*C*, p. 15). Nothing shocks, or even interests, Marlow very much in *Chance*—certainly not human nature, which he ceases to encounter on any but a mocking or trifling level. Conrad's mistake, like Shakespeare's in *Merry Wives of Windsor*, consists of reducing to domestication the natural scope and conflict of a profoundly mistaken moral spokesman; a mellow Marlow speaks to our deepest needs and joys no more than does a Falstaff playing at love.

Marlow seeks not only depth but scope as he journeys from "Youth" to *Chance*, yet Marlow has come full circle by *Chance*. *Chance* is far longer than "Youth" but attains no greater depth, for, as Conrad's defensive Preface implies, its amplitude depends largely on verbiage. The problem may be seen as focusing on the fact that *Chance* begins at the end not of *Lord Jim* but of "Youth." Marlow concludes "Youth" by asking rhetorically, " 'wasn't that the best time, that time when we were young at sea; young and had nothing, on the sea that gives nothing, except hard knocks—and sometimes a chance to feel your strength—that only—that you all regret?' " (*Y*, p. 170); and he begins *Chance* by agreeing with Powell "that the happiest time in their lives was as youngsters in good ships, with no care in the world . . ." (*C*, p. 4).

Marlow's attitude towards the sea represents a singular failure to evolve. Upon failing his first test, the youthful Jim scorns "the spurious menace of wind and seas. He knew what to think of it. . . . he exulted with fresh certitude in his avidity for adventure, and in a sense of many-sided courage" (*LJ*, pp. 6-7). We expect *Chance*'s Marlow to sound a good deal different, but halfway through his final narrative Marlow himself echoes Jim's naive assertion that the sea is "unchangeable, safe . . . sheltering man from all passions, except its own anger"

(*C*, p. 292). Surely one of Jim's functions is to complete the process that Kurtz began: Marlow's initiation into disillusionment, his alienation from earlier visions of youth and sea. He speaks of Jim's being " 'the sort whose appearance claims the fellowship of those illusions you had thought gone out, extinct, cold . . . ,' " and then of the destruction of that fellowship.

> "Surely in no other craft as in that of the sea do the hearts of those already launched to sink or swim go out so much to the youth on the brink. . . . In no other kind of life is the illusion more wide of reality—in no other is the beginning *all* illusion—the disenchantment more swift—the subjugation more complete. . . . He was there before me, believing that age and wisdom can find a remedy against the pain of truth. . . . I was aggrieved against him, as though he had cheated me—me!—of a splendid opportunity to keep up the illusion of my beginnings, as though he had robbed our common life of the last spark of its glamour." (*LJ*, pp. 111-13)

After such an anguished outcry, it is no wonder that the opening note of *Chance*, sounding as it does like the end of "Youth," rings false.

In both "Youth" and *Chance* Marlow wryly but enviously shakes his head over the bravura successes of youth, but such nostalgia, while valid once, becomes brittle and artificial after the confrontations with youth's flagrant excesses of ideas and imagination, and its consequent heart-rending doom, in *Heart of Darkness* and *Lord Jim*. Like "Youth" and unlike *Heart of Darkness* and *Lord Jim*, *Chance* lacks a moral core and Marlow a moral stance. The problems of its plot are situational; they bear no relationship to the crisis of nightmare and conscience that Marlow, along with Kurtz and Jim, experience in *Heart of Darkness* and *Lord Jim*. Though used in various ways, "chance" primarily means coincidence rather than providence, happenstance rather than moral and symbolic aptness.[12] Thus Powell tells us that he got his first chance by chance, a casual display of verbal irony indicative of the novel's level of profundity and wit. The story is the vehicle not for symbolic, philosophical, or moral exploration, but for what Marlow calls "the commonest sort of curiosity" (*C*, p. 40), for he finds what he narrates only mildly interesting, and his lack of temperamental involvement utterly denies any tension at the novel's core.

The tone of *Chance* is one of casual and bland superiority, and Marlow exhibits intense emotion rarely and incongruously, as when he rails out against confessions after presumably having sought to elicit Flora's. He says, " 'Never confess! Never, never! . . . a confession of whatever sort is always untimely. The one thing which makes it supportable for a while is curiosity. . . . And all of them [confessors] in their hearts brand you for either mad or impudent. . . .' " The narrator says, "I had seldom seen Marlow so vehement, so pessimistic, so earnestly cynical before" (*C*, p. 212). Marlow may be correct about his motivation, but curiosity is an oddly feeble basis on which to construct the vast edifice of *Chance*.

In the analogous passage in *Lord Jim*, Marlow also contemplates himself as confidant, wondering what loosens men's " 'tongues at the sight of me for the infernal confidences; as though . . . I didn't have enough confidential information about myself to harrow my own soul till the end of my appointed time. . . . I am not particularly fit to be a receptable of confessions' " (*LJ*, p. 28). Marlow's conclusion here is presumably wrong, and in fact he later qualifies it: " 'I would have been little fitted for the reception of his confidences had I not been able at times to understand the pauses between the words' " (*LJ*, p. 90). Marlow asserts that " 'My weakness consists in not having a discriminating eye for the incidental' " (*LJ*, p. 80), but he implies the opposite when he proclaims his admiration for the French lieutenant's discrimination. Yet with all their contrarieties, such pronouncements are not simply misleading—they are profoundly, supremely misleading, and they express something central and significant about Marlow in the same way as does the confession passage in *Hamlet* that this self-judgment seems to echo. Hamlet defines himself to Ophelia: "I am myself indifferent honest; but yet I could accuse me of such things that it were better my mother had not borne me: I am very proud, revengeful, ambitious, with more offences at my beck than I have thoughts to put them in, imagination to give them shape, or time to act them in. What should such fellows as I do crawling between earth and heaven: We are arrant knaves, all; believe none of us" (III, i, 123-32). The uses of literary sources are subtle and powerful in *Lord Jim*; in *Chance* they are cheap and superior, as when Marlow refers to Flora and de Barral as " 'Figures from Dickens—pregnant with pathos' " (*C*, p. 162).

Marlow's attitudes toward *Chance*'s central concerns—the sea and women—are also disturbing, for his complacent categorization of each confronts endless contradictions while remaining unchanged. As with *Typhoon*'s Captain MacWhirr, the sea in *Chance* is defined as free from all moral challenge, "free from the earth's petty suggestions" (*C*, p. 310), offering professional satisfaction plus adventure with its simple, direct claims (*C*, pp. 31-32). Thus, life on the *Ferndale* must be seen as aberrant, its unrestfulness atypical of the sea but very like that associated with the land. This aberrance is compounded by the marriage of Flora and Anthony, for another of Marlow's *ex cathedra* pronouncements blithely generalizes about marriage and then marriage at sea:

> "With what we know of Roderick Anthony and Flora de Barral I could not deduct an ordinary marital quarrel beautifully matured in less than a year. . . . If you ask me what is an ordinary marital quarrel I will tell you, that it is a difference about nothing. . . . There are on earth no actors too humble and obscure not to have a gallery, that gallery which envenoms the play by stealthy jeers, counsels of anger, amused comments or words of perfidious compassion. However, the Anthonys were free from all demoralizing influences. At sea, you know, there is no gallery. You hear no tormenting echoes of your own littleness there. . . ." (*C*, p. 326)

Once again, Marlow remains unperturbed by the failure of his definition and picture to square with each other.

Marlow maintains that he is out of his element on land (*HD*, p. 179; *C*, pp. 33-34), and he is certainly out of his depth with women, although early in *Chance* he asserts the opposite: " 'There is enough of the woman in my nature to free my judgment of women from glamorous reticency. . . . A woman is not necessarily either a doll or an angel to me. She is a human being, very much like myself' " (*C*, p. 53). Actually, this asserted affinity, this wilful misuse of his "one of us" thesis, serves merely as license for Marlow's endless pronouncements in the face of ignorance and gross inconsistency. Occasionally he sees women as superior to men, but his basic attitude toward them in *Chance*, in fact through all his narratives, is one of condescension.

Marlow then offers us a telling abstraction that gives the show away: " 'You say I don't know women. Maybe. . . . But I have a clear notion of *woman*' " (*C*, p. 353). Of course Marlow has nothing of the kind; he not only knows far less than he asserts, but he cannot keep his assertions straight. Thus, he defends his lie to Kurtz's Intended at the end of *Heart of Darkness* by insisting that he had a duty to keep from her a truth that, as a woman, she would have found "too dark— too dark altogether . . ." (*HD*, p. 256). But in *Chance* he reverses the formula while managing to remain equally patronizing: " 'I call a woman sincere when she volunteers a statement resembling remotely in form what she really would like to say, what she really thinks ought to be said if it were not for the necessity to spare the stupid sensitiveness of men. . . . We could not stand women speaking the truth. . . . It would cause infinite misery and bring about most awful disturbances in this rather mediocre, but still idealistic fool's paradise in which each of us lives his own little life. . . . And they know it. They are merciful' " (*C*, p. 144). Trying to determine his complexly ambivalent attitude toward Jim, Marlow reveals something of his own depths: " 'It is when we try to grapple with another man's intimate need that we perceive how incomplete, wavering, and misty are the beings that share with us the sight of the stars and the warmth of the

sun. It is as if loneliness were a hard and absolute condition of existence . . .' " (*LJ*, p. 155). This sort of intensely personal confrontation
with human relationships lies at the polar extreme from the "common
curiosity" that motivates Marlow in *Chance.*

In his "Author's Note" to "Youth," which appears five years after
Chance, Conrad identifies Marlow as his *alter ego* from first conception to last farewell. Conrad is credible when he denies having merely
used Marlow, when he denies that Marlow is a charlatan, "a clever
screen, a mere device, a 'personator,' a familiar spirit, a whispering
'daemon.' " Their relationship, he continues, grew "very intimate in
the course of years. . . . The man Marlow and I came together in the
casual manner of those health-resort acquaintances which sometimes
ripen into friendships. This one has ripened. For all his assertiveness
in matters of opinion he is not an intrusive person. He haunts my
hours of solitude, when, in silence, we lay our heads together in great
comfort and harmony; but as we part at the end of a tale I am never
sure that it may not be for the last time. Yet I don't think either of us
would care much to survive the other."[13] Conrad's statement has a
poignant validity whose outline has become clear in retrospect, for
though Conrad lives and writes until 1924, both Marlow and his
important writings are behind him by *Chance* in 1913. And this fact
seems more than coincidence, no more mere chance than Jim's ar-
rival in Patusan or the marriage of Flora and Powell through Marlow's
intercession. Jim's death seems to necessitate that of Marlow as artist;
Marlow's demise signifies that of Conrad as artist. Art imitates life
and life returns the compliment.

Conrad had reached a dead-end from which, apparently, there
could be no returning. Marlow's rites of passage from "Youth" to
Lord Jim expand parameters and deepen vision, but *Chance* depicts
a narrowing, a domestication, as Marlow shifts from morally involved
participant to fussily detached busybody making banal pronouncements: " 'Pairing off is the fate of mankind' " (*C,* p. 426). Marlow's
curiosity in *Chance* lacks empathy, the deep solace and despair of
his earlier narratives—Flora, after all, is much younger, alien in
temperament as well as inferior in sex. Unlike Powell, Marlow
doesn't take her seriously until the very end, and even then he manipulates her with condescending superiority and against his own initial condemnation of such interference (*C,* pp. 23-24). Marlow in-
trudes at the end to change the shape and direction of Powell's and
Flora's lives, but apparently without the conviction that his is a significant action. And that the consequences may be presumed unequivocal-

ly fortuitous, like Marlow's banality throughout, suggests that Conrad himself respects and shares Marlow's cheery and dull complacency. No wonder Conrad abandons him here—no beyond is possible once he ceases to take him seriously.

One central question remains concerning the Marlovian narratives. Is Marlow himself aware of and controlling the attitude implicit in his perspective, and thus as cynical as *The Secret Agent*'s narrator from first to last? Or is he as unconscious of many of his words' implications as is the professor of languages who narrates *Under Western Eyes*? By and large, *Chance* does not raise such questions because in it Marlow's sarcasm and sympathy are both distinct and superficial. But *Heart of Darkness* and *Lord Jim*, which are, in Booth's word, "seamless," remain two of Conrad's inscrutable fictions because they both raise such questions and seem to deny all the possible answers. Yet whether or not Marlow is fully a party to the plot, Conrad is surely at great pains to frustrate the part of us craving certitude. In one sense, Conrad (an ironist in all his major fiction) is simply having fun at our and Marlow's expense; yet he is also recognizing that our deepest experiences never sort themselves out neatly: they berate and confound us with their multiple moral claims: they perversely demand contradictory responses of us—and in the process truth and validity must sort themselves out as best they can. Our most difficult and important task may well be to dismiss the ambivalent "Possibly" Marlow offers *Lord Jim*'s "privileged man" as wholly inadequate, and yet to perceive that it lies at the heart of truth—if, that is, one may even speak of truth as having a heart. Marlow's journey, though it finally loses the momentum that is its *raison d'être*, derives its validity by becoming what it seeks—the way into the self-confronting realm of modern art and life, where the artist, burdened by tradition like all of us, nonetheless asserts his claim to "making it new," to striking out for unknown territories of the human psyche like the bold, free, but criminal Leggett of Conrad's "The Secret Sharer." Marlow agrees with Jim that his clean slate is a magnificent chance and then adds, "but chances are what men make them, and how was I to know?" (*LJ*, p. 209). The only answer to such a question must be the quest implicit in the question.

NOTES

[1]All quotations from these four works are from the following editions: "Youth" and *Heart of Darkness*, in *Great Short Works of Joseph Conrad* (New York: Harper & Row, 1966), pp. 143-71, 175-256; *Lord Jim* (New York: Holt, Rinehart, 1963); *Chance* (New York: Norton, 1968). References to these works will be made in the text as follows: *Y, HD, LJ, C.*

[2]Wayne C. Booth, *The Rhetoric of Fiction* (Chicago and London: University of Chicago Press, 1961), p. 346.

[3]The term "multifarious narrator" is taken from Robert Scholes and Robert Kellogg, *The Nature of Narrative* (New York: Oxford Univ. Press, 1966). It is intended to replace "omniscient" since even the most objective and removed commentator "is not everywhere at once but now here, now there, now looking into this mind or that, now moving on to other vantage points. He is time-bound and space-bound as God is not" (pp. 272-73).

[4]See Jocelyn Baines, *Joseph Conrad: A Critical Biography* (New York: McGraw-Hill, 1967), p. 205.

[5]R. W. B. Lewis, *The Picaresque Saint* (Philadelphia and New York: Lippincott, 1959), p. 197.

[6]Marlow never seems to learn the lesson of appearances. His initial reaction to the French lieutenant is that "he looked a reliable officer . . . he was seaman-like" (*LJ*, p. 120). Marlow happens to be right in this case, as Jim happened to be right about the *Patna*'s captain; but such judgments reduce values to a dangerously myopic conflating of morality and esthetics.

[7]At the end, as Marlow writes to the "privileged man," Jim is even further removed from us, even more an artifice of others' constructing. Marlow says, " 'It is impossible to see him clearly—especially as it is through the eyes of others that we take our last look at him' " (*LJ*, p. 294). Oddly, as Marlow would have it, the more Jim becomes shaped and final for some, the more he becomes inconclusive process for others.

[8]Joseph Conrad, *Under Western Eyes* (New York: Anchor Books, 1963), p. 1.

[9]This encounter, like Marlow's earlier one with Kurtz's Intended, also emphasizes that "one of us" is a sexual as well as a racial distinction.

[10]It is no mere coincidence that Jim, become a killer, replays with uncanny exactitude the Stein role, as Marlow describes it. " 'He held his shot, he says, deliberately. He held it for the tenth part of a second, for three strides of the man—an unconscionable time. He held it for the pleasure of saying to himself, That's a dead man! . . . He found himself calm, appeased, without rancour, without uneasiness, as if the death of that man had atoned for every-thing' " (*LJ*, p. 261).

[11]Sherwood Anderson, "The Book of the Grotesque," *Winesburg, Ohio* (New York: The Viking Press, 1967), p. 25.

[12]See, for example, *Chance*, pp. 16, 126, 272, 311, 328, and 446.

[13]"Author's Note," to "Youth," quoted in "*Heart of Darkness*": *An Authoritative Text, Backgrounds and Sources, Essays in Criticism*, ed. Robert Kimbrough (New York: Norton Critical Editions, 1963), p. 155.

Joseph Conrad:
Polish Cosmopolitan

Adam Gillon

ABSTRACT

Ironically, Conrad's Polish heritage is largely responsible for his not being a Polish writer, though the influence of Polish literature and cultural background on his work cannot be questioned. But Conrad is not a citizen of the world, in the political sense of the term "cosmopolitan." Unlike Madame de Staël, he professed no multiple allegiances, nor did he advocate internationalist views. And, unlike Beckett and Joyce, two cosmopolitans who rebelled against their native tradition but remained essentially Irish, Conrad is not a Polish novelist, critics in Poland notwithstanding. Only one short story, "Prince Roman," has a Polish theme and a Polish setting. Paradoxically, however, his cosmopolitanism stems from his psychological awareness of being an *émigré* even after he has established himself as an English citizen and writer. Like Joyce, Conrad rejects the comforts of belonging to a group. He confesses his sense of "secret bitterness and complex loyalty"; he stands alone and apart both as a man and as an artist, but he does not have Joyce's view of himself as "a crucified victim of his country's hatred." Conrad's "standing jump out of his racial surroundings and associations" is partly responsible for a veritable gallery of "displaced persons" in his fiction, who are engaged in an agonizing quest of their psychic identities as they battle against the hostility of the world and against the darkness within themselves. In his depiction of global settings, of multinational and multiracial protagonists, Conrad exhibits contradictory attitudes. He excoriates Western imperialism and materialism, while remaining a staunch Anglophile; he admires the East from the naive perspective of a Romantic, idealizing the natives, then utters stock sentiments of ethnic and racial prejudice. His literary heritage is another important factor which has shaped Conrad's cosmopolitanism, especially the influence of several Polish, Russian, French and English authors. Mickiewicz, Słowacki, Dostoevsky, Tolstoy, Turgenev, Maupassant, Flaubert, Trollope, and Dickens are some of these writers; but it is Shakespeare who has exerted the most overwhelming impact on the novelist. Conrad's fictional world is animated by a truly Shakespearean preoccupation with "the 'ideal' value of things, events, and people." The Shakespearean mortar that binds together the bricks of Conrad's imagination is an important aspect of the story-teller's universal appeal. A close study of Conrad's text shows extensive borrowings of Shakespearean phrases, epithets, images, cadences and significant thematic affinities with the plays. The reception of Conrad's work in different parts of the world is a further indication of his cosmopolitan stature. It is also an acknowledgment of Conrad's humanism, cogently expressed in his admonition to H. G. Wells: "You love humanity but think they are to be improved. I love humanity but know they are not!" (AG)

Conrad described Henry James as being "*cosmopolitan*, civilized, very much *homme du monde* and the acquired (educated if you like) side of his temperament—that is—restraints, the instinctive, the nurtured, fostered, cherished side is always presented to the reader first. Of course he does not deal in primitive emotions. I maintain he is the most civilized of modern writers."[1] F. R. Leavis referred to Conrad as a "cosmopolitan of French culture and French literary initiation . . . ."[2] Conrad links cosmopolitanism with being cultured and civilized; Leavis confines the cosmopolitan aspect of Conrad to the French culture only. Though each of these statements applies to Conrad to some extent, the nature of Conrad's cosmopolitanism suggests far greater complexity; for it is both personal and literary. Conrad was *homme du monde*, but not in the way he saw James; he was not the affluent, polished traveler, the sophisticated expatriate, spanning the vast gap between America and Europe, nor was he a citizen of the world, in the political sense of the term "cosmopolitan."

Unlike Beckett and Joyce, two cosmopolitans who rebelled against their native tradition but remained essentially Irish, Conrad is not a Polish novelist, critics in Poland notwithstanding. Paradoxically, however, his cosmopolitanism stems from the psychological awareness of being an *émigré* even after he has established himself as an English citizen and writer. Like Joyce, Conrad rejects the comforts of belonging to a group. He stands alone and apart both as a man and as an artist but without Joyce's view of himself as "a crucified victim of his country's hatred."[3] In his fiction Conrad has created a veritable gallery of "displaced persons" who are engaged in an agonizing quest of their psychic identities as they battle against the hostility of the world and against the darkness within themselves. In his depiction of global settings, of multinational and multiracial protagonists the novelist exhibits contradictory attitudes. He excoriates Western imperialism and materialism, while remaining a staunch Anglophile; he admires the East from the naive perspective of a Romantic, idealizing the natives, then utters stock sentiments of ethnic or racial prejudice. These contradictions stem largely from his Polish background which, ironically, is responsible for his not being a Polish writer, though the impact of Polish literature on his work cannot be questioned. The Polish heritage, again, shaped his literary cosmopolitanism—hence I choose to call him a Polish cosmopolitan. The heritage of Apollo Korzeniowski, his father, meant an atmosphere of intense nationalism, a hatred of Russia and a love of French Romanticism and Shakespeare. "My main task," he wrote, "is to bring Konrad up as neither a democrat, aristocrat, demagogue, Republican, monarchist, nor as a flunkey or servant or any of these—but only as a Pole."[4] While Conrad held patriotic feelings in high regard, he reacted to his father's revolutionary persuasion with political conservatism, a denunciation of socialism and of the "illusion" of international fraternity.

> I cannot admit the idea of fraternity, not so much because I believe it impracticable, but because its propaganda (the only thing really tangible about it) tends to weaken the national sentiment, the preservation of which is my concern.[5]

However, Conrad the novelist did little if anything to preserve this national sentiment. His Polish critics often observed that he had a truly dual nationality: in his mannerisms, his cultural and literary heritage Conrad was Polish; but he was also a loyal subject of the Queen and a sincere admirer of England. Yet he felt at home neither in Poland nor in England. In his native country he was accused of treason, unfaithfulness and desertion. In England he had never been fully accepted as a *national* writer. In 1907, for example, when he had finally established himself as a novelist, some of his readers could still view him as un-English. Angered by the unfavorable critical comments about *The Secret Agent*, Conrad wrote to his friend, Garnett:

> I've been so cried up of late as a sort of freak, *an amazing bloody foreigner writing in English* (every blessed review of S.A. had it so—and even yours) that anything I say will be discounted on that ground by the public.[6]

And in 1908 Conrad complained bitterly to Garnett about a writer in the *Daily News* "who calls [me]—God only knows on what provocation—a man without country and language." Yet this is precisely what the term *cosmopolitan* implies: to be a citizen of the world, to have *all* countries but no country. Conrad did not relish the idea, and went on to say:

> It is like abusing a tongue-tied man, for what can one say. The statement is simple and brutal; and any answer would involve too many feelings of one's inner life, stir too *much secret bitterness* and *complex loyalty* to be even attempted with any hope of being understood. I thought that a man who has written the *Nigger, Typhoon, The End of the Tether, Youth,* was safe from that sort of thing. But apparently not.[7]

The "secret bitterness" and "complex loyalty" form the basis for Conrad's subsequent literary cosmopolitanism. The Polish romantic poets could write of their native land because their patriotism has a physical pivot: they were profoundly attached to some parts of their country. Conrad, on the other hand, never had a chance to develop this kind of sentimental attachment. By the time he was fifteen, the family had lived in Debreczynka, Nowofastow, Wologda, Czerniakhov, Kazimierowka, Lwów and Cracow.

His quixotic dreams of a seafaring career could not be reconciled with the ideals of Polish patriotism, with which his father had tried to imbue him. Nor could those dreams be realized in the city of Cracow, or anywhere else in Poland. Moreover, Conrad was a lonely and somewhat capricious child, and he rebelled against the environment, against political indoctrination and the dullness of his high school studies. The discontented, solitary boy must have regarded himself as different from or superior to the local Galician Philistines.

Thus, his conflict with the community began in Poland. Like the knight of La Mancha, Conrad could not be a good citizen of his country. Ironically, it is this sense of alienation that eventually produced the result of cosmopolitanism in Conrad's fiction: his avoidance of national or parochial themes. "I verily believe," Conrad wrote, "mine was the only case of a boy of my nationality and antecedents taking a, so to speak, standing *jump out of his racial surroundings and associations.*"[8]

The motives for Conrad's emigration were not simple. There was the initial desire for the sea, which, in a landlocked Poland, meant leaving his country. But Conrad also disavowed his Catholic religion, and he ignored his uncle's suggestion that he contribute travel articles to the journal *Kraj* (Country). From the distance of his self-imposed exile Conrad toyed with the notion of Panslavism—a union of all the Slavic people, advocated by Russia. In 1881 Bobrowski wrote to his nephew, expressing his pleasure at Conrad's concern about Poland, but lecturing him on his naive misconceptions about Panslavism: "Russia only understands by Panslavism the Russification of all other Slav nations and their conversion to the Orthodox Church."[9] Bobrowski explained to young Conrad that Polish culture was "more advanced" and that Polish national history was "more ancient" than Russia's. Conrad forgot all about this theory, but he also gave up his Polish nationalist dreams. Only towards the end of his life did the then-famous novelist revert to Polish nationalism when he made his political proposal in a "Note on the Polish Problem," published in the *Times* in 1916. In his letter Conrad suggested that Poland be dissociated from its Slavic neighbors since it was identified with Western political and cultural traditions. Three years later, he expressed intransigent nationalist views in an essay "The Crime of Partition," in which he made sweeping territorial claims on Poland's behalf and upbraided the Western Powers for their sacrifice of Polish interests.

But Conrad's nationalism was rather ambivalent. Maria Dąbrowska, a noted Polish novelist, agrees with Jessie Conrad's portrait of her husband as "a foreigner in England," who has never lost his "inner Polishness"—a man marked by a paradoxical dichotomy of character. If Conrad was a true Polish patriot, as some critics claimed him to be, his was indeed a strange kind of nationalism, for "he could not be held within his own nationality; he adopted another one, and considered 'national egoism' repulsive."[10]

The African and Asian tales reflect Conrad's sentiments about nationalism. In *Heart of Darkness* he condemns Belgian imperialism; in *Almayer's Folly* and *An Outcast of the Islands* his treatment of national identity shows that there can be no true allegiance in colonial society. Thus, for example, Lingard hoists the English flag above Sambir; Willems, after he gets through the Pantai estuary, hoists the Dutch flag; Abdulla, the Arab claiming British citizenship, displays the British flag; Almayer, who is Dutch, also flies the British flag, defending his disloyalty in pragmatic terms: "What have you ever done to make me loyal? You have no grip on this country" (*AL*, p. 138). These tales, like many others, have nothing to do with *one* national theme, but, curiously, Conrad quite often vividly depicts specific characteristics of various nationalities.

It is as if Conrad wanted to make sure to lend his narratives "a local habitation and a name." In *Lord Jim*, for instance, the author repeatedly describes his characters in terms of their national origin. Even in the "Author's Note" we have an Italian lady reader who found the novel morbid and is chastised for it by Conrad, both as a woman and on account of her ethnic background: "making due allowances for the subject itself being rather *foreign* to *women's normal sensibilities*, the lady could not have been Italian. I wonder whether she was European at all. . . . No *Latin temperament* would have perceived anything morbid in the acute consciousness of lost honor" (*LJ*, p. ix; italics mine). In Conrad's cosmopolis women are often presented as a national group with distinct deficiencies. Perhaps that is why only a few of his women are round, three-dimensional figures, and he appeals to many critics as a writer celebrating manliness or, more precisely, the comradeship of men. When Conrad tags his characters with the

Symposium speaker: Adam Gillon. (Photographed by Billie W. M. Wolfe)

label of a national identity, he tends to make sweeping generalizations. Thus, writing to Garnett in 1911, he scolds his friend, again linking the Italians and the women: "are you *like the Italians* (and *most women*) *incapable of conceiving* that anybody ever should speak with perfect detachment, without some subtle hidden purpose, for the sake of what is said, with no desire of gratifying some small personal spite —or vanity. . . ."[11] Mariani, whose bar the chief engineer frequents, is "the Greek or Italian." Moreover, he is "that unspeakable vagabond Mariani."

The Germans fare worse. Conrad does not conceal his hostility towards "*that race* planted in the middle of Europe, assuming in grotesque vanity the attitudes of Europeans amongst effete Asiatics or barbarous niggers; and, with a consciousness of superiority freeing their hands from all moral bonds" (*NLL*, p. 147; italics mine). He is critical of the naive admiration an American family displays for the Germans: "I had observed long before that German genius had a hypnotising power over half-baked souls and half-lighted minds. There is an immense force of suggestion in a highly organized mediocrity. Had it not hypnotised half Europe?" (*NLL*, p. 159). It is little wonder that some of the fictional Germans are shown as caricatures. The German captain of the *Patna*, from whose thick throat issues "a low rumble" of *Schwein*, is a despicable man who regards the pilgrims aboard his ship as "dese cattle." He does not speak; he growls; he mumbles dismally. His extreme fury is that of the New South Wales German. He shakes his fists at heaven. He is "that greasy beast of a skipper" with "a big cropped head, who screws his fishy eyes at Jim" (*LJ*, p. 126). He is an "odious and fleshy figure . . . the incarnation of everything vile and base that lurks in the world we love" (p. 21).

Schomberg, the hotel keeper in Bangkok, is "a hirsute Alsatian of manly bearing" (*LJ*, p. 198). He appears again in *Victory*: "The keen manly Teutonic creature was a good hater. A fool often is" (p. 26). This Schomberg detests Scandinavians generally, and he vows to destroy Heyst. Conrad heaps derogatory epithets on the man, "his *lurid, heavy Teutonic manner*, so unlike *the picturesque*, lively rage of the *Latin races*" (*V*, p. 106; italics mine). He is also "a bearded creature of Teutonic persuasion, with ungovernable tongue, a noxious ass . . . his thick paw at the side of his mouth" (*V*, p. 20). Conrad uses the same figure in "Falk," where he is again "a brawny, hairy Alsatian, and an awful gossip . . ." (p. 155), and is ridiculed as a coward. But there is also a "good German" in this story, as Norman Sherry refers to him, explaining the resentment against the Germans and that Conrad "was not averse to making fun of them."[12] But Conrad does make fun even of this "good German," Captain Hermann, whose raving is "ridiculous" and "contemptible" and an "odious noise." The very repetition of his name, especially the references to "Hermann's niece" are comic; in fact, the author confesses through the first-person narrator that Hermann "resembled curiously a caricature of a shopkeeping citizen in one of his own German comic papers" ("Falk," pp. 181-82). His language too is supposed to tickle our funny bone: "*Der verfluchte Kerl* came in the morning like a 'tam' ropper" ("Falk," p. 181). But, Sherry is right in considering Stein one of the "good Germans"—a truly positive protagonist. Conrad does retain his sense of balance, however; though Stein's origin is also Bavaria, his German exclamations and comments, e.g., "*Ja, ja, gewiss, schrecklich. . . . Ach so . . .* " are neither offensive nor comic, perhaps because he is portrayed so sympathetically.

Other characters in *Lord Jim* get similar treatment. Chester is "a west Australian" (p. 161). The lieutenant who boards the *Patna* is only the *French* lieutenant whose speech is also sprinkled with words and epithets in his native tongue. The chief clerk is "an obliging little Portuguese half-caste with a miserably skinny neck" (*LJ*, p. 37). There are also "an old Scotsman," Egström, "a raw boned, heavy Scandinavian, with a busy manner and immense blonde whiskers" (p. 191), Siegmund Yucker "(native of Switzerland), a gentle creature ravaged by a cruel dyspepsia . . . " (p. 198), "a cross-eyed Dane of sorts whose visiting card recited his misbegotten name: first Lieutenant in the Royal Siamese Navy" (p. 199), and "a boat-load of Chinamen, bound, as likely as not, on some thieving expedition" (p. 199).

"A Chinaman," declares Jones in *Victory*, "is unfathomable" (p. 268). "It's impossible to tell one Chinaman from another," states Heyst, the Swedish hero of the novel. "One Chinaman looks very much like another" (p. 182). The Ariel-like Wang (because of his propensity for soundless appearance and vanishing) is, properly, enigmatic, inscrutable and, unlike Ariel, unfaithful to his master. Describing the ladies' band in *Victory*, the author remarks, "One could not tell *what nationality* these women were, except that they were of all sorts" (p. 72; italics mine).

Why does Conrad so frequently pinpoint the ethnic identity of his characters? And when does he choose not to do so? Obviously, there must be method in his "madness." Captain O'Brien, Symons, Blake, Brown, Brierly and, of course, Jim himself do not have their nationality pointed out. Is it because Jim is, in Marlow's eyes, "One of us?" After all, "he stood there for all the *parentage* of his kind" (p. 43;

italics mine). Marlow's national origin is not mentioned either. Apparently Conrad does not choose to harp on the nationality of characters who hail from the British Isles since they show their national origin by merely speaking, while more exotic figures, no matter how minor, are "tagged" in a Dickensian manner with a readily recognizable label.

Conrad habitually views people in terms of nationality, perhaps because of his own national ambivalence, his own inner conviction of being a foreigner. Hence there is unintentional irony in Conrad's poking fun at foreigners who fracture the English syntax and split the ears of *echt* Englishmen with their raucous and unholy pronunciation of English. His own use of English syntax and English vocabulary often reveals Polonisms, and he spoke such heavily accented English that Bertrand Russell was shocked by its "guttural" aspect when he met the novelist in person. Another reason for the presence of Conrad's own brand of Dogberries is the time-honored tradition of distorted language as a comic and dramatic device. Dialect, peculiar grammatical construction, foreign words and phrases lend Conradian characters an air of verisimilitude.

Moreover, the sounds of German, Italian, French, Spanish or Malay enhance the effect of symbolic universality, as does the practice of withholding a character's name from the reader. In *Heart of Darkness*, for example, Marlow's name requires no national amplification. Kurtz, on the other hand, whose name is German for *short*, does; his hybrid imagination is "that patchwork of all Europe," which has contributed to his making. His young romantic admirer is a nameless *be-patched* Russian; the girl who loved Kurtz is an equally nameless "The Intended." The "gorgeous apparition of a woman" from the jungle has no name either, but the weight of brass ornaments on her neck is matched by the volume of Conrad's adjectival embellishments heaped upon her: savage, superb, wild-eyed, magnificent, ominous, stately, tragic, brooding, unswerving. The story opens and closes with the tableaux of Marlow's silent listeners and his own Buddha posture. Each of the auditors is "one of us" to the member of the group who introduces Marlow and mentions the bond of the sea between them. He describes Marlow as "the only man *of us* who still 'followed the sea' " (p. 48; italics mine), and bestows brief "occupational" epithets upon the other three: the Director of Companies (also "our captain"), the Lawyer, and the Accountant. Their nationality, presumably, is British.

Though the Russian mumbles and stammers something about "brother seaman" (*HD*, p. 138), when he first speaks to Marlow, he is

"the harlequin." " 'You English?' he asked, all smiles. 'Are you?'
I shouted from the wheel. The smile vanished, and he shook his head
as if sorry for my *disappointment*" (*HD*, p. 122; italics mine).
Throughout the novel this adherent of Kurtz remains "the Russian"
in motley, without a proper name but endowed with the now familiar
wealth of epithets: enthusiastic, fabulous, inexplicable, bewildering,
unscathed, and be-patched.

The dramatic use of foreign speech is further enhanced by expressions of ethnic prejudice reflecting the characters' rather than Conrad's own convictions, as with Schomberg, Donkin or Razumov. Similarly, the purpose of the parenthetical foreign language version of a
speaker's English is to reinforce his national authenticity. Such is the
case with the French lieutenant in *Lord Jim*: " 'I have rolled my hump
(*roulé ma bosse*),' he said, using the slang expression with imperturb-
able seriousness, 'in all parts of the world' " (p. 146). The global
peregrinations of this good man, apparently, gain credence because
Conrad uses two languages rather than one. The Frenchman's exclamations also serve as comic relief from the oppressive sadness of
the Jim-Marlow exchange, and foreshadow the philosophical stance
of another foreigner—Stein, as if both were qualified to render compassionate and objective evaluations of Jim's conduct. The French
exclamations, "*Que diable! parblue! Eh bien! voilà*," are balanced
by the German and Latin words of Stein: "*Ach so! Ja! Ja! Ach! Wie?
Was? Gott im Himmel! Nicht wahr? ewig usque ad finem. Gewiss.*"
Each of these two foreigners delivers a statement aspiring to universal
truth: " 'That is so,' the Frenchman resumed, placidly. 'Man is born a
coward (*L'homme est né poltron*). It is a difficulty—*Parbleu!* . . .
One's courage does not come of itself (*ne vient pas tout seul*). . . . One
truth the more ought not to make life impossible. . . . But the honour
—the honour—monsieur! . . . The honour . . . that is real—that is!
And what life may be worth, when, . . . when the honour is gone—*ah
ça! par exemple*—I can offer no opinion' " (*LJ*, p. 148). Stein's syntax
and the tenor of his thought are similar: " 'And because you not
always can keep your eyes shut there comes the real trouble—the
heart pain . . . . Yes! Very funny this terrible thing is . . . . The way is
to the destructive element submit yourself' " (*LJ*, pp. 213-14). Such
usage abounds in Conrad's fiction.

Ironically, Conrad's own prejudices, no less than those of his characters, broaden the cosmopolitan range of his vision. The statements
about various nationalities emphasize the global scale of the novelist's
interests. In *Under Western Eyes*, for example, he is concerned with
the Russian people, Russian autocracy, revolution and anarchism.

But, since the action takes place in Switzerland as well as in Russia, Conrad offers a severely critical view of Geneva:

> The respectable and passionless abode of democratic liberty . . . tendering the same indifferent hospitality to tourists of all nations and to international conspirators of every shade. (p. 357)

In the original manuscript there are identical references to America which Conrad regarded with some feelings of hostility, though at one time he himself considered settling in the U.S. In June 17, 1880 Tadeusz Bobrowski wrote to his nephew about his proposed position as assistant to a Canadian called Lascalle who had an investment in railroads. Bobrowski did not reject Conrad's "plans to become a Yankee," but cautioned the youth never to forget "what is due to the dignity of the nation and families to which [you] belong amidst the businesses [sic] of American life."[13] The initial romantic attraction for America, which Conrad obviously regarded as a land of adventure, was subsequently dissipated by his political views, notably his distaste for American activities in South America. Both his correspondence and fiction reflect the changed attitude. In a passage deleted by the Doubleday edition of the letters we read: "If one could set the States and Germany by the ears! That would be *real* fine. I am afraid however that the thieves shall agree in the Philippines. The pity of it."[14] In *The Rescue*, Conrad's dislike of Americans is manifested in the figure of the Yankee gun-monger who hates the Negroes. In *Nostromo*, we have as the chief exponent of "material interests" (seen by the novelist as unmitigated evil), the American millionnaire, Holroyd. This American, like Kurtz, reflects Conrad's emphasis of the mixed national background as an indicator of corruption. Holroyd represents a cosmopolitan multiplicity of ethnic origin: " . . . his parentage was German and Scotch and English, with remote strains of Danish and French blood giving him the temperament of a Puritan and an insatiable imagination of conquest" (*N*, p. 76). In his letter to Cunninghame Graham (26 Dec. 1903) Conrad spoke disparagingly of the "Yankee Conquistadores in Panama."[15] Eloise Knapp Hay suggests the existence of "an unintentional conspiracy among French, English, and American critics and biographers to tone down or to ignore Conrad's insuppressible antipathy to American politics, institutions, and character. Only Conrad's wife Jessie in a few wonderfully graphic anecdotes, manages to convey the depth of it." [16]

As Conrad's flirtation with Panslavism was followed by violent Russophobia, so Conrad's hostility towards America changed drastically after his works began to appear in the States, and especially during his American visit. He was overwhelmed by the warmth of the welcome accorded him, and wrote to Elbridge L. Adams on 31 May, 1923:

> I'm going away with a strong impression of American large-heartedness and generosity. I have *not for a moment felt like a stranger* in *this great country*, about the future of which no sensible man would dare to speculate. But no sensible man would doubt its *significance in the history of mankind*. I am proud to have from it an *unexpected warmth* of public recognition and the gift of precious private friendships.[17]

This reversal is rather typical of Conrad's personality. Rather than disavow a formerly held view, he will ardently proclaim his "reformed" attitude. It is ironical that he used *identical terms* in defense of his Polish-Western origins, as he indignantly protested H. L. Mencken's "harping of [my] Slavonism." Conrad did not think the word could possibly apply to him:

> Racially I belong to a culture derived at first from Italy and then from France; and a rather Southern temperament; an outpost of Westernism with a Roman tradition, situated between Slavo-Tartar Byzantine barbarism on one side and the German tribes on the other; resisting both influences desperately and still remaining true to itself to this very day. I went out into the world before I was seventeen, to France and England, and *in neither country did I feel myself a stranger for a moment*: neither as regards ideas, sentiments, nor institutions. If he means that I have been influenced by so-called Slavonic literature then he is utterly wrong. I suppose he means Russian; but as a matter of fact I never knew Russian. The few novels I have read I have read in translation. *Their mentality and their emotionalism have been always repugnant to me, hereditarily and individually. Apart from Polish* my youth has been *fed on French and English literature. . . .*
>
> *I am a child, not of a savage but of a chivalrous tradition, and if my mind took a tinge from anything it was from French romanticism, perhaps. It was fed on ideas*, not of revolt but of liberalism of a perfectly disinterested kind, and on *severe moral lessons of national misfortune.*[18]

Conrad again protested against being labeled a Slavonic writer in 1924, in a letter to Charles Chassé, suggesting that at most he could be *charged* with "Polonism" which, at any rate, was far removed from Byzantine and Asiatic associations. He contended that he did not know Russian and knew very few works of Russian literature in translation; that "the formative forces acting on [me] at the most plastic and impressionable age, were purely Western: that is French and English . . . ." In the same breath, however, Conrad admits that authors entertain many illusions about themselves and that his claim to Westernism is made simply because he feels himself "profoundly in accord with it."[19]

Despite Conrad's protestations about his ignorance of things Russian, he did write about them with an air of authority, notably in an article "Autocracy and War" (1905), in which he condemned Russian despotism. In the same piece the novelist prophetically describes Germany as "a people trained to the worship of force . . . full of unscrupulous self-confidence . . . ." He warns the world, characteristically turning to French: *"Le Pressianisme—voilà l'ennemi!"* (*NLL,* p. 47). This anti-German feeling comes from Conrad's early educational experience. He grudgingly acknowledges some German virtues, but there is no doubt about the intensity of his antagonism:

> While I was a boy in a great public school we were steeped in classicism to the lips, and, though our historical studies were naturally tinted with Germanism, I know that all we boys, the six hundred of us, resisted that influence with all our might, while accepting the result of German research and thoroughness.[20]

He disliked all subjects except geography, but even this discipline was not taught properly:

> And their geography was very much like themselves, a bloodless thing with a dry skin covering a repulsive armature of uninteresting bones.[21]

Conrad did not hesitate to acknowledge his Slavic foreignness in an English community. In a letter to John Galsworthy (24 Oct. 1907) he writes: "I did not discuss the point for fear that Edward (who declares himself Irish) should tell me that (*as a Slav*) *I know nothing of the English* temper in controversy."[22] In another letter to Galsworthy (6 Jan. 1908), we find this admission of being an alien, provoked by Conrad's disappointment at the commercial failure of *The Secret Agent*:

> I suppose *there is something in me that is unsympathetic to the general public,*—because the novels of Hardy, for instance, are generally tragic enough and gloomily written, too,—and yet they have sold in their time and are selling to the present day.
>
> *Foreignness,* I suppose.[23]

This preoccupation with foreignness colors Conrad's vision in his most ambitious epic novel, *Nostromo,* in which he struggled " . . . for the breath of life that had to be blown into the shape of men and women, of Latin and Saxon, of Jew and Gentile" (*A Personal Record,* p. 98). As there is only *one* Jewish figure in this novel (and only one more in all of Conrad's fiction—the innkeeper Yankel in "Prince Roman," unless we consider the possibility of Stein being Jewish), the novelist must have had a special reason for including him. Especially because Señor Hirsch stands apart from all social classes of Costaguana, being a foreigner *par excellence*. But then hardly any of the leading characters belong in Sulaco—a land, it seems, of no native sons. Thus, Nostromo, Giorgio Viola, his family, and numerous workers on the wharves are Italians; Captain Mitchell's heritage, unmentioned by the author, is undoubtedly English. There are the "European residents," the engineers "aided by the Italian and Basque workmen who rallied faithfully round their English chiefs" (*N*, p. 14). The Company's lightermen are the natives of the Republic who serve under their Italian Capataz. They are, significantly, "an outcast lot of *very mixed blood*, mainly negroes" (*N*, p. 14; italics mine). Although "no one could be more of a Costaguanero than Don Carlos Gould . . . . he was just the Inglez—the Englishman of Sulaco" (p. 47). So are his wife and Monygham, referred to as "the English doctor." Martin Decoud, born in Costaguana, lived in Paris as "an idle boulevardier" and his "life . . . induced in him a Frenchified—*but most un-French—cosmopolitanism*, in reality a mere barren indifferentism posing as intellectual superiority" (p. 152; italics mine). Like the French lieutenant,[24] he uses French phrases by way of a stylistic crutch, e.g., "What do I know of military rifles? *C'est funambulesque!*" (p. 153). Here Conrad observes helpfully: " . . . for the Decoud family—except the old father and mother—use the French language amongst themselves" (p. 153). Decoud is the "nondescript dilettante of life" (p. 153).

The omniscient novelist's voice denigrating Decoud's cosmopolitanism is most revealing, for if any identification can be drawn of Conrad with a character from *Nostromo*, it is with this "adopted child of Western Europe" (p. 156). Decoud loves Antonia, the paragon of patriotism. Conrad confesses to having modeled Antonia on his first love:

> How we . . . used to look up to that girl . . . as the standard-bearer of a faith to which we all were born but which she alone knew how to hold aloft with unflinching hope! . . . She was an uncompromising Puritan of Patriotism . . . . It was I who had to hear oftenest her scathing criticism of my levities —*very much like poor Decoud*—or stand the brunt of her austere, *unanswerable* invective. (Author's Note, p. xiv; italics mine)

Conrad compares himself to Decoud whose cosmopolitanism, like that of Conrad himself, is a manifestation of his separateness. The self-destructive brand of cosmopolitanism is essential in order to underline its opposite—exalted patriotism. What appealed to Conrad so deeply was the girl's power of conviction and her Puritan self-denial. But the model for Antonia "did not quite understand—but never mind" (ibid.). This apologetic note only emphasizes Conrad's dichotomy. Patriotism, solidarity with a social unit, with mankind, fidelity to a cause or to a ship—these are the highest virtues for Conrad, as betrayal is the worst transgression, invariably punished by death, acute suffering or total isolation from the community.

Many critics, myself included, have discussed Conrad's preoccupation with betrayal and his sense of guilt at having "deserted" the ship of Poland.[25] Though Conrad felt a sense of hopeless fidelity to Poland, this commitment contributed to his estrangement from other Poles. He writes of his father's "ardent fidelity" in "Poland Revisited" (1915) as he recalls the funeral procession. He remembers "that appalling feeling of inexorable fate, tangible, palpable, . . . a figure of dread, murmuring with iron lips the final words: Ruin—and Extinction" (*NLL*, p. 171). He describes himself as "the grizzled *foreigner* holding forth in a *strange tongue* to a youth on whose arm he leaned" (ibid., p. 165). A year earlier Conrad explained to a Polish journalist Marian Dąbrowski why the English critics always found "something incomprehensible, impalpable, ungraspable in [me]." He continued by saying:

> You alone, (i.e., the Poles) can grasp this ungraspable element, comprehend the incomprehensible. *This is my Polishness.* The Polishness which I took to my works through Mickiewicz and Słowacki. My father read *Pan Tadeusz* aloud to me, and made me read out loud, not once, not twice. I preferred *Konrad Wallenrod, Grażyna.* Later I preferred Słowacki. Do you know why Słowacki? *Il est l'âme de toute la Pologne, lui.*[26]

Yet he also adds: "for indeed I am an English writer." That he was—an English writer of Polish extraction who did not know much about his native land. When he finally did begin to write about Poland, it was not as a novelist but as a journalist, after his visit to Poland in 1914. The Polish girl he loved in his youth did not understand his motives for leaving Poland. How could she? "It would take too long to explain," he wrote in *A Personal Record* (p. 36), "the intimate alliance of contradictions in human nature which make love itself wear at times the desperate shape of betrayal."

These contradictions in the novelist's nature account for some of his prejudices, such as his anti-Semitism. As I pointed out in my essay "The Merchant of Esmeralda—Conrad's Archetypal Jew,"[27] there is ample evidence of anti-Jewish statements in his letters and fiction, usually allegations of shrewd or unfair business practices and even a pejorative remark about "the Jewish God." If Conrad received his anti-Jewish sentiments from his early background of the Polish-landed gentry in the Ukraine, he also absorbed some literary influences from Polish and English literature, which affected his treatment of his fictional Jews. The reading of Alexandre Dumas's edition of Garibaldi's autobiography also contributed to the portrayal of Hirsch, whose position in the novel is quite poignant although he does not appear to be of any importance in the development of the plot.

Decoud, Nostromo, and Hirsch are all aliens, and all three die violently; all three experience fear and insecurity. Hirsch is drawn from a largely comic literary archetype, Shakespearean and Dickensian, but he is transformed in the novel into a figure that evokes not laughter but shock and indignation. Despite the initial use of stock anti-Semitic epithets, Conrad views Hirsch with ironic compassion. The tortured Jew, suspended in a posture of crucifixion, is a symbolic warning to Nostromo and a sign of profound social disintegration. Hirsch changes from an abject coward to a man brave enough to spit in his torturer's face. That Conrad intended to confer a certain dignity upon the alien Jew in death is clear if one considers the source of this scene—Garibaldi's description of being tortured by the *estrapado*.[28] While Garibaldi's persecutor, Don Leonardo Milan, does not kill Garibaldi after the latter spits in his face, the mere fact that Conrad associated the action of Hirsch with that of a noble revolutionary suggests Hirsch's transformation. Nostromo is deeply touched by Hirsch's death and swears to avenge him. Ultimately, Hirsch joins Decoud and Nostromo almost as an equal.

The other Jew of Conrad's fiction, Yankel, appears in the "Polish" story, "Prince Roman," and is drawn more from Adam Mickiewicz's *Pan Tadeusz* (1834) than from Conrad's memory of any real Jewish innkeeper. This is a "positive," almost sentimental portrayal of the Jew as a Polish patriot. The mainly literary origin of Yankel, apart from the close correspondence with his counterpoint Jankiel of *Pan Tadeusz*, is confirmed by the feeble attempt of the novelist to use supposedly Yiddish words "Tse! Tse!" The very same words or, more correctly, the sounds, since they have no specific meaning, are spoken by a cringing half-caste servant of Renouard in the story "The Planter of Malata." Perhaps, in the subconscious of Conrad, the half-caste and Yankel belonged in the same category, and hence uttered the same words. Yet the artistic conscience of the writer triumphs over the ethnic prejudice of Conrad the man. There is no servility or abjectness in Yankel.

One cannot accuse Conrad of anti-Semitism when, for example, in *Under Western Eyes* Razumov delivers himself of anti-Jewish sentiments which illustrate his agitated emotional state more than Conrad's own feelings. Razumov is Russian, but his name is "the mere label of a solitary individuality." He is "nobody's child" (*UWE*, p. 10). In a sense he is no less lonely and no less of a pariah than Hirsch. *Under Western Eyes* (the original title of the novel was *Razumov*) is Conrad's fictional answer to Dostoevsky, and, in another sense, a fulfillment of his father's wish to write a great Polish novel about the corruption brought upon Poland by Muscovy. In this instance Conrad no longer professes his ignorance about the Russians, for he states (in a letter to John Galsworthy) that in *Under Western Eyes* he tried "to capture the very soul of things Russian—*Cosas de Russia*."[29] And though the Author's Note to the novel contains anti-Russian statements, the work itself supports his avowed claim of "scrupulous impartiality." Conrad shrewdly observes that Russian autocracy and its moral anarchism provoke the "no less imbecile and atrocious answer of a purely Utopian revolutionism . . . . In the strange conviction that a fundamental change of heart must follow the downfall of any given human institutions" (*UWE*, p. x). Conrad would have been shocked, I imagine, if someone had pointed out to him that his thesis is not substantially different from Dostoevsky's *Notes From the Underground*—his fictional answer to Chernyshevsky's "What Is to Be Done?" Conrad's indictment of Utopian Russian philosophy does not blur his compassionate view of the Russian people. The Russians themselves rewarded Conrad (so he felt) by giving the novel "universal recognition" and publication "in many editions" (*UWE*, p. viii). There is little doubt that *Under Western Eyes* was Conrad's artistic response to Dostoevsky's *Crime and Punishment*; there are numerous textual analogies between the two, which I have discussed elsewhere.[30] Of course, this is not the only source of Conrad's book, but it illustrates the influence of Russian literature on the novelist. Conrad detested Dostoevsky, "the grimacing, haunted creature, who is under a curse."[31] He lumped him with Tolstoy whose *War and Peace* and other works he censured severely: "Tolstoy and Dostoevsky deny everything for which I stand."[32] And, as if to counterbalance his extreme judgment of the two Russian giants, Conrad raved about Turgenev, his "chosen master":

> Every gift has been heaped upon his cradle.—Absolute sanity and the deepest sensibility, the clearest vision and the most exquisite responsiveness, penetrating insight and unfailing generosity of judgement, and unerring instinct for the significant, for the essential in human life and in the visible world, the clearest mind, the warmest heart, the largest sympathy—and all that in perfect measure. There's enough there to ruin any writer.[33]

Yet Conrad displays a greater affinity with Dostoevsky and Tolstoy than with Turgenev—sharing their intense treatment of moral transgression. The allusions (in a cancelled passage of *Under Western Eyes*) to Peter Ivanovich as the author of "The Resurrection of Yegor" and the "thrice famous Pfennig Cantata"[34] are satirical barbs aimed at Tolstoy's *Resurrection* and "Kreutzer's Sonata," which Conrad regarded as "monstrous stupidity."[35]

Conrad's extreme literary opinions are not reserved for Russian literature only. It is somewhat jolting to read his comment on a novel by an outstanding novelist of Poland, the *History of Sin* by Stefan Żeromski: "The whole thing is *disagreeable* and *incomprehensible* in comment and psychology. Often it is gratuitously *ferocious*."[36] As I observed earlier, Conrad applies the words "incomprehensible" and "unsympathetic" to his own work, while reserving the compliment of "ferocity" to the Russians and Dostoevsky. Since *Victory* (and, to some extent, "Because of the Dollars") is remarkably similar to Żeromski's novel (as *Lord Jim* is similar to Żeromski's *The Homeless Men*), Conrad's revulsion is as telling as his vehement condemnation of *The Brothers Karamazov*, which sounded to him "like some fierce mouthings from prehistoric ages."[37] One cannot help wondering whether Conrad's critical irritability is not caused by a conscious or subconscious recognition of the profound affinities he shared with these writers. Even more revealing is Conrad's positively fulsome letter to Stefan Żeromski, written on 25 March 1923, in which he acknowledges the latter's "*magnificent* preface to *Almayer's Folly*" (that is to the Polish translation of the book), continuing:

> I asked Angela (Zagórska—Conrad's cousin and his Polish translator) that she would convey expression of *my gratitude* to you for the *great favour* you had conferred on me. I admit that *I cannot find words* to describe my *deep emotion* in reading this appreciation of yours, by which I feel *profoundly* honoured, appreciation coming from *my country*, voiced by you, dear Sir, who are *the greatest master of its literature*.
>
> Please accept, dear and esteemed Sir, my *most affectionate* thanks for the time, the thought and the work you have devoted to me and for your *most sympathetic comprehension* which *has discovered* the *compatriot* behind the author. With *all my gratitude*. . . .[38]

Żeromski's attitude towards Conrad, interestingly enough, was also marked by lack of sincerity. He praised Conrad's work, assuming, incidentally, that Conrad thought in Polish and wrote in English, and pointing out Conrad's "Polish manner of linking words together, the Polish enthusiasm of marveling at the sight of things unknown, mysterious, terrible and lofty." Yet in private, Żeromski referred to Conrad as "that traitor," in a conversation with J. Lechoń, and wrote of Conrad's "desertion"—a favorite charge with some Polish critics.[39] This attitude, however, did not prevent him from writing a favorable preface to the Polish edition of *Lord Jim*, for which Conrad also thanked him in a rather sycophantic letter. By way of a curious coincidence, Lechoń himself also exhibited this ambivalent attitude toward Conrad, not uncommon among Polish critics. He lauded Conrad's artistic achievement, but in a poem entitled "On the Death of Joseph

Conrad," there is not a word about his subject as an artist or an English novelist, or even a *Polish* novelist. It begins with the words: "Your father, too, had a splendid, gloomy burial, / Followed by simple men and dignitaries." The poem is, in essence, a rebuke to Conrad, the Pole, a reminder that " [your] father summons [you] with *Polish* speech / Where the same lighthouse brightens all the seas."[40] Żeromski, despite his admonition, was more generous and, I think, more sensible than Lechoń, in publicly stating Conrad's position in Poland. He counseled his countrymen not to grab an author from the English and make him Polish property, but to return Conrad's spirit to Poland by means of accomplished translations. He recognized the fact that Conrad was as much an English writer as he was a Polish writer.

The notion of Conrad being a bilingual writer has elicited comparisons with Vladimir Nabokov—that brilliant Russian cosmopolitan. Nabokov himself objects to this analogy, observing (among other things) that Conrad never wrote in Polish. He is right in the sense that Conrad never wrote fiction in Polish. There is a fundamental difference between the two, however. Nabokov began his literary career as a Russian novelist writing in Russian. He came to America in 1940 but now lives in Geneva (not one of Conrad's most favorite places, we might recall). He is a linguistic virtuoso, writing original novels in English and then translating them into Russian and vice versa. For the present, final edition of his Autobiography, Nabokov performed an exercise in linguistic acrobatics:

> This re-Englishing of a Russian re-version of what had been an English retelling of Russian memories in the first place, proved a diabolical task, but some consolation was given me by the thought that such multiple metamorphosis, familiar to butterflies, had not been tried by any human before.[41]

Unlike Nabokov, Conrad was no collector of butterflies, although his Stein indulged in this intriguing hobby; nor were his metamorphoses from a Polish scion of "land-tilling gentry"—as he put it—[42] to French sailor and gun-runner, to British sailor, to English novelist a matter of deliberate choice. The suggestions, especially by some early critics, that he *selected* English rather than French or Polish as his artistic vehicle were rejected by Conrad with the customary vehemence and the ambivalence he revealed whenever he had to deal with the questions of his Polishness or his foreignness. Conrad insisted that he did not *adopt* the English language but was adopted by it. Somewhat apologetically, he argued:

> It is very obvious that I *don't possess the English language in any exceptional way*; but that is no reason to doubt my sincerity when I say that it

had possessed and even shaped my thoughts. Idiomatically, I am never at fault, and it is absolutely true that if I had not written in English I would not have written at all.[43]

Does Conrad protest too much? I wonder.

Madame de Staël, whom Conrad calls "that dangerous and exiled woman" (*UWE*, p. 72), wrote in French but professed to have four other countries as her fatherlands: England—*patrie de choix*; Germany—*patrie de sa pensée*; Italy—*celle de sa sensibilité*, and Russia—*celle de son âme*. For Conrad England was the fatherland of choice or adoption; France—his fatherland of sensibility; Poland—that of his soul. As to the fourth allegiance to a fatherland of thought, no one country would qualify since he never indicated a pronounced preference for a thinker or thinkers of one nationality. In fact, Conrad considered thinking an enemy to perfection. Nothing less than the concept of *Weltliteratur* can shed light on Conrad's preoccupation with universally recognized values. Conrad's development as a novelist was from the transmutation of personal experience to the exploration of themes and characters which evolved from his reading rather than from the tranquil recollection of past memories.

Conrad's world is both Eastern and Western. Even when Conrad's knowledge of the East was superficially arrived at through conversations with other sailors, he was, nevertheless, able to reproduce many aspects of it with remarkable fidelity. Conrad the novelist does bestride the world like a Colossus. But it is not only the global settings of his plots, nor the multi-national aspect of his protagonists that provide the universal fictional canvas presented with amazing artistic objectivity. Norman Sherry's two exhaustive studies[44] illumine the quality of Conrad's imagination by showing how the novelist turns his source material into works of art, though, undoubtedly, many Conradian tales, especially those dealing with the Far East and Africa, are based on personal experience. Conrad's truth, as Picasso once observed speaking about the artist's work, is woven out of a "lie"—that is, out of an often inaccurate or distorted statement of fact. Like Shakespeare, Conrad uses his sources not slavishly but always with a sense of his own artistic truth, often presenting composite portraits of men and women.

The documentary reading done by Conrad (or available to him), recorded by Professor Sherry, provides, like the reminiscences of his seafaring years, the raw materials for his fiction. The finished product, however, is much more than plot, story or even theme; it is, above all, the style, le *mot juste* with which Conrad the artist was so concerned. The total artistic value of Conrad's work and particularly the appraisal of his cosmopolitanism and of his universal appeal must needs extend beyond the examination of these raw materials to the scrutiny of his literary sources.

The earliest sources, of course, were from Polish literature. It is revealing that the first critics of Conrad's work in Poland were scholars of *Polish* literature, including such luminaries as Wacław Borowy, Julian Krzyżanowski, Juliusz Kleiner and Joseph Ujejski. Even some outstanding Polish novelists and poets joined the critical ranks of those who study the Polish elements in Conrad: Stefan Żeromski (mentioned above), Maria Dąbrowska and Jan Parandowski. Elsewhere I gave several examples of the Polish spiritual and moral atmosphere in Conrad's work,[45] and pointed out some specific borrowings from Mickiewicz's *Konrad Wallenrod, The Akerman Steppes, Forefathers' Eve, Grażyna* and *Pan Tadeusz*; from Słowacki's *Lilla Weneda, Lambro* and Malczewski's *Maria*; and from Krasiński's *Undivine Comedy*. A strong case can be made for Conrad's work being close to the poetry of the so-called Polish-Ukrainian school of the early Polish Romantics. Similarly, the affinities with some nineteenth- and twentieth-century Polish novelists are manifestly clear to the Polish student of Conrad, e.g., with Bolesław Prus, Henryk Sienkiewicz and Stefan Żeromski. In a recent study, *Conrad in Poland*,[46] Stefan Zabierowski reviews the problems of critical reception of the novelist during the years 1896-1969. Though a great deal of Polish criticism is concerned with the biographical elements in his fiction, or with the person of Conrad the Pole, there are many thoroughly comparative approaches as well, showing how Conrad used his Polish literary sources, one of which was a volume of memoirs by his uncle Tadeusz Bobrowski.

The Polish critics have fought lively battles as to whether Conrad was a Romantic or a Positivist, a Pole or an Englishman of Polish origin. The Positivist critics debunk the methodological elements of the Romantic portrait of Conrad, while their opponents decry the vulgar sociological simplifications of the Positivist conception of Conrad. Some Polish critics, however, have gone far beyond the early parochial view of Conrad or the narrow examination of his work through the prism of Polish literature alone. Roman Dyboski, for instance, considers Conrad's fiction to be

> . . . as much a European act as is Chopin's music. Chopin spoke and speaks to the whole world in the great and old international language of music; Conrad speaks to the readers of all countries in the English language which is spread all over the world today, and reaches places where the masterpieces of the Polish language will never get.[47]

Zygmunt Nowakowski feels that Conrad belongs to another nation or tribe—to the nation of artists: "not to the English. Let us not be poor relatives. Conrad did not remember us in his testament. Our accusations that he did not write in Polish are ludicrous. Conrad in Polish would be an unknown value for the English and thus for the world."[48] Others agree that Conrad cannot be contained within the national boundaries of any one country, being a writer of genius, and a solitary. They see him as a Renaissance man (Wit Tarnawski), a unique artist whose fatherland is the society of seamen, scattered all over the globe.

As we noted above, Conrad objected to H. L. Mencken's emphasis of his Slavic background, but the exotic flavor of his language cannot be explained away, nor the fact that even the hated Russians had their share in the shaping of his growth as an artist. Conrad himself acknowledges that he read a tale by Turgenev in Polish as a child. It is interesting that many European readers regarded Conrad as a Slavic writer. Thus, for example, the Yugoslav reviewer Milan Sufflay refers to Conrad's "Polish and Russian Artistic Blood" in his article.[49] One should not, however, compare the enormous influence of Polish letters on Conrad with that of Russian literature. Conrad did indeed reject Dostoevsky and Tolstoy though he learned something from each of the two. He genuinely admired Turgenev who made a deep artistic impression upon him. The poetical quality and limpidity of Turgenev's style, no less than his preoccupation with outcasts and rebels (e.g., Bazarov), can be traced in Conrad's fiction, from *Almayer's Folly* to *Lord Jim, Under Western Eyes* and *Victory*. Admittedly, though, no close textual study of Turgenev and Conrad has yet been made.

Still, the critics keep harping on Conrad's Slavonism. The Norwegian Ludwig Wollnick perceives Conrad's melancholy fatalism as an inherent quality of his "Slavic soul," while he also observes the influence of Flaubert whose taste for orientalism, barbarism and fatalism Conrad shared.[50] A Chilean admirer, Mariano Latone, believes Conrad conceives life in a *Russian* manner for his characters are "outside the law, they are ex-men," but, mercifully, he notes an essential difference.[51] The Frenchman Edmond Jaloux sees Conradian heroes not as adventurers in the tradition of Smollet or R. L. Stevenson but, rather, as the heroes of Dostoevsky or Gorki.[52] Another early French critic, J. Kessel, in "Conrad the Slav," attributed Conrad's aversion to Dostoevsky to an emotion that was love and hate at the same time. Despite Conrad's denials, he saw strong Slavic elements in his writings, and his typical hero was *déclassé*.[53] There are many similar opinions among the critics who have little or no doubt as to Conrad's distinct Slavic aspect.

But numerous other critics see Conrad as a writer of "European mentality."[54] There are studies of the novelist in practically all European languages, as there are excellent translations of his fiction. This is hardly surprising when we consider the purely literary heritage of Conrad. There is evidence of encyclopedic reading in his correspondence, which may account for the copious literary associations in his novels and stories. Conrad had a wide knowledge of French literature; in his youth he read German literature and the Classics; he also read the Spanish and Italian masterpieces. He knew and admired several American novelists, e.g., James Fenimore Cooper and Stephen Crane, but, characteristically, he displayed hostility to Melville, possibly for fear lest he be identified with the latter's "exotic" themes or because, as in the case of Dostoevsky, he sensed a spiritual or artistic kinship with the writer. And, of course, he was a great reader of English literature.

Many suggestions have been made in the past about the influence of English masters on Conrad, notably Fielding, Walter Scott, Thackeray, Coleridge, Byron, Kipling, Dickens, to mention a few. One writer, however, undoubtedly exercised an overwhelming impact on the novelist—William Shakespeare. In several recent studies of "Conrad and Shakespeare,"[55] I have attempted to illustrate the full extent of Conrad's borrowings from Shakespeare's plays, and the presence of several major Shakespearean themes and images in the novelist's text. Only a few observations can be made within the scope of this discussion.

Curiously enough, even this important literary source goes back to Conrad's Polish background. As a child Conrad read not only his father's translations of Vigny's *Chatterton* and parts of Hugo's *Légende des siècles* and other dramas, but also Dickens' *Hard Times* and Shakespeare's *Comedy of Errors* and *Two Gentlemen of Verona*. "I reflect proudly," Conrad wrote in *A Personal Record*, "that I must have read that page of *Two Gentlemen of Verona* tolerably well at the age of eight" (p. 72). Apollo Korzeniowski also translated *Othello*, *As You Like It*, and *Much Ado About Nothing*. "Books are an integral part of one's life," Conrad reminisced, "and my *Shakespearean associations* are with that first year of our bereavement, the last I spent with my father in exile" (*A Personal Record*, pp. 71-73; italics mine).

There is plenty of "Shakespearean talk," as Marlow puts it, in *Lord Jim* (p. 237) and in many other works of Conrad; there are epigrams from the plays on title pages of *Nostromo*, and the volumes *Within The Tides* and *Tales of Unrest*. Like Lord Jim, who took a penny edition of Shakespeare's Works along as he embarked on his last journey (and trial), Conrad too carried the works of the Bard as *his* literary baggage, both on his seaman's voyages and on his arduous journey as an English novelist. The profusion of Shakespearean language is astounding; it is, indeed, one of the components of the literary mortar that binds together the bricks of Conrad's imagination. A few examples will illustrate my case; the following phrases all come from Conrad's fiction:

> Heaven and earth!... throwing off the mortal coil of shore affairs.... this stale and unprofitable world of my discontent.... the undiscovered country.... kings, palaces, temples, gorgeous.... the main hatch was less substantial than dreams are made of.... What's Hecuba to him or he to Hecuba?... His gorge rose.... It is all in being ready.... There are more spells than you commonplace magicians ever dreamed of.... unsubstantial sensation of a dream.... mortally weary, sick at heart.... the crack of doom.... those grey eyes.... windows of the soul.... to bring out of the lightless void the souls of unnumbered generations.... some have greatness thrust upon them....[56]

Such direct echoes from the plays in the Conradian text are augmented by Shakespearean situations, themes, and rhetorical devices: guilt and remorse; life viewed as a dream (which could also have been suggested by Calderón); the darkness of the human soul; the paralysis induced by a "Hamletian" imagination; the question asked by Hamlet, "To be or not to be?"; "the quarrel in a straw / When honour's at the stake"; the problem of a "wounded name"; the supernatural aspects of human existence; the readiness to die; the sickness of heart; the images of darkness coupled with the opposing images of light; ghosts or spectral apparitions; double and triple parallelisms; Shakespearean metaphors (e.g., a book for a face or human personality); the sombre portrayal of passion; the ironically triumphant death of a hero; the symbolic punishment for a moral transgression; the symbolic upheaval of nature accompanying the violence of men's passions; the tragic and painful lesson that must be learned as the fury of the elements is finally allayed—all these loom large in Conrad's vision of the world.

Like Shakespeare, Conrad often views his protagonists as actors playing their parts, with numerous reference to the *globe* wherein they appear. Though Conrad was not successful as a playwright, many of his novels and stories were conceived in terms of the Shakespearean *theatrum mundi*, a universal theatre of men's strange games. Heroes and cowards; fools and wisemen; harlequins and rulers; masters and servants—Conrad's cosmic stage is filled with such figures, speaking in man's manifold moods, emphasizing the disparity between the appearance of reality and reality itself.

Conrad himself was aware of this dramatic approach in his fiction:

One thing that I am certain of is that I have approached the object of my task, *things human*, in a spirit of *piety*.

The earth is a temple where there is going on a *mystery play*, childish and poignant, ridiculous and awful enough, in all conscience. Once in I've tried to behave decently. I have not degraded any quasi-religious sentiment by tears and groans; and if I have been amused or indignant, I've neither grinned nor gnashed my teeth. In other words, I've to write with dignity, not out of regard for myself, but *for the sake of the spectacle, the play* with an obscure beginning and an unfathomable *denouement*.[57]

Conrad's sense of piety notwithstanding, he failed to fulfill his father's dream of making little Konrad into a good Pole. But he lived up to two of Apollo Korzeniowski's own aspirations. Joseph Conrad rather than his father wrote a novel about the Russians; and he echoed his father's eloquent tribute to Shakespeare by permeating his prose with Shakespearean language, cadences and themes:

Shakespeare! it is enough to pronounce the name and at once *a whole world* of alluring visions deludes the mind. Before one's eyes, the man and the poet, his people and its civilization, and his age stand out—enigmatical and alluring . . . the dramatic work he created shines on the new road he opened up all the more brilliantly, as after three hundred years, he still stands *alone, unique*, and *solitary*.[58]

Fifty years after his death, Conrad too stands alone, unique, and solitary—a novelist who refuses to be pigeonholed into a single critical category; a self-taught English writer without a university education who refused offers of academic degrees; a Pole who refused an offer of English knighthood; a Catholic who questioned the tenets of his faith; a traitor to some Polish patriots; in a sense, a traitor to his own quixotic ideal of seafaring adventure by dint of giving it up for the stationary berth of the writer's galley; yet, at the same time an artist faithful to his craft beyond measure and, faithful to the community of all men.

Perhaps the true meaning of Conrad's cosmopolitanism lies in his unique conception of the world that transcends (as the term must needs imply) national boundaries. His "displaced persons" travel toward a final destination of self-cognition, which brings no reward of "material interests," no triumph except the assertion of some ideal values, notably that of fidelity. The protagonists' Shakespearean "I am not what I am," or "I am what I am," invariably underscores the ever-present threat to man's precarious existence. Yet whether Conrad's task was "delightful or not," he has "always approached [his] task *in the spirit of love for mankind.* And [he has] rather taken it seriously."[59]

The whole world, it appears, has taken Conrad seriously. Not only has this Polish poet of exile and the divided human soul conquered

Europe and the North-American continent, he is read and studied in several countries of South America, in the Middle East, and in the Far East. Articles, masters and doctoral dissertations, textbooks, new translations of his work appear with increasing regularity. As Goethe remarked once, "Shakespeare *und kein Ende*," so we now can say "Conrad and no end" to the profusion of critical exegesis, even a computer-assisted concordance to *Heart of Darkness*. This posthumous success is ironic in the true Conradian sense, since, as in Shakespeare's case, it was never anticipated by the author. After twenty-two years of creative effort, Conrad still felt that he "had not been very well understood." He wrote to Sir Sidney Colvin, customarily lapsing into French:

> I have been called a writer of the sea, of the tropics, a descriptive writer, a romantic writer—and also a realist. But as a matter of fact my concern has been with the "ideal" value of things, events, and people. That and nothing else. The humorous, the pathetic, the passionate, the sentimental aspects came in and of themselves *mais . . . en verité c'est les valeurs idéales des faits et gestes humains qui se sont imposés a mon activité artistique.*[60]

His tragic and ironic vision of life is that of a modern, and the world-wide acknowledgment which it has received is a fitting tribute to Conrad's humanism, cogently expressed in his admonition to H. G. Wells: "You love humanity but think they are to be improved. I love humanity but know they are not!"[61]

NOTES

[1]G. Jean-Aubry, *Joseph Conrad: Life and Letters* (Garden City, N.Y.: Doubleday, Page & Co., 1927), II, 272. Letter to John Galsworthy, 11 February 1899. Italics mine.

[2]F. R. Leavis, *The Great Tradition* (New York: A Doubleday Anchor Book, 1951), p. 229.

[3]Helmut Bonheim, "James Joyce: Nation Versus World," *Proceedings of the IVth Congress of the International Comparative Literature Association* (The Hague: Mouton & Co., 1966), p. 466.

[4]Stefan Buszczyński, "A Little Known Poet—His Position Before the Last Uprising, His Exile and Death," 1970, quoted by Czesław Miłosz in "Apollo N. Korzeniowski: Joseph Conrad's Father," *Mosaic*, 6, No. 1 (1973), 138.

[5]Letter to Cunninghame Graham, 8 February 1899, *Life and Letters*, I, 269.

[6]Edward Garnett, ed., *Letters from Conrad* (London: The Nonesuch Press, 1927), p. 212. Italics mine.

[7]Ibid., p. 223. Italics mine.

[8]Joseph Conrad, "A Personal Record," *Joseph Conrad: Complete Works* (Garden City, N.Y.: Doubleday, Page & Co., 1924), p. 121. Italics mine. Unless otherwise indicated, the page numbers referring to the novels and stories of Joseph Conrad are those of the volumes in this edition. The following abbreviations are used: *Notes on Life and Letters* (*NLL*), *Almayer's Folly* (*AL*), *Lord Jim* (*LJ*), *Victory* (*V*), *Heart of Darkness* (*HD*), *Nostromo* (*N*), *Under Western Eyes* (*UWE*).

[9] *Life and Letters*, I, 66-67.

[10] Maria Dąbrowska, "Pożegnanie z Conradem" (A Farewell to Conrad), *Nowa Kultura* (New Culture), No. 21/478 (Warsaw).

[11] *Letters from Conrad*, letter 20 October 1911. Italics mine.

[12] Norman Sherry, *Conrad's Eastern World* (Cambridge: Cambridge Univ. Press, 1966), p. 48.

[13] Jocelyn Baines, *Joseph Conrad: A Critical Biography* (New York: McGraw-Hill Book Company, Inc., 1960), pp. 64-66.

[14] Eloise Knapp Hay, *The Political Novels of Joseph Conrad* (Chicago: Chicago Univ. Press, 1963), p. 167.

[15] *Life and Letters*, I, 226.

[16] Knapp Hay, p. 167.

[17] *Life and Letters*, II, 315. Italics mine.

[18] Ibid., letter to George T. Keating, 14 December 1922, II, 289. Italics mine.

[19] Ibid., pp. 336-37.

[20] Ibid., p. 289.

[21] Joseph Conrad, *Last Essays* (Garden City, N.Y.: Doubleday, Page & Co., 1926), p. 12.

[22] *Life and Letters*, II, 62. Italics mine. The reference is to Edward Garnett and to Conrad's article "The Censor of the Plays" (in *Notes on Life and Letters*).

[23] Ibid., p. 65. Italics mine.

[24] Another similar device appears in *Nostromo*, where Conrad describes " . . . a stout, loud-voiced lady of French extraction, the daughter, she said, of an officer of high rank (*officier supérieur de l'armée*) . . . " (p. 55). Her use of French phrases also produces a comic effect.

[25] For further discussion see Adam Gillon, *The Eternal Solitary: A Study of Joseph Conrad* (New York: Bookman Associates, Twayne Publishers, 1966) and my "Betrayal and Redemption in Joseph Conrad," *The Polish Review*, 5 (Spring 1960), 18-35.

[26] Marian Dąbrowski, "Rozmowa z J. Conradem" (A Conversation with J. Conrad), *Tygodnik Illustrowany* (The Illustrated Weekly), Warsaw, 18 April 1914, p. 308. Italics mine.

[27] *The Polish Review*, 9, No. 4 (1964).

[28] Norman Sherry, *Conrad's Western World* (Cambridge: Cambridge Univ. Press, 1971), pp. 158-61. I am indebted to Professor Sherry for this analogy.

[29] *Life and Letters*, II, 64.

[30] Adam Gillon, "Polish and Russian Literary Elements in Joseph Conrad," *Proceedings of the VIth Congress of the International Comparative Literature Association* (Belgrade: Université de Belgrade and Swets & Zeitlinger, Amsterdam, 1969), pp. 685-94.

[31] *Life and Letters*, II, 66-67. Letter to Edward Garnett.

[32] Richard Curle, *The Last Twelve Years of Joseph Conrad* (London: Sampson Low, Marston & Co., 1928), p. 120.

[33] *Life and Letters*, II, 66-67.

[34] Baines, pp. 370-72.

[35] Walter F. Wright, ed., *Joseph Conrad on Fiction* (Lincoln: University of Nebraska Press, 1964), p. 31.

[36] Garnett, letter of 2 September 1921, p. 309. Italics mine.

[37] Wright, p. 35. Letter to Edward Garnett, 27 May 1912.

[38] *Life and Letters*, II, 298-99. Italics mine.

[39] Jan Lechoń, a noted Polish poet (who, not unlike Jim, jumped to his death in New York in 1956), told me this personally. The charge of desertion was made by J. N. Miller in "*Słów kilka o Josephie Conradzie i o godności narodowej tu i tam*" (A few Words about Joseph Conrad and about National Dignity Here and There), *Kurier Polski* (The Polish Messenger), No. 232 (1924). See also Witr (W. Zechenter), in "Pamięci Conrada" (To the Memory of Conrad), *Głos Narodu* (The Voice of the People), No. 188 (1924); and, among others, the view of J. Bandrowski in the same article. See also Stefan Żeromski's own "Joseph Conrad," *Wiadomości Literackie* (Literary News), No. 33 (Warsaw, 1924).

[40] Adam Gillon and Ludwik Krzyżanowski, eds., *Introduction to Modern Polish Literature* (New York: Twayne Publishers, 1964; London: Rapp & Whiting, 1966), pp. 431-32. Italics mine.

[41] Vladimir Nabokov, *Speak Memory: An Autobiography Revisited* (New York: Putnam, 1974).

[42] "I would ask you at once to eliminate the word aristocracy, when you see the proof. The name has never been illustrated by a senatorial dignity, which was the only basis of Polish aristocracy. The Equestrian Order is more the thing. Land-tilling gentry is the most precise approach to a definition of my modest origin." Letter to John Galsworthy, 29 October 1907, *Life and Letters*, II, 63-64. Italics mine.

[43] Ibid., II, 296. Italics mine. Letter to Ernst Bendz, 7 March 1923.

[44] Sherry, *Conrad's Eastern World* and *Conrad's Western World.*

[45] See Gillon, *The Eternal Solitary*; Gillon, "Polish Literary Motifs in Joseph Conrad," *The Slavic and East European Journal*, 10 (Winter 1966), 424-39; Gillon, "Conrad in Poland," *Joseph Conrad Centennial Essays* (New York: Polish Institute of Arts and Sciences, 1960), 145-58; and Gillon, "Polish and Russian Literary Elements in Joseph Conrad."

[46] Stefan Zabierowski, *Conrad w Polsce. Wybrane Problemy Recepcji Krytycznej w Latach 1896-1969* (Conrad in Poland. Selected Problems of Critical Reception in the Years 1896-1969), (Gdańsk: Wydawnictwo Morskie, 1971).

[47] Ibid., p. 106.

[48] Ibid.

[49] Milan Sufflay, "O Josephu Conradu. Polska i ruska umjetnicka krv" (On Joseph Conrad, Polish and Russian Artistic Blood), *Obzor*, LXVII:341 (Zagreb, 1926), 3.

[50] Ludwig Wollnick, "Joseph Conrad. En kritisk studie" (Joseph Conrad. A Critical Study), *Edda*, 34 (Oslo, 1934), 183-218, 307-26.

[51] Mariano Latone, "José Conrad," *Atenea*, Santiago de Chile, 30 September 1925, II, 161-72.

[52] Edmond Jaloux, "Joseph Conrad et le roman d'aventure anglais," *Nouvelle Revue Française*, 12 (December 1924), 713-19.

[53] J. Kessel, "Conrad Slave," *Nouvelle Revue Française*, 12 (December 1924), 72-123.

[54] Leonie Villard, "Joseph Conrad et les Mémorialistes," *Revue Anglo-Américaine*, 3 (April 1926), 313-21.

[55] Adam Gillon, "Conrad and Shakespeare; Part One," *Conradiana*, 1 (Summer 1968), 19-25; "Part Two," ibid., 1 (Fall 1968), 15-22; "Part Three," ibid., 1 (Summer 1969), 7-27; "Part Four," ibid., scheduled to appear in a forthcoming issue in 1974 or 1975.

[56] Ibid.

[57] *Life and Letters*, II, 83. Letter to Arthur Symons, 29 August 1908. Italics mine.

[58] Gustav Morf, *The Polish Heritage of Joseph Conrad* (London: Sampson Low, Marston; New York: Smith, 1930), pp. 34-35. Italics mine.

[59] *Life and Letters*, II, 73. Letter to Arthur Symons, August 1908. Italics mine.

[60] Ibid., p. 185. Letter to Sir Sidney Colvin, 18 March 1916.

[61] Hugh Walpole, Journal for 23 January 1918. Quoted by F. R. Karl in "Conrad, Wells, and the Two Voices," *Publications of the Modern Language Association of America*, 88, No. 5 (1973), Notes, 1065.

Conrad, Graham Greene, and Film

Bruce Harkness

ABSTRACT

Joseph Conrad's novels are intensely individualistic. His use of the time shift has its classic illustration in Jim of that novel—ethical questions are forced into the impact of the novel through manipulation of the time sequence. The reader's suspense and the resolution of it do not concern the end of action but the essence of character. How can a good man commit this act; and, furthermore, how can the narrator continue to insist that he is good—"one of us"? After this issue is resolved, Conradian necessities require that Jim relate himself to the total society. What in the abstract the reader would define as an individual problem becomes one of relationship to the total community: thus the famous "solidarity" of Conrad criticism and of his own theory. This progression is apparent in novel after novel; for example, Razumov publicly confesses to the terrorists, whereas it might first have appeared that the confession to Natalia is sufficient. Conrad would have agreed with those anthropologists and social psychologists who maintain that ultimately individual man depends upon community for self-definition. Movies cannot follow this progression; and since films of Conrad's fiction must work on both levels successfully, they have consequently failed. The problem doesn't exist in Graham Greene. Clearly Greene learned from Conrad the technique of the narrator and the technique of the time shift. But in a paradoxical sense Graham Greene rejects the outer society which, for all his pessimism, Joseph Conrad ultimately accepted. Greene's and Hitchcock's comments on the latter's version of *The Secret Agent* (entitled *Sabotage*, 1936) indicate that the movie, while perhaps of some artistic merit, is certainly not faithful to Conrad. (BH)

I begin my observations with a question. And perhaps I shall end there. It has been observed that the time shift in *The Secret Agent* produced a fictional construction virtually impossible for Conrad to dramatize on the realistic stage of his day.[1] But what of film? Conrad's kinds of time shifts have become standard in the movies and were well known to directors and movie audiences long before any of Conrad was filmed. We see these time shifts—if we consider them as technique only—everyday on television or in the movies.

Why then do Conrad's fictions make such rotten movies? As I have implied, they should have been "naturals." Paul Kirschner said it well many years ago: "Conrad's personal techniques can be used by the film to treat his material, [and] it must be added that the material itself is suited uniquely to the film. His novels seem driven toward their climaxes by accelerating engines of suspense, but with no regard for the economies of space and time demanded by the theater."[2]

Yet I would insist that the adaptations of Conrad's novels are in fact bad. Kirschner's statement is hypothetical. Directors should have found the material uniquely suited, but did not. Why? I posit not the time shift but a different *shift* as the cause.

Conrad's use of the time shift has its classic illustration in Jim of that novel—ethical questions are forced into the impact of the novel through manipulation of the time sequence. The reader's suspense and the resolution of it do not concern the end of action but the essence of character. How can a good man commit this act; and, furthermore, how can the narrator continue to insist that he is good—"one of us"? After this issue is resolved, there is another kind of shift. Conradian necessities require that Jim relate himself to the total society. What in the abstract the reader would define as an individual problem becomes one of relationship to the total community: thus the famous "solidarity" of Conrad criticism and of his own theory. The progression is apparent in novel after novel; for example, Razumov publicly confesses to the terrorists, whereas it might first have appeared that the confession to Natalia is sufficient. Conrad would have agreed with those anthropologists and social psychologists who maintain that ultimately individual man depends upon community for self-definition.

If one were to accept for the moment this theory that Conrad's novels shift focus (in meaning and action) from the internal and individualistic—if one accepts this theory—is *that* disjunction the reason his novels make poor films? On the other hand, Graham Greene's novels stay on one plane or the other and make excellent films.

I am trying, thus, to look ever so slightly into the Bluestone kind of cliché that the best novels make poor movies. Can we look beneath this? What is the reason behind the cliché?

To the degree that the dictum is true, what explains it? To some literary critics it is based almost solely on the theory of greater character development. Movies, it is felt, consist almost entirely of action, whereas the great novels consist of "deep" characters. Obviously, there is no full truth in this theory, for both drama and some few films demonstrate that there is no intrinsic conflict between character development and non-novelistic forms. Graham Greene's work itself disproves the theory. Traditionally one distinguishes between the novels and the entertainments on the basis of how fully characters are developed; but both film extraordinarily well.

Let me pause now to confess that I'm rather an old-fashioned kind of critic. "Book into film" is my approach, not a thirty-page semiotic analysis (complete with charts and diagrams) of the gags of Buster Keaton. I can't give the kind of talk which the Professor of Film Theory would mutteringly approve: "Sound, Sound," while the students are bored to sleep. Keaton and Harold Lloyd are funny; that's enough for me.

To recapitulate somewhat, I will say that Conrad's novels seem to be highly individualistic. Their central plot device was well identified years ago by M. D. Zabel—the test of the individual. Sooner or later and mainly unawares, the test is sprung—it may be as purely physical as a Typhoon, but more likely it is also psychological and moral. The interest of the fiction lies in the action and reaction of the central character to the test: will the Captain be true to his inner ideal.

Thus, most often the backdrop of the action serves to highlight the tension of the central character—a novel being simply *character in action* as Conrad called it somewhere. Yet the twist or paradox is that while the problem *seems* to be individual, at some point Conrad always raises it to the social. There is always a shift. It is not enough for Razumov to confess to Natalia. He must also make a public confession.

This change of direction, so to speak, has long been a source of critical difficulty. Very often it contains within it Conrad's "affirmation"—and his inventiveness being limited, the fictive elements of the affirmation never seem to be as expressive as those of the test. The test, and almost universal failure, of the character—in these elements are his genius. Conrad's subsequent relation of the character and the inner tension of the test to the broader society is so suspect that certain critics go so far as to deny it exists. The ending of *Victory* is the famous example, for the victory of Lena over the disillusionment of Heyst is quite unbelievable to many.

Yet this recovery of Heyst is part of Conrad's vision. Monygham is tortured in *Nostromo*, tested, destroyed; but he must relate himself to society as epitomized in his ideal of Mrs. Gould. It is Charles Gould's concept of Honor which Conrad is criticizing rather than Monygham's endurance.[3] The same vision is in *Lord Jim*. Jim must make his achievements in Patusan. Marlow in "Heart of Darkness" must return to Europe.

Without subscribing fully to any theory of objective correlatives, perhaps I can make my point thus. All the correlatives have flowed, one might say, in the direction of an interior conflict and those of the exterior resolution are poorly chosen. *And this element may account for the relatively poor movies which have been made of Conrad's works.*

On the other hand, one would tend to say that Greene's novels are those which seem to stress the social more than do Conrad's. *England Made Me, It's A Battlefield, The Power and the Glory* are examples. Yet looking beneath the appearance, I judge the meaning of the stories to be interior and to remain there. But they are static. Although *The Heart of the Matter* gives plenty of colorful material for the camera to work with, the meaning of the novel deals with Scobie's pity, betrayal, love, and finally relation to God. It is all inward. These novels, admittedly Conradian, make better movies because they stay on the one plane.

Even in the entertainments, where there is little or no character *change*, the point holds. I don't want to bog down in a critical argument over whether Greene's plots are internal to the characters or external. Whatever one's critical judgment on this issue may be, my point just now is that in Graham Greene, the emphasis is *either/or*: in Conrad it is both. Yet while the shift in Conrad gives rise, perhaps, to critical flaws in the novels and in the stories, this shift is *radically* harmful to the film versions.

Here I judge it is impossible to tell whether the fault is essential to the genres or merely a defect in the work of those who adapted the fiction to the film version. I lean toward the former theory, reasoning as follows.

If the fault lay in the adaptors, then perhaps Conrad would be like Henry James, a writer of great novelistic power unable for one reason or another to write well for the stage. But just as Henry James could be well adapted for the stage or for movies (*The Heiress* or *The Turn of the Screw*), perhaps Conrad has simply been unlucky in those who have set to work on his novels. Alas, facts destroy the hypothesis. Who could ask for a better adaptor for story consultant than André Gide? Yet my memory of *Razumov* is one of enormous disappointment. The producer, director, the all-star cast of the latest movie version of *Lord Jim* should have made it a classic of our time. Yet it is dreadful.

I wish to take Hitchcock's version of *The Secret Agent* as my primary example, in part because Graham Greene reviewed it and liked it as Hitchcock if not as Conrad. Unfortunately, it would be a much better example for me, if only I had seen it!

This note does lead me to comment on one aspect of film criticism. What is the text one studies? I have to comment on Hitchcock's movie without having seen it, and yet in a way the film critic has the best textual position. The worst would be that of the drama critic, for what is the text? By one theory, at any rate, the play is reborn at each production and is different each night. The film, on the other hand, is absolute. It is done. It is in the can. With the novel, the position is somewhat intermediate. When textual editors are finished, the work stands absolute, perfected, to be read from the page. In that sense it is a little like the film, which also is finished except for one or two variants—such as edited for television or a nude scene allowed by the censors of one country and not by those of another. There are relatively few of these, and those few are well enough known. More precisely the "master print" of the film pre-exists, and variants flow from it.

But on the other hand, sometimes the other inherent difficulty of film criticism develops—one can't get movies from the distributors, and must base criticism on faulty memories, either one's own or those of other critics. (A shocking illustration will be made later on in this talk.)

This movie was made in 1936, and has virtually disappeared. Why? I hypothesize that it is very poor. The collaboration between Hitchcock and Conrad, again, hypothetically should have been perfect. As a critic has recently said of Hitchcock and Pinter there is a strong similarity; and the point fits the author of *The Secret Agent* even better: "Each in his own way is a master at exploring characters in a commonplace situation which gradually proves a deadly trap."[4]

The movie was updated to the mid-1930's and, as one might expect, does the murder scene very well indeed. Verloc is the manager of the local Bijou and Winnie gets news of her brother's death while she is in the theater. A Silly Symphony is playing—"Who killed Cock Robin?" In spite of herself she giggles.

Later, "as she prepares her husband's dinner, she looks first at the carving-knife, then at [Adolf's] back. After a few moments' hesitation during which he seems to be imploring her to get it over with, she kills him. The scene is played without dialogue—to Miss [Sylvia] Sidney's consternation; this was to be her big moment. Hitchcock persuaded her to play it his way and it was one of the most effective scenes of her career."[5] Hitchcock's own comments on the scene are quite different, though they do emphasize the quite un-Conradian acceptance of his death by Verloc, while M. Truffaut's comments do mention the Conradian likeness between Winnie and Stevie. Their description also confirms Kirschner's belief that the cutting from one person to another, to the wall, to the knife, is essentially filmic in Conrad's own version. But while the technique is similar, the ends pursued and the meaning evolved (especially in Conrad's Verloc's abortive plans to jump up, save himself, by dashing behind the table) are entirely different.

Truffaut said in the interview: " 'Obviously the finest scene . . . is the meal, toward the end of the film, after the bomb explosion which killed the boy, when Sylvia Sidney makes up her mind to kill Oscar Homolka. It has many little details which are references to the dead child and at the end, when she stabs her husband it is less murder than suicide. Oscar Homolka lets Sylvia Sidney kill him, and at the very time that she is stabbing him, she is uttering soft plaintive cries— that's admirable.' " Hitchcock responded:

> That was the whole problem; the sympathy of the audience had to be with Sylvia Sidney, Verloc's death had to be accidental, and therefore it was essential for the audience to identify with Sylvia Sidney. In that situation, we don't expect the audience to be afraid but to want badly to be killers; that is more difficult. This is how I went about it.
>
> When Sylvia Sidney brings the plate of vegetables to the table, she is really obsessed by the knife, as if her hand were going to grab it, independently of her will. The camera focusses on her hand, then her eyes, then her hand again and once more her eyes, to the point when her gaze suddenly realises what the knife means. At that moment, I put in a perfectly ordinary shot of Verloc eating his supper, absent-minded as ever. Then I return to her hand and the knife.
>
> The bad way would have been to expect Sylvia Sidney to convey all that was going through her mind by the expressions on her face, but I dislike that. In real life, people do not have all their feelings visible on their face; I am a director and I try to expose to the audience by purely cinematic means this woman's state of mind.
>
> Now the camera is on Verloc, then it goes to the knife and then back to Verloc, to his face. Suddenly you realise that he has noticed the knife and knows what it means. Suspense has been created between the two characters and there between them lies the knife.
>
> Now, thanks to the camera, the audience participates in this scene and, above all, the camera must not suddenly become distant and objective, for fear of destroying the emotion which has been created. Verloc gets up and walks around the table, but in so doing, he walks directly towards the camera in such a way that those in the cinema feel they must draw back

to make room for him. If the scene works, the spectator must instinctively draw back into his seat to let Verloc pass in front of him; once Verloc has passed in front of us, the camera pans again on to Sylvia Sidney and to the knife, the focal point. And then the scene continues, as you know, until the murder.

The first task is to create emotion and the second, to preserve it.[6]

It is interesting to note the way Hitchcock treated the bombing itself, in view of the comments yesterday during the question and answer period on Jeffrey Smitten's paper. The criticism was made somewhat along these lines. Having set Stevie loose with a bomb to walk through the city, Conrad is obliged to develop "the Big Scene." Conrad's having the bombing offstage constitutes a violation of the well-made naturalistic novel. What does Hitchcock do?

In a remarkable sequence there is "the protracted journey of Mrs. Verloc's young brother through London, unwittingly carrying a bomb under his arm to be left at Piccadilly Circus tube station. Delays on the way—he gets involved with a salesman demonstrator, pauses to watch the Lord Mayor's Show go by—increase the suspense as the time for the bomb to explode approaches. He is on a bus when it happens and all the passengers are killed. Hitchcock's view of this sequence is that it was one of his biggest errors of judgment—after the suspense build-up the explosion is anti-climatic. It is like letting the buzz-saw kill the girl strapped to the log—something that is never done in the cinema."[7]

The above observation certainly implies that Hitchcock fell into the cinematic trap of showing something simply because it can be shown; since one doesn't have the offstage of a play, one tends to show too much.

Indeed, the whole suspense in the Hitchcock version is backward. It is the keenest feeling of suspense in the audience since they know of the time bomb, and the boy believes it an ordinary package. But that suspense is backward from that of the novel. In Conrad's *Secret Agent*, we know the bomb has exploded and that Stevie was killed. Then we read all the scenes leading up to the bombing, and see Winnie's crazed devotion and her secret bargain with Verloc. Our suspense creates of her the heroine and is a kind of moral suspense—what will she do when the truth strikes home at her. We see it circling ever closer, what will she do?

Suffice it for the moment to say that I must assume the film to be poor. Graham Greene was more than charitable in his review. He is no great fan of Hitchcock, seeing him as merely clever: "His films consist of a series of small 'amusing' melodramatic situations: the murderer's button dropped on the baccarat board; the strangled organist's hands prolonging the notes in the empty church; the fugitives hiding in the bell-tower when the bell begins to swing. Very perfunctorily he builds up to these tricky situations (paying no attention on the way to inconsistencies, loose ends, psychological absurdities) and then drops them: they mean nothing: they lead to nothing."[8]

But in *Sabotage*, Greene felt, Hitchcock "for the first time . . . has really 'come off.' " Greene observes:

> *Sabotage* is not, of course, Conrad's *Secret Agent*. That dark drab passionate tale of Edwardian London could never find a place in the popular cinema. . . . This melodrama is convincingly realistic, perhaps because Mr. Hitchcock has left the screenplay to other hands.
>
> The story retains some of the ruthlessness of the original. Mr. Verloc, no longer an *agent provocateur* but a straightforward destructive agent of a foreign Power, keeps a tiny independent cinema in the East End, and the film opens with his secret return home one night during a sudden blackout. . . . Mr. Verloc has succeeded in getting sand into the Battersea generators, but his employers are dissatisfied: he is told to lay a bomb in the cloakroom at Piccadilly Circus on Lord Mayor's Day. Mr. Verloc's friends fail him, and he is himself closely watched by the police, and he has to entrust the bomb to his wife's small brother, who, delayed by the procession, is blown to fragments with a busload of people. Mrs. Verloc, after hearing the news, passes through the little cinema hall to her living-room. A children's matinee is in progress and Walt Disney's *Cock Robin* is on the screen. She is pursued by the children's laughter and the diminishing repetitions of the song, "Who killed Cock Robin? Who killed Cock Robin?" This ingenious and pathetic twist is stamped as Mr. Hitchcock's own, but unlike so many of his ideas in the past it is an integral part of the story: it leads on to the admirably directed scene when Mrs. Verloc, serving dinner to her husband, finds herself against her own will continually picking up the carving-knife—to serve the potatoes, to scoop up the cabbage, to kill Mr. Verloc. The happy ending of course, has to be contrived: Mr. Verloc's body is plausibly disposed of: a young detective is there to marry her: but this is all managed with the minimum of offense.[9]

This is typical Graham Greene film criticism. Essentially he liked the cinematic or the filmic, much preferring cheap detective stories such as the Charlie Chan series to the flamboyant and pretentious Art film or the Cecil B. De Mille extravaganza. He believed that a strong story line was essential, and could not be compensated for with strong acting or perfect direction. While he disliked heartily the "money men" controlling the film industry, there was a strong realistic element in his criticism which knew that films had to appeal to millions and millions of viewers. Hence contrived happy endings were acceptable provided a director somehow held down the offense, perhaps by indicating he didn't really believe in this element of the movie.

But note that at least in this review Graham Greene is not setting a double standard, if I may pun; he wishes simply a good movie.

I want a good movie that is Conradian. And despite Graham Greene, I wonder if, aside from a scene or two, this is really a good movie.

Variously entitled, *Sabotage* in England, *A Woman Alone* in the United States, and perhaps also *I Married A Murderer* it seems impossible to find. Made in 1936, it is only two years older than *Razumov* and ought to be available from distributors. I presume its quality must be poor.

On the other hand, while Greene's films may not always be as good as his fiction, some are magnificent—"The Basement Room" for example. And all are well above the tolerable.

Both writers *should* have been the sources of good film. More than that, the reasons are similar. I was struck by their likeness again, at this year's Modern Language Association meeting. The Seminar on Film there was on Graham Greene and more than one of the papers, but especially those of Professors Welsh and Barrett, likened once more the authorial eye of Greene to the moving camera of film-making. Greene's angle of vision is that of the director.

What struck me most was the remarkable similarity of tone to that used in Paul Kirschner's 1957 article on "Conrad and the Film." The parallel is especially striking in Kirschner's discussion of the murder scene in *The Secret Agent*.

Conrad *should* have been the source of great movies. Why not? Let us look at "Heart of Darkness" and *The Secret Agent* for an answer and then return to "The Third Man" and "The Secret Sharer"—both dealing with the double character in their own ways.

I must break off here a moment to give as briefly as I can my interpretation of "Heart of Darkness" and *The Secret Agent*, especially their endings. I interpret them as much darker, much more bitter, and Conrad himself as much more pessimistic than do, for example, Norman Sherry and Zdzisław Najder.

Sherry, for example, believes that we don't quite know, in the final sense, what Conrad would have said of Lord Jim's father, the safe and secure Parson from the countryside of England.[10] I think that the framework of "Heart of Darkness" tells us very precisely—and I suspect Sherry agrees with me, had he time for elaboration.

"This also has been one of the dark places of the earth." The Thames. London. London now. London at the time of the Romans. Lubbock now. Given the proper conditions, each and every man will fail the test, surrender to the fascination of the abomination which is chaos and mud and old night.

Certainly a dedication to the concept of Honor, *pace* Zdzisław Najder, would not have saved the Parson any more than it saves

Charles Gould or the characters in *The Duel.* I obviously interpret Conrad as guying the British Code with its stiff upper lip. I also interpret Conrad as "putting down" the Glorious concept of Honor.

But to return to "Heart of Darkness." It is clearly Marlow's story and, as I have said, has its path plotted in his inwardness. And one's interpretation of the Lie at the end of the story is quite otherwise. Marlow is identified with Kurtz in several different ways in the story. Kurtz is the heart of darkness and the end of Marlow's voyage, which is also to the center of the universe. First Kurtz is "equated" with the heart of Africa and darkness and the universe; then Marlow is equated with Kurtz: He too is a voice only,[11] one who confuses the beating of his own heart with that of the conventional symbol of the jungle, the native drum (p. 58). Eventually he, like the savages, worships Kurtz and in this act their intimacy is laid.

The course of the meaning of the story is to strip away all illusions and all those cloaks of time that our civilization covers us with. The direction of the journey is eventually to Kurtz, the God of evil and savagery. Starting with imperialism, all civilization is a sham and fraud, says the story.

My reading is quite literal at this point. Even the Idea behind civilization does not redeem. Principles won't do. When one gets to the heart of the universe, it is completely evil. Kurtz sees the ultimate truth: it is not that man has an evil side. It is that in his essence Kurtz is evil. Marlow is evil. All men are evil. And finally that evil is the essence of the universe. For E. M. Forster in *A Passage to India* the rock of the cave may be neither good nor evil, but chaotic—a distortion and ambiguity which renders all the accents whether of love or of evil to the dull sound of "boum" or "ou-boum." But for Conrad the very rock itself is evil.

Kurtz's vision is entire. His stare "could not see the flame of the candle, but was wide enough to embrace the whole universe, piercing enough to penetrate all the hearts that beat in the darkness." Evil is all that there is. Suddenly comes the final twist, the reversal. Kurtz's soul had looked within itself and gone mad, yes; the evil is within, not just in the wilderness. Yet how could Kurtz still struggle with himself—" 'I saw the inconceivable mystery of a soul that knew no restraint, no faith, and no fear, yet struggling blindly with itself' " (p. 59).

For the mystery is not that man is evil, shocking as that might have been to Conrad's Victorian audience; but that somewhere beyond this essential evil, Man is good—shocking as that might be to Conrad's present-day audience. Kurtz had summed up the whole universe, had penetrated "all the hearts that beat in the darkness" and had summed them up in his final cry—"The Horror! The Horror!" But it is significant that Marlow swears this is *an affirmation*. It was " 'a moral victory paid for by innumerable defeats, by abominable terrors, by abominable satisfactions. But it was a victory!' " (p. 63).

The source of this affirmation remains a mystery. If the whole course of the story until its last half dozen pages (of 69) has been to expose the phoniness of civilization and to condemn the universe and man's heart through all time and space as evil, what is the ground of Kurtz's criticism? If I understand the terms of Ivo Vidan's essay, the source of Kurtz's authenticity is mysterious.

Logically, his struggle cannot happen. Logically, his affirmation could not be. If Kurtz is entirely evil, he cannot judge himself as The Horror. Yet he does. It is rather like an opposite paradox, as has been said elsewhere, of the Garden of Eden. Some interpreters hold that Adam, being all good, could not be tempted, that temptation only makes sense from the fallen point of view. So Kurtz, being all evil, could not condemn himself. Yet if we allow this mystery, all else makes sense. What makes even harder sense, perhaps, is Marlow's action thereafter. He remains loyal to Kurtz and to Kurtz's victory.

Having seen that Kurtz, that all men, that he himself, are evil, having seen that society, and European civilization most of all, is evil, a charade, he returns to that society. Marlow's response, having seen the truth, is to live as if it were not so. He lies for Kurtz. He soothes the Intended. He becomes a hypocrite.

This is the very rottenness of the Manager. Such is evil which Marlow sees through even at the start of the story. Obviously *hypocrisy* cannot be the message of the fiction, and it is not.

The difference between the manager and the others is that Marlow knows the truth of man's evil and cautiously, carefully, committedly, acts otherwise. He knows the streets of Brussels could crack open above the abyss, but lies to Kurtz's betrothed. His first step toward a return to society is the lie, denying the reality of the darkness.

"Deliberate hypocrisy," may be a weak term to express the concept, but I am not sure I can find a better phrase. The problem, of course, is that through time, of which we are all Playthings, one begins to believe the lie if one lives it. The tension of walking those streets as if they were safe, as if Kurtz's last words were not echoing in the darkness, is too great. A man like Marlow begins to believe the lie, gradually to endanger himself and slip over into unconscious acceptance of falsehood—to become like his aunt.

This is, I believe, the final message of the framework of the story. That framework not only says that the story is timeless and universal and that the heart of darkness is to be found in Roman Britain as well as Africa and in today's London, and today's Lubbock. The message of the framework is of Marlow's second solution.

As Stein says in *Lord Jim*, there is no cure for your humanity short of death: " 'One thing alone can us from being ourselves cure!' The finger came down on the desk with a smart rap. The case which he had made to look so simple before became if possible still simpler— and altogether hopeless. . . . 'Yes,' said I, 'strictly speaking, the question is not how to get cured, but how to live.' . . . 'How to be!' "[12]

One cannot change one's ultimate nature. How is Marlow in "Heart of Darkness" to be, knowing the truth? How? Lie to society and one's self and pretend it is good. How to prevent one's self from gradually coming to believe this lie? Periodically to re-immerse one's self in the Heart of Darkness by retelling the story. The trick is to realize the moment that one is slipping, beginning to accept the phony, and prevent that slip by telling the truth once more. The final circling round of "Heart of Darkness" is Conrad's statement of the practical efficacy of the Writer's Art. Like Marlow, the artist has a voice too, and his is "the speech that cannot be silenced."

How could this be filmed? The only version I know of was on television. It did well enough with Kurtz, reasonably well with Marlow; but it made no attempt to work with the elements of the story when Conrad shifted to the "recovery," to the affirmation, to the re-acceptance of society.

The same course of meaning is observable in *The Secret Agent*. Winnie, like Kurtz, has a final moment which contains a hushed but vibrating note of revolt, and in that an affirmation. I expect it is less generally accepted that Winnie is the protagonist of the novel, though Conrad in describing its genesis says: "At last the story of Winnie Verloc stood out complete from the days of her childhood to the end. . . . *This* book is *that* story." If Verloc were the central character, the story should end with his death as—in effect—the shortened magazine version, the original version, did. Only in Winnie's death is the novel ended.

It is odd how misunderstood her death is. To at least one critic, Conrad robs her of any dignity and tragic stature. She is simply a low woman, in a panic, withdrawing in fear, who hears the stewardess and steward talking "in audible whispers (for she seemed past hearing) of St. Malo and the Consul there, of communicating with her people in England." The suicide to this critic, then, is simply a jump away from the police.

I believe it to be just the opposite. The imagery surrounding Winnie's final moments is remarkably similar to that of Kurtz. She is lying looking into the dark in one of the hooded seats on a cross-channel steamer. "Her eyes were open, but she would not answer anything that was said to her." She finally penetrates to the bottom of the affair and sees there not just the gallows which she had imagined as her punishment for having killed her husband. She also sees "madness and despair," in the words of the bomb-making Professor.

Conrad is very definite. Her suicide is not a meaningless act of fear. It is quite the opposite. Winnie loves life, could not have committed suicide—"You must kill me first," she says to Ossipon—rather than let the police catch her. "I couldn't do it myself—I couldn't, I couldn't —not even for what I am afraid of [the gallows]."

"How could I be such a coward!" she cries. "She lamented aloud her love of life, that life without grace or charm, and almost without decency, but of an exalted faithfulness of purpose, even unto murder. And, as so often happens in the lament of poor humanity rich in suffering but indigent in words, the truth—the very cry of truth—was found in a worn and artificial shape picked up somewhere among the phrases of sham sentiment."

It cannot be, then, that Winnie's motive is fear. Ossipon, the man who deserted her, knows better, and through his thoughts the point is made explicit: "But Comrade Ossipon knew that behind that mask there was struggling against terror and despair a vigour of vitality, a love of life that could resist the furious anguish which drives to murder and the fear, the blind, mad fear of the gallows. He knew. But the stewardess and the chief steward knew nothing, except that when they came back to her in less than five minutes the lady in black was no longer in the hooded seat. She was nowhere. She was gone. It was then five o'clock in the morning, and it was no accident either. An hour afterwards one of the steamer's hands found a wedding ring left lying on the seat. It had stuck to the wood in a bit of wet, and its glitter caught the man's eye. There was a date, 24th June, 1879, engraved inside. '*An impenetrable mystery is destined to hang forever. . . .*'"

Her most deliberate death has a meaning which can be inferred from the deliberate hiding of her wedding band.[13] Finally having looked into life and finding its essence in madness and despair, this ignorant woman cannot like Kurtz condemn it as horrible. She is no universal genius. All she can do is revolt. She rejects Verloc, to whom she was married for seven years, and rebels against life by jumping overboard. She is, in her ignorant way, returning the ticket as does Ivan in *The Brothers Karamazov*. But Conrad has the insentient heroine, who can only act, and that wholly offstage. Her soul rejects a world which is ultimately horrible. At first she sees life in Sunday-supplement terms, and the reward of her acts being the gallows with the drop of fourteen feet. But then she sheds this phoniness and penetrates all, in the darkness, like Kurtz. Kurtz condemns himself and thus is triumphant over the evil. Her silent death ironically reaffirms her humanity. It is as if she saw the truth of the world in madness and despair—and said, if that is the way life is, "I won't play." In a world of madness, her death shines as a tribute to the mystery of affirmation.

If there is only madness and despair, how to be? She refuses to accept that life; she denies it, like Marlow with his Lie. But she has not the voice of a Kurtz or of a Marlow. She is a modern heroine. The heroine of common means—as earlier she "lamented aloud her love of life, that life without grace or charm, and almost without decency, but of an exalted faithfulness of purpose, even unto murder. And, as often happens in the lament of poor humanity rich in suffering but indigent in words, the truth—the very cry of truth—was found in a worn and artificial shape picked up somewhere among the phrases of sham sentiment" (p. 298).

That was her voice before the betrayal by Ossipon. When finally deserted, all she can do is act and not speak. In her deliberateness she rejects Kurtz's universe of evil.

It is a muted affirmation, a mysterious one—but like Kurtz's, a victory over the forces of evil. Her "vibrating note of revolt" is not audible, but like his, affirms.

The affirmation is, in Conrad, always a turning toward society, toward solidarity. The power of the story largely lies in the inner struggle and recognition of truth, but that truth finally turns outward. Razumov lives on in Russia.

Perhaps the point is clearest in "The Secret Sharer." The theme of the story, as we all know, turns on how faithful the Captain will prove to be to his ideal conception of himself. He learns from Leggatt that he too has the murderous instinct for violence within him. He is ultimately the opposite of his ideal. But that vision is not enough for Conrad. The problem is, how to live, having learned that truth? This is the Captain's final problem, Stein's problem posed for Jim. Conrad perhaps never found a good way of dramatizing his solution. Perhaps he could only assert it, as at the end of *The Nigger of the "Narcissus."* There he asserts the solidarity of the crew and that it has wrung out a meaning for itself from life.

Thus there is the obscurity of the hat upon the water at the end of "The Secret Sharer." Critics differ widely on its meaning. I believe it to be the bringing together of the instincts of violence and pity, as Leggatt saves the ship by passing underneath the hat in swimming away. And it permits the Captain to return to the skills of seamanship, to bring his ship round, to rebuild his society on shipboard. For the problem was not just truth to his inner ideal. That inner ideal itself is ultimately dependent upon the solidarity of the crew.

But notice how imperfect the image is when translated to the screen. The film of "The Secret Sharer," with James Mason in the lead role, is, I suspect, the best "translation" of Conrad to the other medium. Yet the fact that this crucial ending is changed has been noticed many times in criticism. We get the image, finally, of two old grizzled Gabby Hayes types, saying to each other, "Yep, that boy certainly can sail a ship!" (In the movie, the ending represents a watering down of even the simpler question than the Captain poses at the beginning about his crew—they had only to be equal to their jobs. A slick pilot!)

The whole problem doesn't arise in Graham Greene, for the drama is carried out at the one level *or* the other. While it appears that the drama of Jim, of Marlow, of Kurtz, of Heyst, of Winnie, is within—in the final twist the conflict and its resolution lies in their relationship to the outer society. While it appears that Scobie's drama is in his relationship to Helen, to his wife, to his servant—what finally matters is solely his relationship to God. Marlow's only significant relationship is first to himself, then to Society.

As an aside one might observe that often in Greene there is the use of a kind of initiate, rather in the Hemingway manner but at a deeper level. A contrast represented, for example, by the Boy in *Brighton Rock* who carries the truth, the knowledge of good and of evil. To him the falsity of Ida is contrasted. Her knowledge is simply of right and wrong. It is as if the Boy were a kind of Marlow who did not have to do anything with Kurtz's knowledge.

In Graham Greene, in short, the inner awareness either does not change, remaining static through the story and novel; or does not have to be related in action to the total society. Hence the ending of "The Third Man" is excellent in the film. Holly and Harry alternate as it were, are sharers in an oblique sense, with (or of) the girl. As was pointed out at the recent Modern Language Association Film Seminar I referred to above, the point is excellently made in Anna's confusing the names, and even Holly doing so at least once. The likeness is also mirrored in the automobile scenes and in Holly's making certain moves identical to those of Harry Lime. (The two men share the same events on several occasions, by a jump in time.)

But Anna understands evil, understands Harry Lime, and finally rejects the pulp-novel world of Martins. The drama is an external one, highlighted by touches of contrast and of sharing alike in the inwardness of the characters; but the knowledge of good and evil remains static: there is no change for Holly nor for Anna. There is no deepening awareness for her, and what slight increase in knowledge there is for him subserves the outer action of the plot. It is the opposite of the fiction of Conrad.

I wish I had the time and space to work through the movie version of *An Outcast of the Islands*. I suspect this is the second best of the movie versions of Conrad; and it is a pleasant critical coincidence, so to speak, that Carol Reed made both *The Third Man* and this movie. But its success comes, I think, from a perhaps deliberate shift of objective correlatives to the external level. For example, as John Gordan once said, instead of a Lingard searching his way through thousands and thousands of silent, tiny waterways, a maze that might have been a symbol of the inward psychological problems stymieing Lingard's growth, the whole success of his seamanship is changed. There are wonderful filmic versions of the bow of the ship shaving rocky coasts in the foam of a breakwater. These details make a good movie, but were not the symbols for the inner tension of Conradian fiction. Similarly, the actress who played Aïssa was magnificently sensuous but scarcely a Conradian character!

Carol Reed's collaboration was at its best with Graham Greene, in *The Third Man*, where the elements of tragedy had been carried another full, downward step into the meanness of modern life. If Greek tragedy chose a hero better than ourselves whose fall is great, the naturalists and Conrad after them extended the range of suffering humanity to a Winnie Verloc. In Graham Greene's *The Third Man*, the lament of "poor humanity rich in suffering but indigent in words" is not even allowed a cry of truth in "the phrases of sham sentiment."

The world is evil but about all that can be done is to walk on by. There is no impenetrable mystery to be summed up as "the horror." Life can be meanly summed by Calloway/Callaghan—"Poor all of us, when you come to think of it."[14]

NOTES

[1]Jeffrey R. Smitten and Adam Gillon agreed on this point during the discussion following Smitten's paper, "Flaubert and the Structure of *The Secret Agent*: A Study in Spatial Form."

[2]Paul Kirschner, "Conrad and the Film," *Quarterly of Film, Radio, and Television*, 11 (Summer 1957), 353.

[3]This point was explored by Irmina P. Pulc in the discussion session following Zdzisław Najder's paper, "Conrad and the Idea of Honor."

[4]Alan Brody, "The Gift of Realism: Hitchcock and Pinter," *Journal of Modern Literature*, 3 (April 1973), 159.

[5]George Perry, *The Films of Alfred Hitchcock* (New York: E. P. Dutton, 1965), p. [56].

[6]F. Truffaut, *Le Cinéma Selon Hitchcock* (Paris: Editions Robert Laffont, 1966), pp. [79]-82. I wish to acknowledge with thanks Professor John R. Kane of the Kent State University, French section, who provided the translation.

[7]Perry, pp. 55 f.

[8]*Graham Greene on Film*, ed. John Russell Taylor (New York: Simon and Shuster, 1972), p. 75.

[9]Ibid., pp. 122-23.

[10]See Norman Sherry's essay in this volume.

[11]Joseph Conrad, "Heart of Darkness," in *Conrad's "Heart of Darkness" and the Critics*, ed. Bruce Harkness (San Francisco: Wadsworth Publishing Co., 1960), p. 31. Other references to "Heart of Darkness" are from this edition and are cited parenthetically in the text.

[12]Joseph Conrad, *Lord Jim* (New York: Doubleday, Page and Co., 1925), p. 212. I am using the Kent Edition, checked against the Heinemann. Unless otherwise noted, all references to Conrad are to this edition and are cited parenthetically in the text.

[13]Joseph Conrad, *The Secret Agent*, p. 309.

[14]Graham Greene, *The Third Man* and *The Fallen Idol* (London: Heinemann, 1958), p. 148.

James Wait as Pivot: Narrative Structure in *The Nigger of the "Narcissus"*

Marion C. Michael

ABSTRACT

Several critical studies have offered valuable insights into Conrad's use of James Wait as the artistic focus of *The Nigger of the "Narcissus."* On the other hand, criticism has either badly represented the matter of the two narrators in *The Nigger* or have chosen completely to ignore it. Important to the theme of this novel is Conrad's conception of Wait as both victim and exploiter of a real illness. When Wait joins the "Narcissus," he is a dying man. Fearing to die, however, he convinces himself that his real illness is pretense, nothing more, by which he can escape his duties aboard ship. Thus, ironically and paradoxically Wait makes his imminent death an accomplice in what becomes a complex act of self-deception. It is primarily in terms of this self-deception that one achieves an understanding of Conrad's statement that Wait is "merely the centre of the ship's collective psychology and the pivot of the action." Wait comes to own a complex and varying monopoly of the emotions of the crew of the "Narcissus." Their feelings about Wait constantly shift—one way, then another. Their failure to understand the truth of Wait's dilemma leads to the mutiny. And it is only after the mutiny is put down that they realize that Wait is in fact dying. The narrative shifts in *The Nigger of the "Narcissus"* have been variously described as "flaws" or "inconsistencies." However, as attested to by the evidence of authorial revisions, the alternations between the crewman narrator, with his limited knowledge, and the omniscient narrator, with his full knowledge, provides the aesthetic distance from which the reader views events and interpretation of events ironically. Conrad strove deliberately to authenticate his narrative simultaneously on two levels of meaning. (MCM)

In an obvious moment of pique, Conrad in 1902 declared to William Blackwood that fiction "is not the haphazard business of a mere temperament. There is in it as much intelligent action guided by a deliberate view of the effect to be attained as in any business enterprise."[1] Conrad then went on to protest:

I am long in my development. What of that? Is not Thackeray's penny worth of mediocre fact drowned in an ocean of twaddle? And yet he lives. And Sir Walter, himself, was not the writer of concise anecdotes I fancy. And G. Elliot [sic]—is she as swift as the present public (incapable of fixing its attention for five consecutive minutes) requires us to be at the cost of all honesty, of all truth, and even the most elementary conception of art? But these are great names. I don't compare myself with them. I am *modern*, and I would rather recall Wagner the musician and Rodin the Sculptor who both had to starve a little in their day—and Whistler the painter who made Ruskin the critic foam at the mouth with scorn and indignation. They too have arrived. They had to suffer for being 'new.' And I too hope to find my place in the rear of my betters. But still—my place.[2]

Similar assertions about the aims of art abound in other letters and in Conrad's prefaces to individual works. Surely, it is sometimes difficult to separate the chaff from the grain in Conrad's statements about fiction. However, while admitting to the good common sense of D. H. Lawrence's precaution that a reader must trust the tale, not the teller, I obviously proceed in this discussion under the assumption that Conrad's statements about art offer a more illuminating insight into his aims and achievements than is generally recognized. Taken together, these statements, made throughout Conrad's life, show an abiding concern with the potentials of narrative technique in the delineation of the human dilemma. This is a concern that becomes, perhaps, the primary ethic of Conrad's fiction, but that emerges, certainly, as its singlemost distinguishing characteristic. In fact, as revealed in the fiction itself, it is this concern, expressed in Conrad's words as "a deliberate view of the effect to be attained," that leads us as close as anything else to understanding why he refused to compare himself with Thackeray, Scott, Eliot and protested "I am modern." Though other Conrad novels would surely serve, an analysis of the structure of *The Nigger of the "Narcissus,"* published in 1897, early in his career, provides an immediate test of Conrad's claim.

Before I proceed directly to the subject of my discussion, the narrative structure of *The Nigger of the "Narcissus,"* I ask your patience with one brief aside. Much of the evidence which has been brought to bear upon the arguments that are to follow is drawn from an examination of the variant states, both pre-publication and published, that delineate the history of the development of the text of *The Nigger of the "Narcissus"* and provide the basis upon which someday an authoritative edition of the novel will be published. In fact, following the lead of John Gordan, who in 1940 in *Joseph Conrad: the Making of a Novelist,* first examined the relationship of the holograph manuscript of the *Nigger* to several of its published states, Kenneth Davis and Donald Rude of Texas Tech University are well along in their work to produce such an authoritative edition. Their efforts, like the efforts of all textual critics, reveal that a study of the variant states in the growth of a novel bring one as close to an understanding of its aesthetics as any other critical discipline. Unfortunately, however, the age of enlightened tolerance toward the textual critic has not fully arrived. He is still too often denounced as a "comma counter," or as one whose critical vocabulary in his response to literature is limited to a discussion of accidentals. Such an attitude is wrong. If I may be permitted to say it, there is often in textual criticism a terrible accuracy that some find offensive. However, the statements which Fredson Bowers makes about the study of the variant stages in the development of a poem apply to the textual study of all forms of creative literature:

> If anyone inquires what all this has to do with the independent life of a poem as we have it in the form that the author wanted to present it to the world, I think we can answer that we are likely to know an adult better if we have followed him through all stages of his childhood. Though a poem, like a man, may stand rejoicing in finished maturity, we must surely understand it with superior intimacy if we have watched its growth and seen its perfection in the very act of shaping. There is such a thing as love, I should urge, in our response to a perfect poem. The current games of intellectual chess, of subjectively drawn tensions, ambiguities, and *discordia concors*, too often overlook or overlay that simple act of love, which the textual critic may help us toward in his concern for the childhood and adolescence, awkward or charming, of the living seed of a writer.[3]

In the discussion which follows, my own purpose in citing textual variants is not to account for the historical development of the text of *The Nigger of the "Narcissus,"* but to employ the evidence of these variants as representative of Conrad's attempt to achieve a successful blend of form and idea.

No matter what direction it may eventually choose to take, critical attention to *The Nigger of the "Narcissus"* must at some point deal with Conrad's conception of James Wait's psychology, with the extent to which Conrad makes Wait the artistic focus of the novel, and, perhaps most important, with the two narrative voices through which events and interpretations of events are rendered. Although Walter Wright, John Gordan, and Jocelyn Baines, among others, have offered valuable commentaries on Wait's psychology and on Conrad's use of Wait as artistic focus, these commentaries have been by no means full enough. Further, critics have for the most part either badly represented the matter of the two narrators in *The Nigger of the "Narcissus"* or have chosen completely to ignore it.

Certainly *The Nigger of the "Narcissus"* contains beautiful descriptive passages; but in the main it follows the pattern of what de

Maupassant described as the novel of pure analysis, or that novel in which the writer reveals "the smallest evolutions of a soul, and all the most secret motives of our every action . . . ."[4] Central to this pattern in *The Nigger* is Conrad's rendering of Wait as a person who makes his imminent death an accomplice in what becomes a complex act of self-deception. Nothing could be more distant from the truth than Wilfred Dowden's statement that "the fact or fiction of Wait's illness is a small point and does not in the least affect the theme of the book."[5] When Wait joins the "Narcissus," he is a dying man; but to hide from himself the fact of a real illness, he affects a friendly relationship with death and parades it unceasingly before the crew. In doing so, he convinces himself that his attitude is mere pretense, nothing more, by which he can escape his duties aboard the "Narcissus." Walter Wright has pointed out how important even Wait's cough becomes as a means of sustaining the pretense:

> He does not want pity because he is dying; he must secure it on false ground in order to believe that he is really not. Consequently, when racked by his cough, he adds an extra, voluntary display. By insisting on coughing he can avoid recognizing how bad his illness would appear stripped of pretense.[6]

John Gordan, in *Joseph Conrad: The Making of a Novelist*, has cited several instances of holograph revisions which emphasize Conrad's presentation of Wait as both the victim of a real illness and, owing to Wait's fear of death, the exploiter of an imaginary one.[7] In the holograph Conrad first wrote concerning Wait, "Life seemed an indestructible thing. It went on in darkness, in sunshine, in sleep; tireless, it hovered affectionately around the legend of his death." He then altered "the legend of his death" to "the imposture of his ready death" (p. 112). Similar additions to the holograph occur later in the narrative. During the height of the storm, Wait is momentarily forgotten by the crew. Finally, someone remembers him alone in the cabin, the water-jammed door preventing his escape. With great difficulty and at the risk of their lives, five of the crew members manage to break the bulkhead and rescue him. In rendering Wait's reaction to the rescue, Conrad first wrote, " 'Now after I got out of there!' he breathed out weakly." He then revised the statement to read, " 'Now after I got myself out of there!' he breathed out weakly" (p. 76). By the addition of a single reflexive pronoun, Conrad depicts Wait's amazing self-confidence in the face of what ordinarily would be an awareness of imminent death. In another instance, revisions made in "To My Readers in America," a special preface written for the American collected edition of *The Nigger*, clearly focus on Conrad's conception of Wait's psychology. In the initial attempt Conrad wrote, "But James Wait afraid of death and making her his companion was a man of character." The revised passage reads, "But James Wait afraid of death and making her his accomplice was an imposter of some character."[8] As developed in the novel, Wait's attitude toward death is both paradoxical and ironic in that Wait, whose name becomes a token of procrastination in the face of an inevitable certitude, invokes as an agent of deception that which for a fact is already in progress, and his flaunting of his imminent death as a means to fool the crew results ultimately only in self-deception. It is in terms of this self-deception that one achieves an understanding of Conrad's statement that Wait is "merely the centre of the ship's collective psychology and the pivot of the action."[9]

The extent of the self-deception is clearly revealed in Wait's relationship with Donkin, who must have represented to Conrad the archetype of the shiftless seaman. Conrad presents Donkin consistently as a person who knows all about his rights as a seaman, but nothing of his duties. To promote insurrection, Donkin appeals to the naive instincts of the crew of the "Narcissus" through a false show of concern for their welfare. In the many revisions made in the variant states of *The Nigger*, Conrad worked carefully to present Donkin's sinister, brooding and despicable traits of character. On his last visit to Wait, Donkin intends to rob Wait's sea chest. Seeing Wait immobile on the bed, Donkin hopefully imagines him already dead. In the holograph Conrad first wrote:

> Jimmy did not move but glanced languidly out of the corners of his eyes.—
> "Calm?" he asked.—"Yuss" said Donkin and sat down on the box.

He then expanded the last sentence of the passage and with remarkable economy depicted Donkin's sinister state of mind:

> "Yuss" said Donkin very disappointed and sat down on the box. (p. 164)

When he revised *The Nigger* for the collected edition, Conrad continued to give careful attention to depicting Donkin's sinister qualities. The earlier reading, "his hate for every man looked out through his eyes," becomes in the collected edition, "his hate for every man dwelt in his furtive eyes."[10]

Both Wait and Donkin, by playing upon the naive sentiments of the crew, offer an insidious threat to the solidarity of the crew and thus to the peace of the ship. But the difference between the two men is carefully delineated along with their interdependence. The discussion which Jocelyn Baines offers of the relationship is sound as far as it goes, but it requires expansion. Baines contends that the threat offered

Luncheon guests: From left to right Zdzisław Najder, Irmina P. Pulc, and Ivo Vidan. (Photographed by Billie W. M. Wolfe)

Symposium speaker: Marion C. Michael. (Photographed by Billie W. M. Wolfe)

by Donkin is crude compared to Wait's, which is complex and subtle, and that Wait is able to create a situation, while Donkin is able only to take advantage of it.[11] The point is clearly demonstrated in the mutiny scene. Donkin has been able to condition the crew for a mutiny by his talk of higher wages and injustices, but he is not able to bring the men to the point of the mutiny until their resentment is aroused by Captain Allistoun's treatment of Wait. Then, when Donkin throws the belaying pin at Allistoun, Donkin is disowned by the crew "because he has overstepped the tacitly accounted bounds of what is permissible."[12] The relationship between the two men is, however, worked out on a somewhat more complex basis than Baines' discussion shows. Donkin, no matter how he understands Wait's relationship with death, exploits the situation as a pretext for registering grievance and aggravating trouble. But the fact that Wait recognizes in Donkin what Wait believes himself to be, a person capable of inventing all sorts of dodges to escape work, complements and strengthens Wait's self-deception, helps him to cling more firmly to his lie. Wait can find only comfort from Donkin's derisive attitude. Donkin calls Wait a "black fraud" and abuses the crew for being "taken in by a vulgar nigger" (p. 41), and for this kind of derision Wait paradoxically rewards Donkin with a warm jersey. At one point in the novel, Donkin reproaches Wait with the extra work Wait's malingering gives the watch, and in recounting Wait's reaction, Conrad first wrote in the holograph, "But Jimmy seemed to revel in that abuse." He then expanded the sentence to read, "But Jimmy positively seemed to revel in that abuse" (p. 47), thus giving stronger emphasis to Wait's psychological dependence upon Donkin.

In his study of the holograph of *The Nigger*, John Gordan turned up a cancelled passage that suggests Conrad's original intention to have the attentive and emotional Belfast cause Wait's death by talk of doctors.[13] After he cancelled the passage, Conrad continued in the holograph to render the scene in Chapter V in which Donkin visits Wait for the last time. There are many possible reasons for the cancellation. A likely reason, however, is that Conrad decided he could increase the subtle, brutal irony of the scene if the person who had been the greatest boost to Wait's ego should suddenly, by withdrawing his friendly derision, shake Wait's steadfastness and thus, at least indirectly, cause his death.

The relationship between Podmore and Wait, a subtle mixture of comedy and inadvertent brutality, shows Conrad's consistency in using Wait as the pivotal point for revealing the psychology of the crew. Through revision in several states of *The Nigger*, Conrad carefully built up Podmore as the canting and conceited moralist. He first wrote in the holograph:

> The cook approached to hear and stood by beaming with the inward consciousness of his faith, like a conceited saint mindful of approaching glory.

He then revised "mindful of approaching glory" to "unable to forget his glorious reward" (pp. 32-33). Other passages from the variant states of the novel show Conrad's care in presenting Podmore as a religious fanatic. In the holograph Conrad had Podmore say to Wait:

> "Don't you see fire.... don't you feel it. Blind, *full* choke-full of sin!" (p. 126)

Later the expanded the passage for the serial edition:

> "Don't you see the fire ... don't you feel it? Blind, chock-full of sin. I can see it for you. I can't bear it. I hear the call to save you. Night and day."[14]

Further expansion took place for the collected edition:

> "Don't you see the everlasting fire ... don't you feel it? Blind, chockfull of sin! Repent, repent! I can't bear to think of you. I hear the call to save you. Night and day." (p. 116)

When he revised *The Nigger* for the collected edition, Conrad achieved one of his finest touches of irony in revealing Podmore's posturing of Christ. Podmore's fame with the crew rests primarily on his being able to make coffee for them during the storm. When in Chapter IV he visits in Wait's cabin, Podmore is caught up in the tide of his emotions and is reminded of his remarkable feat. The holograph reads:

> He was a voice—a fleshless and sublime thing as *like* that memorable night —the night when he went over the sea to make coffee for suffering perishing sinners. (p. 126)

For the collected edition Conrad expanded the adjective clause to read: "when he went walking over the sea to make coffee for perishing sinners."[15]

The scene in Chapter IV between Podmore and Wait becomes ironically brutal especially in the light of Wait's self-deception, and it is in this scene that the psychological lines of the novel begin to coalesce. Podmore's talk of hell fire and death forces Wait to the wall; and, rather than admit that he is really sick, he demands his immediate return to duty. When Captain Allistoun refuses to meet the demand, the crew, because they have been falsely conditioned by Donkin's talk of their rights and because they have been unable to make up their minds about Wait, oppose Captain Allistoun's authority. Thus, the mutiny is precipitated.

The mutiny comes as a climax of the fact that throughout *The Nigger* Wait owns a complex and varying monopoly of the emotions of the crew. Because they are uncertain about Wait, they allow themselves to be corrupted. Though suspicious of Wait, they can find no safety in scorn, and their misplaced pity would be a threat to their childish dignity. Their feelings about Wait constantly shift one way, then another. Belfast would "knock his ugly black head off—the skulking dodger!" (p. 37). Yet he steals the officer's Sunday fruit pie "to tempt the fastidious appetite of Jimmy" (p. 38). Archie refuses to provide music for songs because Wait has lectured him about the noise. No one can drive nails to hang his clothes on. Watches are called man to man in whispers in order not to disturb Wait's sleep. Wait becomes the master of every moment of the crew's existence and, owing to Belfast's theft of the pie, the destroyer of mutual confidence between officers and men. The naive emotions of the crew, their uncertainty about Wait, coupled with Donkin's tutelage about rights and Podmore's forcing Wait to demand to be returned to duty, bring the crew to the mutiny. The mutiny is put down, and the crew realize the subtlety of Wait's imposture and understand his fear only after the Captain's stinging lecture, the shaming of Donkin, and Singleton's assurance that in ordering Wait to continue to lie up the Captain "has something on his mind" (p. 130). Thus, ultimately Donkin's threat to the peace of the ship is proved impotent, but in a different way Wait triumphs. The crew, now amazed at Wait's self-deception, set about to support it, and so strong is the bond of the sentimental lie that the crew actually feel cheated at Wait's death. Though there are deplorable aspects to the changes in title, the publication of the first issue of *The Nigger of the "Narcissus"* in America under the title *The Children of the Sea* was in some respects appropriate.

Conrad presents Captain Allistoun as a confident and stern officer who is able to deal with any problem arising aboard ship. His behavior during the storm is unimpeachable. He refuses to cut the mast, and his officers support his conviction that the crew are to take care of the ship and cannot expect to be taken care of at the ship's expense. His handling of Podmore's sanctimonious rantings, of Donkin's throwing the belaying pin, and of Wait's demand to return to duty reveals his knowledge of what is necessary to keep the crew in line. The best thing for Podmore is to threaten him with the pump. Allistoun has only the bitterest contempt for Donkin and succeeds in humiliating him before the crew, thus destroying completely Donkin's effectiveness as a breeder of insurrection. His problem with

Wait, however, is more complex. When Wait is frightened by Podmore and demands to be returned to duty, Allistoun tells him, " 'There's nothing the matter with you, but you choose to lie up to please yourself—and now you shall lie up to please me' " (p. 120). Then in his remark to Mr. Baker, Allistoun reveals his compassion and understanding and, as Gordan has stated, gives a name to what is for Wait a "nameless fear":[16]

> "Did you think I had gone wrong there, Mr. Baker?" He tapped his forehead, laughed short. "When I saw him standing there, three parts dead, and so scared—black amongst that gaping lot—no grit to face what's coming to us all—the notion came to me all at once, before I could think. Sorry for him—like you would be for a sick brute. If ever creature was in a mortal funk to die! . . . I thought I would let him go out in his own way. Kind of impulse." (pp. 126-27)

Only Singleton remains untouched by Wait's imposture. His theory that Wait will die at the very first sight of land—for this is the tradition of the sea—is borne out only by coincidence. He is, of course, important to the dramatic structure of the novel in that as the old man of the sea he assuages the crew's pent up emotions at the critical time of the mutiny. On the other hand, Singleton is of special significance in the novel because the experience of the storm does not leave him unchanged. His more than thirty hours at the wheel during the storm make him aware of an uncomfortable truth: that "Old Singleton" is something more than an honorific title and that he has grown too old for the hardships of the sea.

Conrad intended that psychological development in *The Nigger of the "Narcissus"* be understood in terms of the two narrative voices through which events and interpretations of events are provided for the reader. A misunderstanding of the two narrative voices has all too often led to undeserved condemnation of the novel's structure. What John Gordan glossed over as "an inconsistency"[17] and Harold Davis has called "curious slips" [18] that represent structural faults is in fact a deliberate attempt by Conrad to provide a dual perspective from which the reader views events ironically. Conrad is intent upon authenticating his narrative as it exists simultaneously on two different levels of meaning.

In *Almayer's Folly*, which appeared two years before *The Nigger of the "Narcissus,"* Conrad by the inversion of normal time sequence in the presentation of narrative provides a frame in which psychological movement and emotional response are of primary concern. In *Almayer's Folly* Conrad by shifts to time past provides fragments of information that serve to place in ironic perspective events presented in time present. The inversion of time in *Almayer's Folly*, a method which he was to use with even greater artistic effect in *The Secret Agent*, places a strong emphasis on the underlying human situation and releases the reader's emotions, as Donald Davidson stated as early as 1925, "for the suspense of an evolving character rather than for mere incidental outcome."[19] Recently, Eudora Welty described the method in her statement that fiction "can set a fragment of the past within the frame of the present and cause them to exist simultaneously."[20] Time is linear, or sequential, in *The Nigger*, but through the use of two narrative voices Conrad achieves a deeper psychological penetration than that of *Almayer* and reveals a greater complex of relations. *The Nigger* is told omnisciently down to the point early in Chapter Two where in the use of the pronoun *our* a crewman narrator emerges: "Along the main deck, Mr. Baker grunted in a manner bloodthirsty and innocuous; and kept all our noses to the grindstone, being—as he once remarked—paid for doing that very thing" (p. 31). From this point on, there are constant shifts in the novel between the crewman narrator and the omniscient narrator, with the crewman narrator revealing himself by the use of a collective *we*, *us*, or *our*. He becomes *I* in the final pages after the members of the crew go their separate ways. At times in the novel Conrad allows the crewman narrator to make evaluative statements that perhaps go beyond what one would ordinarily expect to be his true capabilities—judging, of course, by one's built-in notions of the intellect of seamen. For instance, he comments that Donkin's is one of those natures which "forget that under extreme provocation men will be just—whether they want to be so or not" (p. 40). In this respect the crewman narrator performs in a manner similar to that of Ishmael. Yet, unlike Melville, Conrad in all instances limits his crewman narrator to reporting events in which he actually participates or which he hears about. He can recount the rescue of Wait from the cabin because he is one of the five crewmen who go to Wait's rescue. Thus, he becomes narrator-agent, producing a measurable effect upon the course of events in the novel. On the other hand, on the basis of information received from Knowles, he can report that Wait, in a private interview with the Captain, coughed over the Captain's meteorological journals (p. 45).

However, the crewman narrator is by no means limited to a mere reporting of narrative events or to an occasional philosophical speculation. He is capable of doubt and uncertainty and thus of the dramatic potential for change and for growth in understanding. For instance, as general spokesman for the other members of the crew he reflects in his comments both his and their initial uncertainty about Wait's dilemma. Early in the novel he comments on Wait's relationship with death:

No man could be suspected of such monstrous friendship! Was he a reality
—or was he a sham—this ever-expected visitor of Jimmy's? We hesitated
between pity and mistrust, while on the slightest provocation, he shook
before our eyes the bones of his bothersome and infamous skeleton. (p. 26)

Then, after the mutiny, when he, like other members of the crew, has
realized that Wait is for a fact dying, the crewman narrator comments:

Falsehood triumphed. It triumphed through doubt, through stupidity,
through pity, through sentimentalism. We set ourselves to bolster it up,
from compassion, from recklessness, from a sense of fun. Jimmy's steadfastness to his untruthful attitude in the face of the inevitable truth had the
proportions of a colossal enigma. . . . (p. 138)

It is a natural outgrowth of his limiting his crewman narrator to
realistic vision and inference that Conrad renders through an omniscient narrator such scenes as Podmore's and Donkin's visits to
Wait's cabin. Involved, however, in this narrative technique is something more than mere consistency. It is, in fact, these alternations in
the angle of vision that are the chief source of irony in the novel, for
Conrad never in the novel intends for the reader to identify his own
responses to Wait solely with those of the crewman narrator. By pro-
viding the reader with a dual perspective, Conrad creates ironic distance between the limited notions of the crew, with all their doubts
and uncertainties about Wait, and the wider range of understanding
about Wait that belongs to the omniscient narrator. Although later
revisions in the printed text of the novel reveal Conrad's attempts to
give his use of the two narrative voices clearer meaning, the idea to
provide a dual angle of vision occurred to Conrad in the earliest
draft of the novel. In fact, the dramatic and ironic effect of the use of
the two narrative voices is revealed in a passage that Conrad created
in the holograph, reworded, and then let stand with only minor revision for the collected edition. In the passage, occurring early in the
novel, the "Narcissus" is a week out of Bombay, and the crew are
suspicious of Wait's attitude toward death, not certain whether he has
merely invented a ruse for escaping work or is for a fact dying. They
are in no way aware of the subtlety of his imposture.

One morning as we were washing decks Mr. Baker called to him. "Bring
your broom over *there* here Wait." He *moved* strolled languidly.—*What's
Move yourself man!"* yourself! Ough! *cried* grunted Mr. Baker—What's
the matter with you hind legs? He stopped dead short. He gazed slowly
with *prominent* eyes that bulged out, with an *audacious and sad expression* expression audacious and sad. "It isn't my legs," he said "it's my
lungs." Everybody listened. "What's—Ough! What's wrong with 'em" in-
quired Mr. Baker. *Hand* All the watch stood around on the wet deck and
with brooms or buckets in their hands. He said mournfully: "Going—or
gone. Can't you see I'm a dying man? I know it!" Mr. Baker was disgusted.

"Then why the devil did you ship*ped* aboard here? he said. "I must live till
I die—musn't I? he replied. The grins became audible. "Go off the deck
—get out of my sight!" said Mr. Baker. He was nonplussed. It was a unique
experience. James Wait, *was* obedient, dropped his broom and *obediently*
walked slowly forward. A burst of laughter followed him. *All hands* too
funny. All hands laughed . . . They laughed! . . . Alas! (pp. 45-46)

The shift from the *we* of the first sentence to *they* of the last would
perhaps appear to some abrupt and awkward; but in the light of the
aesthetic distance which it provides, the shift reveals, nevertheless,
Conrad's attempt to achieve his avowed aim of appealing to a "sense
of pity, and beauty, and pain" and "by the power of the written word
to make you hear, to make you feel . . . before all, to make you *see*"
("Preface," pp. xii and xiv). In one of her more sensitive responses to
Conrad's art, Virginia Woolf declared that Conrad "sees once and he
sees for ever."[21] No matter how one judges the success of the two narrative voices in particular, it is hoped that he would concede that the
overall artistic integrity of *The Nigger of the "Narcissus,"* centering
as it does on experimentation with narrative technique, and pointing
clearly to the even more complex narrative methods of later novels
such as *Lord Jim* and *Under Western Eyes*, represents one of Conrad's
finest achievements.

This afternoon I would hazard the assertion that with the death of
Casper Almayer at three a.m., April 24, 1894, the modern novel
was born.[22] It was a precocious child. In 1924, the year of Conrad's
death commemorated in this symposium, Virginia Woolf declared,
". . . we are trembling on the verge of one of the great ages of English
literature."[23] As far as modern fiction is concerned, she did not realize
that the age was already in its maturity.

NOTES

[1]William Blackburn, ed., *Joseph Conrad: Letters to William Blackwood and
David S. Meldrum* (Durham: Duke Univ. Press, 1958), p. 155.

[2]Ibid. (Conrad's italics)

[3]Fredson Bowers, *Textual and Literary Criticism* (Cambridge: Harvard
Univ. Press, 1959), pp. 17-18.

[4]Guy de Maupassant, *Pierre et Jean*, trans. Clara Dell (New York: P. F.
Collier and Son, 1902), p. lii.

[5]W. S. Dowden, *Joseph Conrad: The Imaged Style* (Nashville: Vanderbilt
Univ. Press, 1970), p. 50.

[6]Walter Wright, *Romance and Tragedy in Joseph Conrad* (Lincoln: Univ.
of Nebraska Press, 1949), p. 172.

[7]John D. Gordan, *Joseph Conrad: The Making of a Novelist* (Cambridge:
Harvard Univ. Press, 1940), pp. 148-50. Several of the holograph passages
cited in my study were first cited and discussed by Gordan; however, since
my own independent study of the holograph turned up passages that were not

pertinent to the scope of Gordan's study, I have, in lieu of referring to Gordan, in all instances merely given holograph page numbers within the text of my discussion. I am grateful to the Rosenbach foundation for permission to examine the holograph and to quote from it. It is, of course, impossible within a printed text to reproduce all of the characteristics of holograph revision, especially those of a Conrad holograph. In all instances, I have aimed at clarity and accuracy. I have avoided the inevitable *sic* where the errors in Conrad's use of English are quite obvious. The italicized words in holograph quotations represent Conrad's own cancellations of text.

[8]The original draft of this special preface is laid in with the Rosenbach holograph of *The Nigger*. This revision occurs on page 1 of this draft.

[9]"To My Readers in America," *The Nigger of the "Narcissus"* (New York: Doubleday, Page & Co., 1926), p. ix. Unless otherwise indicated, all references to the printed text of the novel are to this collected edition. Therefore, in such citation hereafter, only page numbers will be given within the text of the paper.

[10]Conrad revised *The Nigger* for the collected edition by working in longhand on the face of a copy of the Popular edition, published by Heinemann in 1910. On the flyleaf he identified this volume, now in the Keating Collection at Yale, as the "Corrected Text for the collected edition. J. C." This expansion of the description of Donkin appears on page 213 of this text and is printed in the collected edition. I am grateful to Yale University for permission to examine this text. At this time Kenneth W. Davis and Donald W. Rude of Texas Tech University are preparing an authoritative edition of *The Nigger*. However, they have not yet determined the exact relationship of the revised 1910 edition to the various collected editions.

[11]Jocelyn Baines, *Joseph Conrad: A Critical Biography* (New York: McGraw-Hill Book Co., 1960), pp. 184-86.

[12]Ibid., p. 186.

[13]Gordan, pp. 147-48.

[14]*New Review*, 17 (Nov., 1897), 494.

[15]This expansion, like the earlier one cited, occurred in Conrad's reworking the 1910 Popular Edition (p. 171).

[16]Gordan, p. 149.

[17]Ibid., p. 54. I briefly developed this point in my share of the comments in "Currents in Conrad Criticism: A Symposium," *Conradiana*, 4, No. 3 (1972), 14.

[18]Harold Davis, "Shifting Rents in a Thick Fog: Point of View in the Novels of Joseph Conrad," *Conradiana*, 2, No. 2 (1969-70), 23.

[19]Donald Davidson, "Conrad's Directed Indirections," *Sewanee Review*, 33 (April-June, 1925), 165.

[20]Eudora Welty, "Some Notes on Time in Fiction," *Mississippi Quarterly*, 26 (Fall, 1973), 485.

[21]Virginia Woolf, "Mr. Conrad: A Conversation," *The Captain's Death Bed and Other Essays* (New York: Harcourt Brace and Co., 1950), p. 80.

[22]John A. Gee and Paul J. Sturm, ed. and trans., *Letters of Joseph Conrad to Marguerite Poradowska, 1890-1920* (New Haven: Yale Univ. Press, 1940), pp. 65-66.

[23]Virginia Woolf, "Mr. Bennett and Mrs. Brown," *The Captain's Death Bed and Other Essays* (New York: Harcourt, Brace and Co., 1950), p. 119.

Conrad and the
Idea of Honor

Zdzisław Najder

ABSTRACT

"Honor" is a Janus concept: it implies both a consciousness and a reputation, both a feeling of accomplishment and its public acknowledgement. For centuries, it formed the center of an ethos based on stern principles to be adhered to irrespective of circumstance and consequences. Other ideals of this ethos are courage, duty, fidelity, patriotism, and solidarity. In its social origins bound up with noble warriors, later with knights, landed gentry, and aristocracy, the idea of honor also greatly contributed to the development of the consciousness of human dignity in other, emancipating classes. It became "democratized" in France as result of the Revolution and the Napoleonic wars, and about the same time in Poland as result of wars of national independence. Although in France its influence was severely curtailed by the flourishing of bourgeois morality, in Poland (where the national culture has always been dominated by a gentry mentality) it remained a leading moral ideal. Conrad belongs to the tradition of the ethos of honor both as a Polish nobleman by birth, and as a writer consciously carrying on, in the midst of a reign of middle-class literature, the ancient heritage of Homer, the *Chanson de Roland*. Shakespeare, Calderón, Cervantes, Stendhal, Mickiewicz, and de Vigny. True to this heritage, he explored not only the triumphs of honor, but its dangers and pitfalls. He also pioneered, in literature, the shedding of the social ramifications of honor; most of his heroes are neither noblemen, nor military figures. Although the structure of his ethics has been frequently misunderstood by writers and critics conditioned by utilitarianism, Conrad as a moralist has left a powerful legacy, to which, in their different ways, Faulkner and Hemingway, Saint-Exupéry and Camus owe much. (ZN)

It is evident that the idea of honor was very important for Conrad as a person and stands at the heart of ethical problems that he raised in his books. Some of his contemporaries, such as Wells, noted this fact with an ironical shrug; others, such as Cunninghame Graham, with admiration. But, even though the fact itself has been registered by many critics, the function and implications of the idea as present in Conrad's work remain by and large unanalyzed. When Conrad deals with honor in its simple form, as in "The Duel," *Chance*, or *The Rescue*, there is little chance for misinterpretation. But whenever the problems raised become more intricate and a deeper comprehension of the whole ethos of which honor forms the center is required confusion arises, for instance in interpretations of the final part of *Lord Jim*, or of the predicament of *Nostromo*.

Many critics simply fail to identify the moral and literary tradition to which Conrad belongs, and persist in interpreting him in the terms of, and as within, the conventions of middle-class nineteenth-century prose. And if one does not know the history and logic of the concept of honor, he certainly cannot appreciate what was new in Conrad's handling of it. Some of his greatest admirers, like Faulkner or Camus, seem to have seen it quite well, but we are unable to comprehend their links with Conrad as long as we do not place the connection in a historical perspective. Therefore, if we wish to understand more clearly what Conrad as a moral writer was about, we have first to ask what were the origins and the history of the idea of honor, and what are the ramifications and implications of this concept. Unfortunately, this is not a subject much written about. Apart from C. B. Watson's excellent book *Shakespeare and the Renaissance Concept of Honor* (where, however, only the intellectual, and not the literary, tradition is presented),[1] most other studies are fragmentary and limited in scope.

We have to look into the history of "honor" because it is neither a simple, psychologically definable ideal (like truthfulness or mercy), nor, in spite of some appearances, a formal concept—like the categorical imperative, which it resembles in its absolute stringency. The categorical imperative says only that one must not advocate any moral rules which he is unwilling to regard as universally binding; the content of these rules, however, remains open. The ideal of honor, on the contrary, requires not simply that one remains faithful to his principles and defends them in spite of any odds, but it also determines, to a large extent, the kind of principles he ought to stick to. Thus, for instance, when in Conrad's *Under Western Eyes* the General, to whom Razumov denounces Victor Haldin, talks of himself as of a defendant of "fidelity" and "honour,"[2] the reader is supposed to feel no doubt that the scene is ironical and that the General has no right to his claim of representing these values.

Perhaps the most striking thing about honor is that it is a "Janus-concept": it has to have its public face (reputation) and private face (consciousness). This characteristic and essential duality has been present in the ideal since its very beginnings, which go back at least to Homeric Greece. Honor consisted then of rewards and reputation on the one hand, and of a consciousness of accomplishment and dignity on the other—or, to put it differently, of external marks of honor and a feeling of inherent worth. Of course, the external aspect was the earlier one. As Conrad wrote: "We are children of the earth. It may be that the noblest tradition is but the offspring of material conditions, of the hard necessities besetting men's precarious lives. But once it has been born it becomes a spirit."[3] What began as a matter of material prizes and acquired authority developed quickly into an answer to the perennial question: what makes life worth living? Already in the *Iliad* we see Achilles asking himself: is it preferable to live a long, safe, and obscure life, or to meet an early death adorned with honor and glory? As we know, he chose the latter.

The answer to this question, offered by the ideal of honor, has been repeatedly stated. Its essence is best visible in the paradoxical formula that to give your life a meaning you must act as if your life by itself has no value.

Honor is, therefore, basically a secular ideal. Glory, its crown, results in secular immortality. As Balzac wrote, "La gloire est le soleil des morts."[4]

The idea of honor has been bound with a specific concept of man and his nature. Man is seen as an individual person, not as a particle in a crowd (and, by the same token, society is not a simple sum of its members). He possesses a free will and can use it. But he is not "naturally" good: there are higher and lower elements in him, and he has to be carefully educated. This idea of man is in some respects similar to the Christian one: personalism and man's inborn defectiveness, obligation to fight his lower inclinations—all that made possible a coexistence (by no means peaceful) of the chivalric ethos and Christianity.

Jean-Jacques Rousseau eloquently proclaims almost the very opposite of this idea of man. He insists on the natural goodness of man, goodness marred by civilization and restraints. He stresses the importance of emotions and intentions, rejects discipline, and suggests that the uniqueness of the individual makes general rules of conduct absurdly cruel. Rousseau calls the following principle his "great moral lesson": "to avoid those situations in life which bring our duties into conflict with our interests."[5] What is perhaps most striking in this "lesson" is that Rousseau calls it "moral" while it seems, in fact, to be an exhortation to shirking. But for Rousseau our interests—and feelings, instincts, passions, propensities—were inherently good; duties were not. The great patron of the Declaration of the Rights of Man postulated, in the words of Anatole France, "an excessive and unfair separation between man and the gorilla,"[6] idealizing the former. In spite of appearances, the ethics of honor and the chivalric code make more modest claims concerning human nature.

For the concept of man implied by the idea of honor, Pindar's formula "become what you are" is superbly characteristic. Rousseau, while liberating man from external constraints, makes him a prisoner of his own character. The Pindarian tradition, on the contrary, while subjecting man to external obligations, restraints, and rules, makes him internally free: he can shape, mould, and model himself; he is an object of his will and aspirations.

Within the ethics of honor, a morally relevant act is taken to have, in principle, irreversible consequences. Originally, it was understood to influence, literally, the very essence of a man. A man who lost his honor would become qualitatively different—as if another person, or rather, de-personalized. Later this magical conception was toned down, but the basic idea that moral implications of behavior are qualitative, not quantitative, and that once an act is committed there is no way to erase it, remained among the fundamental differences between this ethic and, for instance, utilitarianism with its quantitative and cumulative approach. Here we see another analogy with Christian morality and its doctrine of mortal sin.

Irreparable, or reparable only through special, great acts of regaining honor lost (and not by acts of repentance or material retribution), are the misdeeds of the heroes of medieval romances, of Shakespeare, Mickiewicz, and Conrad. And when André Malraux, in his famous preface to Faulkner's *Sanctuary*, identified "his only true subject" as *l'irrémédiable*, he put his finger on the very spot where, in Faulkner's work, the traditions of honor and of Christianity converge.[7]

The ideal of honor did not originate and exist in isolation: it formed the central part of a whole ethos. For lack of a better name we may call it the "chivalric ethos," although it is much older than medieval chivalry, has survived it, and did not stop developing long after the last knights disappeared from courts and battlefields.

It has been a matter of pride, within this ethos, to be judged by severe standards. Legendary and half-legendary heroes were set as examples to follow. Since reputation was a component of honor, the opinion of one's equals was of a paramount importance. What distinguished this reverence of public opinion from crude opportunism was the fact that both the individual and his community were supposed to adhere to identical ideals and neither of them established rules at will. The community was an arbiter, not a lawmaker. Therefore, a man could claim that his arbiters were wrong. Thus, for instance, Achilles' wrath was not, as it may seem today, an expression of egocentric pride, but of a consciousness of injustice.[8]

The direct opposite of honor is shame, and the fear of shame was considered praiseworthy. Ajax invokes his comrades-in-arms: "My friends, be men and think of your honour. Fear nothing in the field but dishonour in each other's eyes. When soldiers fear disgrace, then more are saved than killed."[9] Aristotle maintained that courage instigated by shame was more valuable than courage elicited by fear of punishment.[10]

Courage is, in fact, a necessary concomitant of honor. And not only military courage. If a steady link between self-esteem and public esteem is essential for honor, then only a man who is ready to stand up and fight against any infringement of his reputation can be honorable. Other implications of the ideal are perhaps less obvious but no less important. The immediate consequences of an act are irrelevant for evaluating it as honorable or dishonorable. Whether the hero won or lost, whether he gained wealth or ruined his family, whether he saved his life or died, whether his glorious death was of any help to the cause he defended—nothing of that really counts. What matters is fidelity to a principle. (However, fidelity to principles can be defended on practical grounds, by pointing at their far-reaching consequences.) This impracticality of honor is most obvious in the disregard of material advantages. "For if, Socrates, there be one point in which the man who thirsts for honour differs from him who thirsts for gain, it is, I think, in willingness to toil, face danger, and abstain from shameful gains—for the same of honour only and fair fame."[11]

Honor is, as I have said, theoretically and basically a conservative ideal, but with a paradoxical rider. Although since the earliest times honor was considered a monopoly of the well-born and privileged, this ideal has also been, for well over two thousand years, used as a weapon against inequality grounded in differences of birth and class. The more forcibly it was argued that honor and virtue were the basic characteristics of the nobility and that the nobles morally deserved to be nobles, the easier it was to turn the tables and ask the question: why should good men of humble birth or profession be considered "lower" and unworthy of honor? Thus the argument that the well-born are at the top because they are better would repeatedly turn out to be a double-edged one: by establishing honor and virtue as criteria of nobility it made, by definition, all virtuous and honorable men equal to the nobles. Furthermore, the ideal of honor gave birth to, and then fostered the idea of human dignity; but once this idea had taken shape, it became impossible to keep it within socially closed confines.

Seen from this angle, the Renaissance was perhaps the most important period in the development of the concept of honor. In spite of the proliferation of statements about a gulf separating the aristocratic and the lower classes, the stress on virtue as the basis of nobility and on honor as a mark of virtue prepared theoretical ground for a social emancipation of the ideal. (The intellectuals were the first to profit from this process.) Robert Ashley, in the best known English Renaissance definition of honor, does not mention social origin at all: "*Honor* therefore ys a certaine testemonie of vertue shining of yt self, geven of some man by the iudgement of good men: For when any one ys of such and so apparant vertue that he turneth others into admiracion and love of him, yf as the shadow followeth the body so prayse and reverence followeth him, then he ys called honorable, and the same which is geven unto him as an approbacion of his vertue is termed *Honor*."[12]

At the same time, the ideal of honor, within the medieval chivalric code at least overtly "Christianized," revealed more fully its secular essence and loosened its links with religious beliefs. Reformation and Counter-Reformation theologians were quick to assail the vogue of honor.[13] However, more momentous was the spread of the bourgeois ethos of capitalism, based on work, usefulness, and profit. It brought along more palpably attractive possibilities of vertical social change and drove the ethos centered around honor into a valiant retreat.

The next stage of development came with the French Revolution and the Napoleonic Wars. Suddenly, every Frenchman became officially capable of honor; military glory, previously exclusive to the aristocracy and landed gentry, became attainable to all *citoyens*. Then the Romantic vogue of chivalry spread across Europe at the same time as did new liberal and democratic tendencies, and an Italian *carbonaro* felt that he could vie in his thirst for honor with any *marchese*.

Let us now focus on Conrad's mother country, which occupies in the history of the idea of honor a rather peculiar position. It is unusual for two main reasons. (1) The nobility-gentry class (within which there was no legal stratification) was in Poland exceptionally numerous and formed some 10-12% of the population.[14] Thus a large section of the population, proportionately larger than the enfranchised electorate in England up until 1867, consisted of fully privileged men, adhering—at least in principle—to the typical values of the nobility. (2) After the partition of Poland between Russia, Prussia, and Austria at the end of the eighteenth century, there was a long line of uprisings and wars of national liberation (1794, 1806, 1830, 1846, 1863). For several generations, military virtues remained in the forefront of national values; all Poles were assumed to be under an obligation to fight or work for national independence; by and large, the emancipating classes joined in and combined their struggle for social equality with the struggle for national identity; individual honor was generally identified with fulfilment of patriotic duties.[15]

This was the tradition to which Konrad Korzeniowski was born as a Pole. But as a writer, Joseph Conrad also belonged to a tradition—an ancient tradition of literature steeped in the idea of honor. The *Iliad* and the *Chanson de Roland* belong to it, and it boasts of such names as Calderón and Cervantes, Shakespeare and Tasso, Stendhal, Mickiewicz and de Vigny. To conceive of this tradition as of one simply extolling the glories of honorable and heroic deeds is as naive as to suppose that most dramas and novels concerned with the power of love culminate in scenes of happy matrimony. Rather, it probes the implications of the ideal, it explores both its splendors and its dangers and excesses, pitfalls and perversions. The writers saturated with chivalric ethos seem to describe and analyze most frequently either the duality of honor and the resulting conflicts between its private and public side, or the tragic practical consequences of a strict adherence to the ideal.

It is perhaps not the impracticality of honor that makes it and its literary presentations so frequently difficult to comprehend for the modern public. More often, the confusion stems from the failure of contemporary readers to realize that—for all its fascination with the *beaux gestes*, flourish, and glory—this is not a cheerfully optimistic tradition. The view of life, historically and philosophically associated with the idea of honor, does not entail a belief in a universal and just order of things. On the contrary, it is essentially a tragic outlook[16]—if only because it makes all value of a man's existence reside in his actions and the resulting reputation and consciousness, but at the same time commands man to throw away, at any moment of challenge or test, "the dearest thing he ow'd / As 'twere a careless trifle."[17] The more a man achieves, the greater he succeeds in becoming, the more we lose by his death; but to shun death means to destroy one's greatness.

Turning now directly to Conrad, we may ask two kinds of questions: what was his personal attitude toward the ideal of honor? And what role does this ideal play in his works? Of course, I can only sample the issue involved and try to give fragmentary answers.

To Conrad, whose father was, in the long line of his ancestors, the first to be employed (as administrator of a country estate), the choice of occupation was, even if unconsciously, a matter of special concern. Whatever a nobleman would do was supposed to be meaningful not primarily in the sense of being profitable; and his accomplishments could not be judged by the simple standard of material rewards. Therefore, the decision to become a sailor and live a life filled with risks and exacting duties, subject to a paramilitary code of behavior, was in a sense quite consistent with Conrad's background.[18]

It is worth noticing here that Conrad does not idealize work; just the contrary, he presents it as a hard necessity, even a curse. What he does idealize is *duty*. This is the standpoint from which he looks with such a scorching disdain at all these Donkins, Ossipons, and Verlocs who manage to wheedle out a living without honest work.

Conrad was strongly opposed to the typically middle-class and capitalistic tendency to regard success as the measure of worth. To separate the value of one's achievements and activities from the profits and rewards was for him a problem of immediate personal concern. Writing his famous Preface to *The Nigger of the "Narcissus"* he penned a few sentences which he then grudgingly deleted upon the advice of his friend Edward Garnett:

> For in art alone of all the enterprises of men there is meaning in endeavour disassociated from success, and merit—if any merit there be—is not wholly centered in achievement but may be faintly discerned in the aim.
>
> For, art is long and life is short, and ideals are practically unreachable except by the very great who can commend the sanction of recognized success. To others the consciousness of a worthy aim is everything; it is conscience, dignity, truth, honour—the reward and the peace.[19]

Garnett quite mistakenly took these statements to be self-defensive, an apology for lack of success; while in fact they expressed a positive programme of a non-pragmatic approach to artistic work.

In a letter to Arthur Quiller-Couch, sent in response to this critic's appreciation of the *Nigger*, Conrad wrote that a "solitary writer," such as himself, when working "thinks only of a small knot of men—three or four perhaps—the only ones who matter."[20] These "select few," mentioned in several other letters, formed the group of the arbiters of his achievement—of his literary "honor." But they did not form a coterie. Conrad's contempt for the "mass public" was simply a result of his exasperation at being financially dependent on its favor. But it never marred his "subtle but invincible conviction of solidarity" with "all humanity," about which he wrote in the quoted Preface. He never addressed himself to a caste; he toiled for a few friends—and at the same time for all men.[21]

Now let me give but two examples of the use to which we can put the concept of honor in analyzing Conrad's novels. *Lord Jim*, of course, comes first to one's mind. In assessing Jim's behavior, most critics consider primarily the practical consequences of his actions. They point at, e.g., the disastrous results of Jim's decision to let Gentleman Brown leave unharmed, and deem it to be not only a fatal error but also a sign of weakness. But are we supposed to judge the hero simply by the practical outcome of his moral decisions? If we go back to Jim's original crime, his desertion of the *Patna*, we notice that the evaluation of Jim's act does not at all hinge on its consequences. Had Jim stayed on board, it would not have made the slightest difference to the situation of the boat and her passengers. His remaining on the *Patna* would not have saved a single life if the steamer went down. But still we, like the court, condemn him for his escape.

At the end of the novel, after Brown kills Dain Waris, Jim decides to go and face Doramin as a matter of principle. But his decision could also be based on practical considerations: the only alternative open to him was to fight—and kill more innocent people. Here the principle of honor, of taking full responsibility for one's word, coincides with simple concern for preserving human lives.

It is often maintained that Brown appealed to Jim's weakest and most shameful side, to a common bond between two fallen men. This is a misunderstanding, based on a failure to grasp what is the moral structure of the story, and on taking Brown's own point of view too seriously. (Perhaps Conrad exaggerated here in his attempt to make the reader get at the truth by himself; we learn many things Jim did not know about and naively wish that he avoided the trap.) In fact, Brown appeals to what is *best* in Jim, to this trait which constitutes the difference between him and an average autocrat: to the principle of fairness, implied by honor. Anyway—and this is a point most critics seem to have missed—it is not Brown, but Cornelius, spared by Jim's humanitarian pity, who causes the catastrophe.

Seen in the terms of honor, the basic conflicts in *Lord Jim* are between motives, principles, and consequences of action. In *Nostromo* we see another characteristic tension: between the public and the private side of honor. When the action begins, there exists a correspondence between Nostromo's reputation and his consciousness of his own worth. Then there develops a dialectical interplay of these two factors, and Nostromo passes through a phase of false fear of losing his "image" to the state of guilt-ridden and dishonorable fame. His vice is vanity: excessive deference to public acclaim. Seen in this light, his melodramatic death appears strikingly apt: he dies as a result of an error of the same kind within which he lived, of mistaking external marks for the whole truth.

Apart from using honor as his pivotal moral concept and presenting its various aspects and entanglements, Conrad pioneered in his fiction the shedding of social class ramifications of this ideal. Most of his heroes are neither noblemen nor soldiers. With him, honor has finally lost its status of a privilege and has become a right, if not a duty.

What I have said above represents only a bare outline of the topic indicated by the title. To discuss it in any detail would require considerably more space—in fact, a whole book. This applies particularly to the more recent developments.

The legacy of Conrad-moralist seems to have been picked up, in their different ways, by writers such as Camus, Faulkner, Hemingway, Malraux, Saint-Exupéry. Each of these names raises its specific problems. For instance, in Hemingway's work we would have to penetrate through the thick plumage of showing-off and pose to the hard body of ethical stance. One of the many books on Malraux bears the title *The Honor of Being a Man.*[22] But perhaps Malraux's concept of man belongs rather to the tradition of Nietzsche, a tradition which, in its radical individualism and total disregard for society and its inherited values, stands in sharp opposition to the ethos of honor? Faulkner's *Absalom, Absalom!* has been called "a puritan tragedy." But is not the Sutpen family saga also a tale of the myth of chivalry enacted, a drama of honor real and apparent, in a word: a tragedy of a search for honor? And was not Faulkner's morbid fascination with puritanism at least partly due to the paradoxical affinities between the puritan ethos and the concept of man inherent in the ethics of honor? The work of Saint-Exupéry—particularly his ideas of human solidarity and of the "*solitude fraternelle*," his stress on action and responsibility —resembles Conrad most obviously. But strangely little has been written about this resemblance; and we would have to ask, for instance, to what extent Saint-Exupéry's religious beliefs constitute a difference between him and the sceptic Conrad. Camus said once that "honor, like pity, is an irrational virtue that carries on after justice and reason have become powerless."[23] But what is the role of the idea of honor in Camus' own work? I think it is certainly present in *The Plague*—but to go beyond this bland statement would take another paper.

However, in order not to end this one with a string of question marks and topics for future study, I shall give an example, symbolic in its conciseness, of the continuity of the tradition I have briefly described.

In the last paragraph of his famous Nobel Prize address, Faulkner tried to sum up his message. Ian Watt, in one of the best pieces ever written on Conrad, has pointed out that the crucial passage in the first part of this paragraph, the passage expressing Faulkner's belief that man will endure and prevail, closely echoes a fragment in Conrad's essay on Henry James.[24] Faulkner's passage echoes it not only in its images, but in the very cadence of phrases. And in the other part of this last paragraph, Faulkner formulates his answer to the question of the purpose of a writer's work: "The poet's, the writer's, duty is . . . to help man endure by lifting his heart, by reminding him of the courage and honor and hope and pride and compassion and pity and sacrifice which have been the glory of his past."[25]

In another place, Faulkner describes his quest for that answer, the quest which lasted "until suddenly one day I saw that that half-forgotten Pole had had the answer all the time. To uplift man's heart . . . ."[26] That half-forgotten Pole (today still the most popular novelist in Poland) was Henryk Sienkiewicz, whom Faulkner had read as a young man. He goes on to explain this answer: "This does not mean that we are trying to change man, improve him, though this is the hope—maybe even the intention—of many of us. On the contrary, in the last analysis this hope and desire to uplift man's heart is completely selfish, completely personal. He would lift up man's heart for his own benefit because in that way he can say No to death."

Saying "No" to death is, in fact, what the ethic of honor is about.

Thus we have here, within the space of a few sentences, a linking together of Polish literature—of all modern literatures probably the one most obsessed by the idea of honor—with the work of the greatest of contemporary American writers. It shows that the tradition to which Conrad belonged and which he greatly enriched, is very much alive and transcends national boundaries.

NOTES

[1]Curtis Brown Watson, *Shakespeare and the Renaissance Concept of Honor* (Princeton: Princeton Univ. Press, 1960).

[2]*Under Western Eyes* (London: Dent, 1947), p. 51.

[3]*Notes on Life and Letters* (London: Dent, 1949), p. 183.

[4]*La Recherche de l'Absolu* (Paris: Hachette, 1960), p. 153.

[5]*The Confessions* (New York: The Modern Library, n.d.), p. 56.

[6]*The Opinions of Jérôme Coignard*, trans. Mrs. Wilfrid Jackson (New York: W. H. Wise, 1930), p. 23.

[7]André Malraux, Preface to *Sanctuaire*, trans. R.-N. Raimbault and Henri Delgove (Paris: Gallimard, 1933).

[8]See Werner Jaeger, *Paideia: The Ideals of Greek Culture*, trans. Gilbert Highet (New York: Oxford Univ. Press, 1945), I, 10-11.

[9]Homer, *The Iliad*, trans. E. V. Rieu (Baltimore: Penguin Books, 1966), p. 106.

[10]*Nicomachean Ethics*, III, 8.

[11]Xenophon, *Works*, trans. H. G. Dakyns (London: Macmillan, 1897), III, pt. 1, 262.

[12]Robert Ashley, *Of Honour*, ed. Virgil B. Heltzel (San Marino, Calif.: Huntington Library, 1947), p. 34.

[13]See Watson, pp. 102-35.

[14]Estimates vary from 8-10% for the entire state to 15-25% for ethnic Poland. See, e.g., Jarema Marciszewski, *Szlachta polska i jej państwo* (Warszawa: Wiedza Powszechna, 1969), *passim*.

[15]See *Conrad's Polish Background*, ed. Zdzisław Najder (London: Oxford Univ. Press, 1964), Introduction, pp. 2-3.

[16]Watson, p. 10.

[17]Shakespeare, *Macbeth*, I, iv, 10-11.

[18]At the same time, however, Conrad took pride in his mercantile as captain of the "Otago" and financial enterprises—a behavior typical for an aristocrat who dabbles in trade and wishes everybody to know that, although it is only his hobby, he is doing very well. It was also typical that Conrad's financial ventures, which would invariably start in a most promising way, almost invariably ended in disaster.

[19]MS of the Preface to *Nigger* is at the Rosenbach Collection, Philadelphia. This quotation appears in John Dozier Gordan, *Joseph Conrad: The Making of a Novelist* (Cambridge, Mass.: Harvard Univ. Press, 1940), p. 238.

[20]See Ian Watt, "Joseph Conrad: Alienation and Commitment," in *The English Mind*, Studies in the English Moralists presented to Basil Wiley, ed. H. S. Davies and G. Watson (Cambridge: Cambridge Univ. Press, 1964), pp. 266-68.

[21]Letter of 23 Dec. 1897, unpublished.

[22]Edward Gannon, *The Honor of Being a Man: The World of André Malraux* (Chicago: Loyola Univ. Press, 1957).

[23]Camus talking to J. Bloch-Michel, *Reporter*, 28 Nov. 1957.

[24]Watt, pp. 277-78.

[25]William Faulkner, *Essays, Speeches, and Public Letters*, ed. J. B. Meriwether (New York: Random House, 1965), p. 120.

[26]Ibid., p. 181.

Photograph of an original acrylic on canvas painting (36″ x 48″) of Joseph Conrad, displayed during the symposium. (Artist, Paul R. Milosevich)

The Imprint of Polish on Conrad's Prose

I. P. Pulc

ABSTRACT

Though Conrad's prose has often struck the English ear as somewhat strange, while sounding familiar to Polish readers, surprisingly little has been done to uncover the qualities that create this impression. Traces of Polish can be most easily discerned in Conrad's diction, for throughout his writing career Conrad weaves Polish sayings, idioms and metaphors into the fabric of his language. However, it is the Polish warp of his sentence, interlaced with its English weft, that gives Conradian prose its special character. Conrad's descriptive style, particularly, bears a strong imprint of Polish rhetorical habits. His fondness for such figures as the asyndeton, the anaphora and triple parallelism, which are commonplace in Polish writers of the nineteenth and twentieth centuries but unusual in British novelists of the same period, engenders his distinctive syntactical patterns. And at times these patterns reveal what is perhaps Conrad's most exotic trait as a stylist—his affinity for falling rhythm, the dominant rhythm of his native tongue. (IPP)

Readers who know Polish have long sensed a kinship between Conrad's English prose and his native language. Yet nearly half a century after his death, the Polish "tonality"[1] of his style still remains to be plumbed. So far only three critics have endeavored to move beyond mere generalizations to specific examples of Polish influence on Conrad's diction and syntax, and even their efforts, while enlightening, have been either too casual or too limited to give a fair measure of Conrad's debt.

The pioneering work was that of Gustav Morf. In his book, *The Polish Heritage of Joseph Conrad*, written more than forty years ago, Morf tilts boldly, if somewhat recklessly, with the complex issue of Conrad's polonisms. Charmed by the exotic novelty of Polish speech during his stay in Poland, he imputes to it all sorts of special virtues, without demonstrating convincingly that they actually exist. Such sweeping statements as his claim that "Proverbs, proverbial sayings, and picturesque expressions . . . take in Polish a much greater place than in any language of the West"[2] are at best debatable. What Morf fails to consider is that any foreign language may well seem remarkably vivid to the new speaker; even the most hackneyed phrase wears its original freshness for him at first, since he can readily discern its figurative underpinnings, no longer perceived by the natives. Thus newcomers to English are often delighted by the commonplace tag, "as the crow flies," which appeals to them as a picturesquely terse way of indicating the shortest distance—just as once colorful but now worn-out Polish sayings appeal to Morf. Likewise, a stock comparison which for Morf is a fine example of Polish expressiveness, "one needs it like a gap in the bridge" (*potrzebne jak dziura w moście*, literally "needed like a hole in the bridge"), does not strike a Pole as any more vivid than its equivalent, "one needs it like a hole in the head," may be for an English speaker.[3] Since Morf's untempered enthusiasm leads him into dubious generalizations about the character of Conrad's mother tongue, his comments on the effect of Polish linguistic norms on Conrad are not always plausible. Despite this handicap, however, his study is important for prying open a hitherto untouched subject. Furthermore, as I shall have occasion to note later, he does ferret out several genuine polonisms from Conrad's writings.

Shortly after the appearance of Morf's book, A. P. Coleman published an article on the negative aspects of Conrad's indebtedness to Polish.[4] Confining his remarks to one fairly late and unevenly written novel, *Chance*, Coleman scans the damaging imprints of Conrad's linguistic heritage on his English word order, and catalogues the errors in usage and style caused by sporadic surfacing of Polish grammatical forms. More recently, a Polish scholar, Róża Jabłkowska, has offered a brief supplement to Morf's and Coleman's studies in her biography of Conrad.[5] Regrettably, she merely lists a few additional polonisms that she has uncovered, and does not always distinguish between exclusively Polish expressions and those that are common property of several European languages, including English.

Ultimately, then, none of these three writers provides an accounting of Conrad's Polish debts that is thorough enough to warrant a judgment on the extent of his conscious or unconscious dipping into the treasury of his first language as he molded an alien speech to his literary needs. The aim of my paper is to lay some of the groundwork on which such a judgment could be based. On the simplest level, this will mean gathering together and sorting into categories Conrad's borrowings from his Polish vocabulary—a task which I shall take up first. But the Polish tonality of Conrad's prose is less a matter of transposing Polish idioms into English than an effect of Polish rhetorical habits, which, it would seem, Conrad could never wholly shed. Consequently, my main concern here will be the possible relationship between some of the common rhetorical procedures of both literary and colloquial Polish, and Conrad's syntactical choices and distinctive prose rhythm.

I

Roughly speaking, the locutions which Conrad culls from his mother tongue fall into three types: idiomatic phrases and sometimes single words that retain their foreign flavor when rendered literally into English; similar borrowings, as well as stock similes and metaphors, that fit well into their new surroundings and even gain fresh vigor from the transplantation; and Polish proverbs that have no precise equivalents in English.

So far only one member of the first group has come to the attention of English readers. Morf points out that two of the comments voiced by Conrad's characters in "The Duel" and "The Warrior's Soul"— " 'There's some milk yet about that moustache of yours, my boy' " (*A Set of Six*, p. 197) and " 'Some of you had better wipe the milk off your upper lip before . . . passing judgment' " (*Tales of Hearsay*, p. 1)—are actually allusions to a Polish saying, "to have milk under the nose" (*mieć mleko pod nosem*), which disparages youth.[6] In her Polish book, Róża Jabłkowska cites a couple of examples that must sound quite bizarre to an English reader: "in the force of his age" and "forget my tongue in my head."[7] The first phrase is a literal translation of the Polish idiom, *w sile wieku*, corresponding to the English "in the prime of life"; Conrad uses it twice, in his very first literary production, "The Black Mate," and in a much later, though not much more important, story, "The Tale" (*Tales of Hearsay*, pp. 87 and 72). The second expression is also an exact rendering of a stock Polish saying, *zapomnieć języka w gębie*, except (as Róża Jabłkowska does *not* point out) for one word, "head." While the Englishman simply loses his tongue if startled or embarrassed, the Pole in a like situation forgets his tongue in his *mouth*.

Curiously enough, many of Conrad's most obvious polonisms, stowed in his better known works, have gone unobserved. When handling idioms that are fairly close in both English and Polish, Conrad sometimes falls into the trap that probably no one who is well versed in two or more languages can wholly avoid—the unconscious replacement of a part of an idiomatic expression from one language with that of another. The phrase "heavy mourning" (*ciężka żałoba*), which supplants the customary English locution, *deep mourning*, in *A Personal Record* (p. 71) illustrates this sort of transfer. So does another example from the same work, "my hired home" (p. 113), since in English *hire* is not normally used in reference to dwellings, while the corresponding Polish verb, *wynajmować*, can govern houses, rooms, furniture, vehicles and people with equal propriety. In *Under Western Eyes*, "handgrasp" (p. 238) is a literal translation of the Polish idiom, *uścisk ręki* (more often *dłoni*, i.e., the palm of the hand), that matches the English *handshake*. But the substitution is apt here, I think, for Conrad is describing the seasoned revolutionary activist Sophia Antonovna, and "handgrasp" connotes a decisiveness and virility that the common English term fails to suggest.

Some critics, unfamiliar with Polish, are quick to pounce on Conrad's second language, French, as the source of his stylistic anomalies.[8] Certainly, Conrad's works do contain gallicisms, especially *The Arrow of Gold* and *The Rover*, which are set in France.[9] An interesting instance of a gallicism also occurs in *The End of the Tether*, where Conrad describes a storeroom on the *Sofala* as "that Capharnaum of forgotten things" (p. 322). At least one of Conrad's readers was sufficiently puzzled by the reference to seek a gloss from *The New York Times Book Review*, when it still carried a section of literary queries. This particular question was never answered in the *Review*, but *capharnaüm* is the French term for what the British call a lumber room, or a place for odds and ends, and Conrad seems to be using the word in this sense.[10] However, some of the expressions that might be attributed to French could have slipped as easily into Conrad's English from his native tongue. The English adjective *clear*, for instance, is not usually applied to clothes, yet in *Nostromo* Mrs. Gould's "clear dress gave the only truly festive note" to the dinner party on the *Juno* (p. 35), and "the clear, light fabrics . . . of her dress appear luminous" to Dr. Monygham during his conversation with her near the end of the book (p. 520). The French *clair* and the Polish *jasny*, both of which translate into the English *clear*, often describe light-colored garments and connote the sort of bright effect that Conrad apparently intends here.[11] A distinctly un-English locution from *Victory* would also be very much at home in Conrad's other two languages. Assessing the situation as he sees Heyst and Lena walk off into the woods, Ricardo decides that "Heyst had gone to combine some fresh move" (p. 341). The verb *combine* makes little sense here unless one recalls its French and Polish meaning, *devise* or *contrive*. Furthermore, the Polish verb *kombinować*, used in this way, has a colloquial flavor that is most appropriate in the context, since Ricardo affects slang. As a sidelight, it might be added that the Polish substantive from this verb, *kombinator* (perhaps best approximated by the English word *schemer*), has a strongly pejorative ring that also suits Ricardo's attitude towards Heyst. An expression in a later novel, *The Rover*, is linked more closely to Polish than to French through Conrad's choice of the governing preposition. The farmhouse where Peyrol settles, Conrad tells us, "commanded on one side the view of Hyères roadstead *on the first plan*" (p. 30). The phrase I have italicized renders exactly the Polish locution *na pierwszym planie*, which corresponds to the English idiom *in the foreground*. The French say *au* (rather than *sur le*) *premier plan*, though of course the French phrase may be translated into English in the same way as the Polish one.

Conrad's most interesting borrowings, however, are not the tell-tale oddities I have dealt with so far, but the perfectly assimilated words and phrases that could hardly strike the English reader as false to his language. More often than not, these expressions are Polish clichés, coaxed back to their original freshness of image by means of translation. Already in his first novel, *Almayer's Folly*, Conrad rescues an attractive, but dying, Polish metaphor, *sheaf of light* (*snop światła*, the idiomatic equivalent of the English *beam of light*). Placing it at the center of one of his best descriptions of nature in that work, he exploits its full pictorial value as a vivid agricultural image, and at the same time transmutes it into a symbol of hope and magnificence for Nina and Dain's love: "Suddenly a great sheaf of yellow rays shot upwards from behind the black curtain of trees" (p. 70). A less striking image, "the high sky without a flaw" (*The End of the Tether*, p. 243), also gives new life to an overused Polish expression; for while the modifying phrase is a common one in English, it is not normally used of the sky, as in Polish. The comparison "cold like a block of marble" (*The Arrow of Gold*, p. 320) presents a similar case, except that it belongs to both Polish and French. In English marble is generally taken as a type of something hard, durable or smooth; the *OED* does not include a single reference to its chilling properties.[12] Occasionally a borrowed figure receives a new twist. A passage in *Nostromo* yields this simile: "drops of perspiration as big as peas" (p. 447). The Polish cliché which Conrad resorts to here involves a different body fluid: *tears big as peas* (*łzy wielkie jak groch*). Other standard, well-worn expressions that Conrad either translates *verbatim* or slightly adapts include the following:

" 'a long individual . . . *as dry as a chip*' "—*suchy jak trzaska* (*Lord Jim*, p. 40)

" 'He wept and blubbered like a child' "—*łkał jak dziecko* (*Lord Jim*, p. 115)

"as naked as a Turkish saint"—*goły jak święty turecki* (*A Personal Record*, p. 52)

"bare like a barn"—*pusty* (i.e., empty) *jak stodoła* (*Under Western Eyes*, p. 216)

" 'alone. . . . Like this finger' "—*sam jak palec* (*Under Western Eyes*, p. 234)

Conrad also draws on Polish clichés in fashioning his own metaphors and similes. A hackneyed Polish comparison, *dziurawy jak sito* (as full of holes as a sieve), underlies this comment about Jim: "His incognito, which had *as many holes as a sieve*, was not meant to hide a personality but a fact" (p. 4). Later in the book, Marlow's impression of the people among whom Jim is living in Patusan—" 'They exist as if under an enchanter's wand' " (p. 330)—recalls a Polish saying *odmienić co różdżką czarodziejską* (to transform something by means of an enchanter's wand). In *Victory*, Ricardo complains that the music his master appears to enjoy is " 'enough to give colic to an ostrich' " (p. 151). While according to the *OED* this bird's digestive powers have long figured in English comparisons, they are affirmed much more succinctly in the Polish phrase *strusi żołądek* (ostrich stomach). Elsewhere an image of destitution—"I hadn't even the bundle and the stick of a destitute wayfarer" (*The Arrow of Gold*, p. 256)—may hark back to the Polish saying *pójść o kiju* (roughly, to go off leaning on a stick, i.e., to become a beggar), although it also calls forth visions from childhood reading of the inevitable poor lad who sets out into the world with all his earthly goods dangling in a small bundle from a stick he carries on his shoulder. Likewise, the description of Shaw in *The Rescue*—"He stared . . . like an offended owl" (p. 466)—may be indebted to the Polish expression *siedzieć jak sowa* (to sit like an owl, i.e., to be out of humor or puffed up).[13]

Not infrequently, too, Conrad falls back on colloquial and literary figures that are common to both Polish and English, and in some cases may well have multilingual status: "like a drowning man clutching a straw," "air thick enough to slice with a knife," "lay hold of a needle in a pottle of hay," "sloe-black eyes," "ribbon of smoke" (foam, forest, etc.), "the thin sickle of the moon," "fell as if cut down by a scythe," and so on. The phrase "under the angle of eternity"[14] also belongs in this group, being, of course, merely a variant of the Latin *sub specie aeternitatis*. It bears a Polish stamp, however, for *pod kątem* or *under* the angle (rather than *from* an angle, as in English) is an idiomatic Polish phrase indicating point of view or aspect. The adjective *superterrestrial* in "the superterrestrial nature of my misery" (*The Arrow of Gold*, p. 247) seems to be a translation of the Polish word *nadziemski* (not *nieziemski*—unearthly—as Róża Jabłkowska would have it[15]), which is neither as clumsy nor as stilted as Conrad's rendering of it in English.

In at least two of his works Conrad appears to be using polonisms with full awareness of what he is doing: the stories "Amy Foster" and "Prince Roman," both of which have Poles as their protagonists. Morf singles out the following phrases from Yanko Goorall's speech as obviously "translated Polish": "the iron track" (*kolej żelazna*) instead of railroad, "multitudes of nations" (*mnóstwo narodu*) to indicate a large crowd, and "steam-machines" (*maszyny parowe*) instead of engines (*Typhoon and Other Stories*, pp. 114-115).[16] As Morf does not mention, but Róża Jabłkowska points out, "Prince Roman" (*Tales of Hearsay*, pp. 29-55) abounds in Polish titles and forms of address.[17] Furthermore, Conrad's portrayal of the Jew Yankel and his inn (pp. 38-39) owes a good deal to a passage in Adam Mickiewicz's *Pan Tadeusz*.[18] Perhaps, too, in fashioning one of his similes in this story —the old servant's words to the Prince, " 'I am over seventy and of no more account in the world than a cripple in the church porch' " (p. 43)—Conrad may have been thinking of the beggars, often maimed or decrepit, who used to gather beside Polish churches, seeking alms.

The last category of Conrad's Polish borrowings, proverbs, is also the smallest. I have come upon only four clear-cut examples. Three of them have been noted by Morf:

"We haven't kept pigs together" (*The Nigger of the "Narcissus,"* p. 23)

"Man discharges the piece, but God carries the bullet" ("Gaspar Ruiz," *A Set of Six*, p. 18)

"when a guest enters the house, God enters the house" (*Victory*, p. 358)[19]

These sayings occur in contexts dealing with foreigners, and so a foreign touch seems appropriate. Still, it is a bit odd to hear an American Negro, James Wait, throw off an old Polish saw in order to keep Donkin at a proper distance. The second proverb, on the other hand, suits the texture of "Gaspar Ruiz" better than its English equivalent, *every bullet finds its billet*, might have done, since it stresses a cruel divine control of the world rather than purely mechanistic fatalism. Heyst's comment on the " 'sacred virtue of hospitality' " is fraught with irony, for his guest is Ricardo; as in the short story, so here too the proverb implicitly negates the existence of a benign Providence that might protect the innocent from villainy. *The Sisters* yields the fourth proverb, which appears in a comment on the hopes that Stephen's father has for his young son: "Everything is possible in Russia; and, as the proverb says: anything may be done—only cautiously!"[20] Róża Jabłkowska also lists the rich student Kostia's words to Razumov in *Under Western Eyes*—" 'I am like a pig at a trough' " (p. 314)—as a possible polonism, and indeed they are akin to various Polish proverbs involving pigs.[21]

The examples I have brought together here do not exhaust the whole store of Polish vocabulary scattered through Conrad's works. Still, my list is long enough, I think, to show that Polish verbal echoes were not necessarily a handicap to Conrad; he could also turn them into an asset. Certainly, his occasional reliance on Polish clichés as a source of his images lends additional support to Donald C. Yelton's suggestion in his *Mimesis and Metaphor* that Conrad had a penchant for refurbishing conventional epithets.[22] Conrad made no secret of this fact himself, vowing early in his writing career, in the famous Preface to *The Nigger of the "Narcissus,"* to bring "the light of magic suggestiveness" to "the commonplace surface of words . . . the old, old words, worn thin, defaced by ages of careless usage" (p. ix). His revival of long-tarnished expressions from his mother tongue with the aid of an alien but hospitable setting of his adopted language gives a new cast to this pledge.

II

But it was "through an unremitting never-discouraged care for the shape and ring of sentences" that he thought he could best imbue his prose with "magic suggestiveness." As he himself once confessed, English prose cadences "quickly awakened [his] love."[23] Yet his own rhythms are obviously different. What we still do not know is in what ways and to what degree. For apart from Coleman's essay, there is no published analytical evidence relating Conrad's stylistic choices to the syntactical patterns of his first language,[24] and Coleman, as I have mentioned before, dwells exclusively on *mistakes* in diction and sentence structure. If we are ever to explain why Conrad's prose has a familiar sound for Polish readers and an exotic ring for English ones even when it is flawless in terms of grammar and idiom, we must look for subtler, non-aberrant effects of Polish rhetoric on his style.

Two questions lead to the heart of this darkness: do Conrad's rhetorical procedures differ significantly from those followed by other major English novelists of Conrad's time, and do they have anything in common with the rhetorical habits of major Polish writers of the same period? To find at least tentative answers, I have examined descriptive passages from several English and Polish novels of the last half of the nineteenth century and, roughly, the first quarter of the twentieth, comparing their authors' modes of expression to Conrad's.

Not surprisingly, an analysis of these selections indicates that what sets Conrad apart from his English fellow-novelists also links him to their Polish counterparts. Still, taking into account the fact that both Conrad and the other English writers were working within the bounds of the same language, one might not have expected the differences to be quite so pronounced. The English novelists on whom I shall concentrate here—Dickens, George Eliot, Hardy, James, Lawrence, Forster and Virginia Woolf—all have distinctive, sometimes idiosyncratic, styles. Even so, all of them, including James, can be held to a certain norm from which Conrad significantly departs.[25] And Conrad's divergence from the basic pattern adhered to by the others involves precisely those elements of style that characterize the Polish passages, taken from such diverse writers as Kraszewski, Orzeszkowa, Sienkiewicz, Prus, Tetmajer, Reymont and Żeromski.[26]

What I am suggesting then, is that Conrad's exoticism as a stylist stems from his choice of syntactical procedures that had a far greater currency in the Polish than in the English of his time. Some of the rhetorical features of his work may seem to hark back to an earlier English prose—the elaborately arranged and balanced Latinate periods of the seventeenth century. But Conrad did not have to seek out such writers as Sir Thomas Browne for his models, though he must have responded warmly to their cadences. Such cadences were already a part of his heritage, for Polish grammar and syntax are based on Latin, and Polish prose has remained considerably more rhetorical than English well into this century. In fact, a good many rhetorical flourishes that would seem too stilted and flamboyant in modern-day English are so tightly woven into the texture of Polish literary prose that they do not strike the reader as special effects. The simple inversion of subject and predicate illustrates how differently the same rhetorical figure can sound in English and in Polish. In English, a phrase like "Howls the great wind," when used in a prose passage, smacks of bombast—the sort of bombast that Dickens found hard to resist, for the words come from his description of Chesney Wold in *Bleak House*. Translated into Polish, these words might not seem well chosen for reasons of euphony, but if "roar" is substituted for "howl," then "ryczy wiatr" (roars the wind) is a better, more forceful way of communicating the phenomenon than "wiatr ryczy" (the wind roars). Now Conrad was too much of a stylist to indulge himself in this type of inversion, despite the example of Dickens. Whatever the truth about his English pronunciation, he could obviously distinguish what might or might not work well in English prose. And by and large, he does not wrench English into unnatural or even merely old-fashioned postures. The rhetorical patterning that he favors is not aberrant in his adopted language; but of course neither is it ingrained, as in Polish. Consequently, it is noticeable without being wrong, and appears remarkable because it is rare and unexpected rather than eccentric.

A standard feat of Conrad's rhetorical legerdemain is the asyndeton, or the omission of conjunctions. In Polish one simply does not feel the same urgency as in English to place an *and* before the final member of a series of words or phrases. No doubt this tendency is encouraged by the relative looseness of Polish syntax. Polish is a highly inflected language, and when the relationship among various words is indicated by their endings, different parts of the sentence can be moved about much more freely than in English. An adjective— or several adjectives—can be placed before or after a noun, depending on the effect desired. And the pronoun can usually be omitted as a subject, for normally in Polish we do not say "I am," but as in Latin rely on the predicate alone—"jestem." This applies to other verbs as well, for the inflection always indicates the person and number.

A consequence of this freedom is a special kind of terseness, a condensation of energy and a narrowing of focus: in Polish one can operate by means of content words (i.e., nouns, verbs, adjectives and adverbs), with just a sprinkling of essential prepositions, much more readily and successfully than in English. And looking at English nineteenth- and twentieth-century literature, one finds that with the sole exception of Dickens' famous description of fog in the opening pages of *Bleak House*, Conrad stands out as the writer who is most apt to use elliptical phrasing until the stream-of-consciousness novelists come along. His favorite kind of ellipsis—the omission of connectives—is probably most frequent and most noticeable in *Heart of Darkness*. For example, one might look at Marlow's recollection of the dying natives at the first inland station:

> "Black shapes crouched, lay, sat between the trees, leaning against the trunks, clinging to the earth, half coming out, half effaced within the dim light. . . ." (p. 66)

Or one of the many descriptions of the jungle:

> "An empty stream, a great silence, an impenetrable forest. The air was warm, thick, heavy, sluggish." (p. 93)

Or the comment near the end of the book about Kurtz's Intended:

"She had a mature capacity for fidelity, for belief, for suffering." (p. 157)

Conrad's other novels and stories also yield many examples of this figure. It can take a very simple form, as in this brief first description of Decoud in *Nostromo*:

... the short, curly, golden beard did not conceal his lips, rosy, fresh, almost pouting in expression. (p. 151)

But it can also become a highly complicated device of emphasis, particularly when combined with anaphora, and often underlies special rhythmic effects, well illustrated by the passage from *Lord Jim* evoking the seascape at the start of the *Patna*'s ill-fated journey:

And under the sinister splendour of that sky the sea, blue and profound, remained still, without a stir, without a ripple, without a wrinkle—viscous, stagnant, dead. (pp. 15-16)

Polish literary prose is full of asyndetons. I shall quote just a few characteristic examples from the writers whom I mentioned earlier.

In the fane of Nijoła flashes of lightning ... extinguished the glow of the holy fire, smoke filled the temple, sparks flew onto the curtains; the red eyes of the statue flashed as if rejoicing at the destruction. (Kraszewski)

Over the distant bend of the Niemen, as if from the water, floated up the fiery sickle of the rising moon, quickly grew larger, grew rounder, mounted, until it hung above the river in a great, blazing shield. (Orzeszkowa)

The day was a fine one, the sky almost cloudless, the pavement without dust. (Prus)

... after a mild, misty night came a day that was windy, at times clear, at times because of clouds which, chased by the wind, galloped over the sky in droves—gloomy. (Sienkiewicz)

Mists piled upon the world. Autumn mists, thick, murky, in which the nearest trees, the nearest houses disappeared unseen. The mountains and the valley drowned in the darkness, the sun vanished in it, as if for ever. (Tetmajer)

Without screams now, without quarreling, without protest, they were packing, taking out vessels, tying up bundles. . . . (Reymont)

Fleeing with huge strides, he jumped over bushes, rotted fences, softened ridges of plowed earth, a ditch still full of ice. He reached the meadows . . . . But suddenly . . . . he saw . . . the river. Swollen to the top of its banks from the spring thaw and flood, full of black, writhing water . . . the deep river barred his way with a semicircle to the right, a semicircle to the left. (Żeromski)

English novelists of Conrad's time and stature for the most part eschew this rhetorical figure. Except for some instances in Henry James, occasional examples in Lawrence, and the special case of Joyce, I have found no asyndetons in the many passages I have examined closely, or in the random samplings of additional descriptions from the works of both major and minor English writers.[27] Indeed, the paucity of asyndetons in English literature is brought home with some force when one leafs through handbooks and dictionaries of literary terms. Most figures listed in them are illustrated by appropriate quotations of English prose or verse. The favorite example of asyndeton, on the other hand, is Julius Caesar's "I came, I saw, I conquered."

A writer who omits connectives is likely to seek other means of linking related phrases. Conrad is quite fond of anaphora, or the repetition of the same word at the beginning of two or more phrases. In English, this figure belongs to older prose and to poetry. It appears in the King James Version of the Bible, for instance in *Ecclesiastes*:

> A time to be born, and a time to die; a time to plant, and a time to pluck up that which is planted. . . . A time to weep, and a time to laugh. . . .

The early Romantic poets liked it, especially Blake and Burns. In the latter part of the nineteenth century, it attracted Tennyson, Browning and Matthew Arnold, and in America, Whitman. It also appealed to such different modern poets as Yeats, T. S. Eliot and Dylan Thomas.

English novelists—aside from Conrad—use it rarely. When they do, it is to stress an accumulation of objects, as in this excerpt from *The Mill on the Floss*, where the preposition *with* is repeated:

> . . . the black ships—laden with the fresh-scented fir-planks, with rounded sacks of oil-bearing seed, or with the dark glitter of coal—are borne along to the town of St Ogg's.

Or it may be to point out specific objects—a sort of writer's substitute for the speaker's sweep of the arm, which E. M. Forster employs in *Howard's End*:

> There were the greengage trees . . . there the tennis lawn . . . there the hedge. . . .

By contrast, Polish novelists value anaphora as a serviceable device of both emphasis and linkage. Some of my earlier quotations, illustrating asyndeton, demonstrate this point as well. I shall cite only three additional, very brief, examples here:

> From many apartments came the sound of grand pianos, from many yards the sound of barrel-organs. . . . (Prus)

> He lay a long time without movement, without the ability to raise his arms, legs, eyelids. (Żeromski)

> . . . from the damp shade under the trees, from moldering leaves, from overgrown nettles rose a heavy, stifling smell in the hot air. (Iwaszkiewicz)[28]

Like his Polish contemporaries in the craft, Conrad often combines anaphora with asyndeton; he is also apt to rely on prepositions to generate his anaphoras, and he sometimes repeats prepositions whereas a native English speaker would be likely to omit them. So in *Lord Jim* he writes,

"The smell of mud, of marsh, the primeval smell of fecund earth. . . ." (p. 331)

rather than "the smell of mud, marsh, the primeval smell of fecund earth." In another, better known, passage from the same novel, recurring prepositions function in a much more complicated way. I have in mind the celebrated description of the seascape at the end of Chapter Two, to which I referred earlier in this paper. Jim's ship, the *Patna,*

. . . held on straight for the Red Sea under a serene sky, under a sky scorching and unclouded, enveloped in a fulgor of sunshine that killed all thought, oppressed the heart, withered all impulses of strength and energy. And under the sinister splendour of that sky the sea, blue and profound, remained still, without a stir, without a ripple, without a wrinkle—viscous, stagnant, dead. (pp. 15-16)

The preposition *under* draws attention to each phrase it introduces, and makes us take notice of what Conrad is doing—how in effect the third phrase brings to a much higher pitch the contrast implicit in the first two. From "serene" we move to "scorching and unclouded" and then to "sinister splendour." Each successive phrase seems to encompass the preceding one. "Unclouded" in the second phrase suggests serenity, but it is coupled with "scorching," and then the physical aspect of the sky, as well as its influence on what lies below, is summed up in the third phrase, "sinister splendour." Finally, the fiery might of the sky is made even more palpable by the brief evocation of the sea, which "remained still, without a stir, without a ripple, without a wrinkle—viscous, stagnant, dead." So a second anaphora has appeared to balance the first, but now it depends on a negative word, on a word denoting lack or absence—here the absence of any motion and hence of life. The second anaphora is, of course, linked to the first by more than symmetry. It is the sea and all upon it that is *under* the sky. By the end of the sentence, the word *under* takes on an additional dimension, for we realize that it describes not only the physical location of two points in space, but a condition of domination and subjugation, the relationship of tormentor and victim, of master and slave. Its conspicuousness as part of an emphatic rhetorical figure helps to bring out this other, more complex meaning and to underscore a characteristic situation in Conradian fiction: the perpetual conflict within the natural world, as well as its hostility towards man.

Anaphora is a refinement of syntactical parallelism, which is a time-honored device, common in spoken, as well as written, English and Polish. Unlike his English coevals, however, Conrad shows a predilection for a specific type of this figure—triple parallelism, which is a type prevalent in Polish literary prose. The quotations from Polish literature, cited above, illustrate it amply. It characterizes the writing of Prus, who is a careful stylist, shunning flamboyance and excess of any kind. It appears in the spare prose of Sienkiewicz, as well as in the lush descriptions of Żeromski and Reymont.[29] Even more significantly perhaps, this rhetorical device had found favor with the writers on whose works Conrad was nurtured—Mickiewicz, Słowacki, Fredro.[30] His own father, too, fancied it to a fault; his play, *Dla miłego grosza*, contains numerous examples of the figure, sometimes as many as three or four in a space of twelve lines.[31]

Conrad loves the device—so much so that triple parallelism can be termed his own special signature in the English novelistic prose of his time. While the other English writers I have referred to do occasionally turn to this figure, they apparently prefer either simple parallelism, or parallel structures consisting of four members.[32] The latter is Hardy's choice in describing Egdon Heath:

> The face of the heath by its mere complexion added half an hour to evening; it could in like manner retard the dawn, sadden noon, anticipate the frowning of storms scarcely generated, and intensify the opacity of a moonless midnight to a cause of shaking and dread.

As for Conrad, you can hardly open a page of description in any of his works without coming upon at least one instance of triple parallelism. Sometimes it is a simple matter of three adjectives following a noun: "The land lay silent, still, and brilliant" (*An Outcast of the Islands*, p. 85), or "the hard ground of Russia, inanimate, cold, inert" (*Under Western Eyes*, pp. 32-33). It can also be a trio of nouns, as when during the storm in *The Nigger of the "Narcissus,"* "Nothing seems left of the whole universe but darkness, clamour, fury" (p. 54). There may be two parallel triadic sets, one of nouns and one of qualifiers; the classic example occurs in *Heart of Darkness*: " 'Trees, trees, millions of trees, massive, immense, running up high' " (p. 95). Predicates and their modifiers cluster in triads, as do various kinds of modifying and qualifying phrases. In "The Lagoon,"

> The mist lifted, broke into drifting patches, vanished into thin flying wreaths. . . . (*Tales of Unrest*, p. 202)

In "Youth,"

> "A magnificent death had come like a grace, like a gift, like a reward to that old ship at the end of her laborious days." (p. 35)

In "The Secret Sharer,"

> ... around us nothing moved, nothing lived, not a canoe on the water, not a bird in the air, not a cloud in the sky. (*'Twixt Land and Sea*, p. 92)

As most of these examples suggest, Conrad reinforces even fairly simple parallelisms with asyndeton, and sometimes with anaphora as well. Quite frequently, he elaborates them into still more complex structures. He may interlock two or more sets of triads, as in the following description from *Lord Jim*, during Marlow's journey down river with Jim, at the end of his visit to Patusan:

> "The light itself seemed to stir, the sky above our heads widened, a far-off murmur reached our ears, a freshness enveloped us, filled our lungs, quickened our thoughts, our blood, our regrets. . . ." (p. 331)

While " 'a freshness enveloped us' " at first glance is merely a fourth phrase paralleling the first three, it is also the beginning of a new triad which merges with a third one—" 'our thoughts, our blood, our regrets.' " Sometimes, too, a triple parallelism is augmented by two additional, extended parallel phrases, as in this excerpt from "The Lagoon":

> In the stillness of the air every tree, every leaf, every bough, every tendril of creeper and every petal of minute blossoms seemed to have been bewitched into an immobility perfect and final. (*Tales of Unrest*, p. 187)

In longer sentences, the basically parallel structure of three sets of phrases is saved from monotony by a slight deflection of the third member. This happens in the evocation of setting which opens Chapter Six of the last part of *Nostromo*:

> The declining sun had shifted the shadows from west to east amongst the houses of the town. It had shifted them upon the whole extent of the immense Campo, with the white wall of its haciendas on the knolls dominating the green distances; with its grass-thatched ranchos crouching in the folds of ground by the banks of streams; with the dark islands of clustered trees on a clear sea of grass, and the precipitous range of the Cordillera, immense and motionless, emerging from the billows of the lower forests like the barren coast of a land of giants. (p. 394)

Parallelism here is sustained by the repetition of *with* (anaphora), and by the three present participles, *dominating*, *crouching* and *emerging*, which constitute the main verbal force of their respective phrases. But the final segment of this tripartite sentence actually consists of two phrases, both governed by the third *with*.

There are numerous other ways in which Conrad manipulates triple parallelism, and examples abound in all of his works, both in descriptive passages and in narrative ones. I shall mention three more here. In the panoramic description from *Nostromo*, part of which I have just quoted, an introductory parallelism takes us in stages to the main object being depicted:

> ... and away there, beyond Rincon, hidden from the town by two wooded spurs, the rocks of the San Tomé gorge ... took on warm tones of brown and yellow .... (p. 394)

Three parallel subjects of an elliptical coordinate sentence mark both the space traversed and the passage of time as Ossipon wanders through London streets near the end of *The Secret Agent*:

> The lights of Victoria saw him, too, and Sloane Square, and the railings of the park. (p. 300)

And a triple set of phrases, each containing two modifiers strictly balanced in syllabic length, emphasizes the ponderous and restrictive atmosphere of the Palazzo Brignoli in *Suspense*:

> Massive and sombre, ornate and heavy, with a dark aspect and enormous carvings, the Palace where little Adéle was living had to Cosmo's eye the air of a sumptuous prison. (p. 80)

Even when he does not use triple parallelism, Conrad is apt to let his sentences divide into three segments. This tendency may remind some readers of the celebrated *coupe ternaire* associated with Flaubert. Although Flaubert's example may well have encouraged Conrad in his predilection for tripartite arrangements, it should be noted that this kind of phrasal configuration is quite common in Polish.[33]

The syntactical patterning of a sentence is obviously what determines its rhythm. Conrad's reliance on rhetorical devices generally avoided by his English compeers save in very special situations is bound to give his prose a different movement from theirs. But it is startling to discover how atypical this rhythm is both in respect to English habits of speech and in respect to English literary practice. Ford Madox Ford, himself a writer of foreign extraction, was puzzled as to how Conrad, whose ear, he thought, "was singularly faulty for ... a great writer of elaborated prose," could produce such splendid cadences.[34] Could it be that Conrad's ear remained attuned to the rhythms of another tongue and that his struggle as an artist was to impose those rhythms on a language not conducive to them? Could it be perhaps that his word order derived from a subconscious pulsation of thought and sound in a different tempo from what he was hearing about him? How else does one explain his astonishing affinity for *falling* rhythms?

In his still indispensable study of prose rhythm, Norton R. Tempest concludes that "*Rising* and *waved* rhythms are the most common measures in English speech; *falling* and *level* rhythms are comparatively rare." Furthermore, he notes that paeons, or feet of four syllables containing a single stress, "are found in abundance in rhythmical or 'numerous' prose" and that "many English writers of highly rhythmical prose show a marked preference for the third paeon (xx/x)."[35] Polish rhythms, on the other hand, are essentially trochaic and amphibrachic, and it is not hard to discern why, when one recalls that Polish is a highly inflected language where nouns that are monosyllabic in the nominative case take on additional syllables with the change in inflection. So the word for home or house, *dom*, becomes a disyllable in the phrase, "I am going home"—*idę do domu.* In the expression, "Peace to this house," it is a trisyllable—*pokój temu domowi.* And since Polish has regular accentuation, the stress falling on the penultimate syllable, practically all two-syllable words are trochees, whereas three-syllable words form amphibrachs.

It goes without saying that Conrad could not impose such a pattern of stresses on English; the most he could do was to bend his adopted language towards an approximation of his preferred metric shape, without straining its own particular normality. What distinguishes Conrad's descriptive prose, in terms of rhythm, from the prose of the other English novelists whom I mentioned at the outset of this discussion is the generally higher proportion of trochaic and dactylic feet in his passages. On the average, these measures account for one-eighth to one-sixth of all metric feet in selections from the seven authors whom I have studied closely.[36] Conrad's usual range is from one-fifth to one-third per passage; moreover, he intersperses level feet among his other measures much more frequently than the others.

If we juxtapose two passages from the novels of D. H. Lawrence and Virginia Woolf, writers whose descriptive prose is no less rhythmical than Conrad's, we find that, despite the individual mood and rhythm of each segment, the ratio of rising and falling measures is quite similar. The first excerpt comes from Chapter XIX ("Moony") of *Women in Love*, the second from the short, middle section of *To the Lighthouse,* called "Time Passes."

Then again | there was | a burst | of sound, |
and a burst | of brilliant | light, | the moon |
had exploded | on the water, | and was flying |
asunder | in flakes | of white | and dangerous |
fire. | Rapidly, | like white birds, | the fires |
all broken | rose | across | the pond, | fleeing |

/ / / /
in clamorous | confusion, | battling | with the flock |
/ / / / /
of dark | waves | that were forcing | their way in. |

/ / / / /
When darkness | fell, | the stroke | of the Lighthouse, |
/ / / / /
which had laid | itself | with such | authority | upon |
/ / /
the carpet | in the darkness, | tracing | its pattern, |
/ / / / / /
came now | in the softer | light | of spring | mixed |
/ / / / /
with moonlight | gliding | gently | as if | it laid |
/ / /
its caress | and lingered | stealthily | and looked |
/ / /
and came | lovingly | again. |

Although in his analysis of prose rhythm, Tempest is chiefly concerned with discursive rather than novelistic prose, his findings hold true for these passages as well. In each of them, rising and waved rhythms clearly predominate; each contains at least twice as many iambs and anapaests as trochees and dactyls, and has very few level measures (spondees and stressed monosyllables). The obligatory third paeons appear in both. Lawrence, particularly, handles his with bravura, placing three of them in a sequence in his first sentence, and letting the fourth one—near the end of the second sentence—spin into "something like an Ionic *a minore*" (xx//), which George Saintsbury saw as the classic function of the third paeon in "those passages which aim at special harmonic effect."[37]

Conrad, too, uses third paeons, though in a much more muted fashion than Lawrence. Often he prefers the second paeon (x/xx), which has less of a rise and more of a fall in its wave. That is his choice in the description of winter landscape in *Under Western Eyes*, a description that also illustrates how densely Conrad can interlace his prose with falling measures.

/ / / /
Under | the sumptuous | immensity | of the sky, |
/ / / /
the snow | covered | the endless | forests, |
/ / / /
the frozen | rivers, | the plains | of an immense |
/ / \
country, | obliterating | the landmarks, |
/ / /
the accidents | of the ground, | levelling |

>   /   /   /   /
> everything | under | its uniform | whiteness, |
> like a monstrous | blank page | awaiting |
> the record | of an inconceivable | history. | (p. 33)

This passage, though unquestionably rhythmical, has only one third paeon, and four iambs and anapaests. But there are seven trochees and three dactyls, together constituting *more* than a third of all the feet in the passage. When one considers, too, that there are four second paeons in this segment, and a longer, seven-syllable foot, which, like the second paeons, has a dactylic ending, then the surge of falling rhythms seems extraordinarily powerful for a passage of English prose. It is not beside the point, surely, to notice that this long sentence also contains two asyndetons and one set of three parallel phrases, as well as two simple parallelisms and a pair of phrases (both beginning with "under"), which, though far apart in the sentence, are nevertheless in a parallel relation to each other.

When there is a larger proportion of rising measures, the pressure of level rhythms often counteracts their force. The following excerpt from the long description in *Nostromo* to which I have referred earlier reveals Conrad's way with spondees and monosyllabic feet.

> The undulating | surface | of the forests | seemed |
> powdered | with pale | gold dust; | and away there |
> beyond | Rincon, | hidden | from the town | by two |
> wooded | spurs, | the rocks | of the San | Tome | gorge, |
> with the flat | wall | of the mountain | itself |
> crowned | by gigantic | ferns, | took on | warm tones |
> of brown | and yellow, | with red | rusty | streaks, |
> and the dark | green clumps | of bushes | rooted |
> in crevices. | (p. 394)

Here rising and falling feet keep to more or less the same ratio as in the excerpts from Lawrence and Virginia Woolf. There are only six trochees to thirteen rising measures. The sentence, however, shows a remarkable concentration of stresses. When added to the six trochees, the five spondees and seven monosyllabic feet raise the number of falling and level measures to near equality with rising and waved feet. But because stresses in this passage cluster in sets of two, three, four and even five, one may go so far as to say that level rhythms dominate here.

Conrad's ability to reconcile his rhythmic preferences and the exigencies of English prose is perhaps best illustrated by the closing lines of *Heart of Darkness*, which Ford praised as "one of the most perfect passages of prose in the language."[38]

> The offing | was barred | by a black | bank |
> of clouds | and the tranquil | waterway, |
> leading | to the uttermost | ends | of the earth |
> flowed | sombre | under | an overcast | sky— |
> seemed | to lead | into the heart | of an immense |
> darkness. | (p. 162)

Though the four trochees and one dactyl equal in number the three iambs and two anapaests, rising feet have a slight edge because of the unquestionable fourth paeon near the end, a possible fourth paeon preceding it (if one does not give "into" a secondary stress), and an imperfect di-iamb earlier in the sentence. Stresses are hardly as pre-eminent as in the passage from *Nostromo*; no more than three occur seriatim and there are no actual spondees. Nevertheless, a nearly absolute equivalence exists between rising and waved measures and falling and level ones, for there are eleven feet of the former to ten of the latter. Consequently, neither kind of rhythm prevails in the passage. Instead, Conrad offers us an almost perfect balancing of the more common and the rarer rhythms of English prose—a balancing that is hardly in the mainstream of English rhythmic tradition, whether one considers novelists contemporary with Conrad, or other writers of highly rhythmical prose, from Browne to Ruskin and Pater.[39]

Conrad's Polish heritage, then, makes itself felt in several ways in his works. Aside from cultural debts, now well known to Conradian scholars, there are the literary borrowings, which have not been as fully explored, and the various traces of Polish speech, some of which I discussed in the first part of this paper—the common metaphors and idioms that Conrad weaves into the fabric of his language. But it is the Polish warp of his sentence, interlaced with its English weft, that gives his prose its special character. The Polish tonality of his writings, while involving a whole range of influences, rises from the very bedrock, the basic rhythms and patterns, of his native language—the language to which, by his wife's testimony, he reverted in times of physical suffering, and to which he apparently turned in the still greater throes of artistic creation.

NOTES

[1] The term is used by Adam Gillon, *The Eternal Solitary: A Study of Joseph Conrad* (New York: Bookman Associates, 1960), p. 43. In addition to Gillon, for general remarks on the influence of his Polish heritage on Conrad, and for specific commentary on his borrowings from Polish literature, as well as his allusions to Polish history and way of life, see the following: Andrzej Busza, *Conrad's Polish Literary Background and Some Illustrations of the Influence of Polish Literature on His Work* (Rome: Institutum Historicum Polonicum, 1966; *Antemurale* X, 109-255); Witold Chwalewik, "Conrad and the Literary Tradition," *Kwartalnik Neofilologiczny* (The *Neophilological Quarterly*), Special Number 1-2 (1958), pp. 29-37; Ludwik Krzyżanowski, "Joseph Conrad's 'Prince Roman': Fact and Fiction," *Centennial Essays* (New York: Polish Institute of Arts and Sciences in America, 1960), pp. 27-69; and Zdzisław Najder, Introduction to *Conrad's Polish Background: Letters to and from Polish Friends* (London: Oxford Univ. Press, 1964), pp. 28-31.

[2] Gustav Morf, *The Polish Heritage of Joseph Conrad* (New York: Haskell House, 1965), p. 209. The book was first published c. 1930.

[3] For the most part, Morf simply translates his Polish examples, without citing them in the original as I do in this paper. Whenever possible, I have checked out the expressions I mention in the course of this study, whether Polish, English or French, in various dictionaries and other works of reference. The *OED* and Stanisław Skorupka's *Słownik frazeologiczny języka polskiego* [Phraseological Dictionary of the Polish Language] (Warsaw: Wiedza Powszechna, 1967-1968), 2 vols., have proven especially useful.

[4] "Polonisms in Conrad's *Chance*," *Modern Language Notes*, 9 (November 1931), 463-68.

[5] *Joseph Conrad: 1857-1924* (Wrocław: Ossolineum, 1961), p. 336.

[6] Morf, pp. 210-11. My page references to Conrad's works are to the New Collected Edition (London: J. M. Dent, 1946-1955), 22 vols.

[7] Jabłkowska, p. 336.

[8] E.g., Albert J. Guerard's remark that an "obvious idiosyncrasy" of Conrad's in "The Lagoon" is his "French positioning of adjectives"—*Conrad the Novelist* (Cambridge, Mass.: Harvard Univ. Press, 1958), p. 67. However, the placing of the adjective after the noun is also common in Polish literary prose and particularly characteristic of ornamental or descriptive writing. See also Najder, pp. 28-29.

[9] Now and then, too, Conrad inserts French words into these two novels for the sake of local color. For instance, "a ci-devant shrine" can be glimpsed from the Escampobar Farm in *The Rover* (p. 30).

[10] Cf. Flaubert's use of this word in *Madame Bovary*, Part Three, Chapter II.

[11] Conrad admitted his occasional reliance on Polish to Cunninghame Graham, when he answered Graham's letter criticizing his use of the phrase

"*Mi alma*" in *Nostromo*. "What misled me," he wrote, "was that in Polish that very term of endearment: 'My Soul' has not the passionate significance you point out. I am crestfallen and sorry." *Joseph Conrad's Letters to R. B. Cunninghame Graham*, ed. C. T. Watts (Cambridge, England: The University Press, 1969), pp. 157-58.

[12] There are a few such references, however, in Byron's Oriental Tales.

[13] Some of the polonisms offered in the preceding two paragraphs are mentioned by Morf, who, however, does not always recognize them as *actual* Polish expressions, believing simply that Conrad formed them on the Polish model. See especially pp. 212-13. As far as I know, the Polish provenance of Conrad's expression, "naked as a Turkish saint," was first noted by Jan Librach in his article, "Mechanizm rewolucji według Józefa Conrada," *Tematy* (New York-London), No. 31-32 (Fall-Winter 1969), 449, n.

[14] First noted by J. H. Retinger, *Conrad and His Contemporaries* (New York: Roy, 1943), p. 111.

[15] Jabłkowska, p. 336.

[16] Morf, pp. 216-17.

[17] Jabłkowska, p. 336.

[18] Busza, pp. 233-34.

[19] Morf, p. 210. He also points out that Conrad "smuggled" the last two into his fiction "under the Russian flag."

[20] Joseph Conrad, "The Sisters," *The Bookman*, 66 (January 1928), 484.

[21] Jabłkowska, p. 336.

[22] *Mimesis and Metaphor: An Inquiry into the Genesis and Scope of Conrad's Symbolic Imagery* (The Hague: Mouton, 1967), p. 134.

[23] G. Jean-Aubry, *Joseph Conrad: Life and Letters* (New York: Doubleday, Page and Co., 1927), I, 206.

[24] See, however, Najder, pp. 29-30, for helpful general comments about the possible effects of Polish on Conrad's literary prose.

[25] The passages I have analyzed closely come from the following novels: *Bleak House* (1853), *The Mill on the Floss* (1860), *The Return of the Native* (1878), *Tess of the D'Urbervilles* (1891), *The Ambassadors* (1903), *Howard's End* (1910), *Sons and Lovers* (1913), *Women in Love* (1920) and *To the Lighthouse* (1927). In addition, I have made a less thorough check of descriptive passages from other novels of the same authors, as well as from the works of other English writers known for their descriptive style, such as Ruskin, Meredith and Pater.

[26] Ignacy Kraszewski (1812-1887), *Stara Baśń* (1876); Eliza Orzeszkowa (1842-1910), *Nad Niemnem* (1887); Bolesław Prus (pseud. of Aleksander Głowacki, 1847-1912), *Lalka* (1887); Henryk Sienkiewicz (1846-1916), *Krzyżacy* (1900); Kazimierz Przerwa-Tetmajer (1865-1940), *Legenda Tatr* (c. 1904); Władysław Reymont (1867-1925), *Chłopi* (1904-1909); and Stefan Żeromski (1864-1925), *Popioły* (1904) and *Wierna rzeka* (1912). As in the case of the English writers, I have looked at additional works of these and other Polish authors. All translations in this paper are mine.

[27] Aside from stream-of-consciousness passages, asyndetons sometimes appear in Joyce when his prose verges on poetry, as in the final paragraph of "The Dead."

[28] Jarosław Iwaszkiewicz, *Opowiadania zebrane* (Warszawa: Czytelnik, 1969), II, 352. There are many other examples in contemporary Polish literature of the rhetorical forms that I discuss in this paper.

[29]For additional examples and commentary see Halina Kurkowska and Stanisław Skorupka, *Stylistyka polska: zarys* (Warszawa: Państwowe Wydawnictwo Naukowe, 1959), p. 217 ff.

[30]Concerning the influence of these and other Polish writers on Conrad, see Busza, p. 171 ff., Najder, p. 15 ff., and Wiktor Weintraub, "Alexander Fredro and His Antiromantic Memoirs," *The American Slavic and East European Review* [New York], 12, No. 4 (1953), 546-48.

[31]Apollo Korzeniowski, *Dla miłego grosza*, ed. Roman Taborski (Warszawa: Państwowy Instytut Wydawniczy, 1964).

[32]Triple parallelism, of a brief, unelaborated kind, seems to be finding more favor in contemporary literature. See for instance Murdoch's new novel, *The Black Prince* (New York : Viking, 1973).

[33]Kurkowska and Skorupka, pp. 219-20.

[34]*Joseph Conrad: A Personal Remembrance* (London: Duckworth and Co., 1924), p. 214.

[35]Norton R. Tempest, *The Rhythm of English Prose* (Cambridge, England: The University Press, 1930), pp. 42, 48 and 135. Tempest's approach to prose rhythm is still the most sensible and useful one, despite newer books on the subject. It is based on the premise that, except in special instances, prose should not be treated like verse. For "since, in prose, there is no metrical pattern to cause interference with the normal speech accents, the basic syllable-grouping is logical, whereas it is metrical in verse. From this it follows that, as a general rule, the rhythm-groups of prose are composed of whole words, and, therefore, in scansion the words are never cut by foot-divisions" (p. 35). In my analyses of prose rhythm, I rely on both his method and his terminology.

[36]They occasionally reach one-fourth in Pater and Joyce, judging from random samplings of their work.

[37]George Saintsbury, *A History of English Prose Rhythm* (London: Macmillan, 1922), p. 452, quoted in Tempest, p. 43.

[38]Ford Madox Ford, *Portraits from Life* (Chicago: Henry Regnery Co., 1937), p. 81.

[39]Admittedly, my samplings of English prose are not large enough at this stage to prove the hypothesis they have generated. Only computer research, I suppose, can amass sufficient evidence for full confirmation. However, if nothing else, the consistency of the results I have obtained from comparatively limited analyses suggests the direction that further studies might take.

The Essential Conrad

Norman Sherry

ABSTRACT

At different stages in his career, Conrad was preoccupied with examining the validity of certain moral assumptions that his characters attempted to maintain against the pressures of a variety of situations and environments. He seemed quite consciously to be approaching the problem of moral validity from a changing standpoint, and the development of his thought can be traced in three of his works: *Lord Jim* (1900), *Heart of Darkness* (1902), and *The Secret Agent* (1907). In these works, Conrad saw such moral assumptions in terms of social ideals embodied in ideal and typical figures who appear in certain environments that demand their special virtues. These characters (except for Jim's father, the old parson) must respond in varying ways to the testing of their moral assumptions by their environments. (NS)

One of Conrad's major preoccupations in his work is with the validity of certain moral assumptions and their relevancy to and ability to stand up to the pressures of a variety of situations and environments. This preoccupation, in Conrad, is inevitably seen against "the immense indifference of things" and demonstrates the "tragic vanity of the blind groping that we call aspiration." It often appears to result in a further demonstration of "that mysterious arrangement of merciless logic for a futile purpose," but within this framework of inevitability and ultimate futility the examination of the moral assumption retains its justification.

It seems to me that Conrad was quite consciously, at different stages, examining this problem of moral validity from a changing standpoint, and the development of his thought can be seen in the three works that I propose to deal with—*Lord Jim* (1900), *Heart of Darkness* (1902), and *The Secret Agent* (1907). I would suggest that

Conrad, in examining certain moral assumptions, saw them, at least in these works, in terms of social ideals embodied in ideal and typical figures, figures seen to be "right" in certain environments demanding those special virtues; and his examination concerned not only the moral assumptions but also the idealized personification of them and the interrelationship of both within the appropriate society.

We can begin with a rather obscure but important figure in *Lord Jim*—Jim's father, the old parson from the red-fronted rectory (an abode of peace and piety), trusting " 'Providence and the established order of the universe, but alive to its small dangers and small mercies' " who advises his son that " 'Virtue is one all over the world' " and that he should " 'resolve fixedly never . . . to do anything which [he] believe[s] to be wrong.' "[1] The old parson's lack of experience beyond his small, secluded and protected world is one of the significant points of the novel, and he stands as a typical and ideal conception of society's belief in the "good man." He is entirely right and appropriate in his place and will never need to question that place.

Beginning with this fixed, narrow and protected concept of virtue, we can move to Captain Marlow in *Lord Jim*, who is as solid in his beliefs and moral assumptions as the old parson, although his experience of life is much wider. He is as much an accepted type as the old parson—an experienced seaman, sober, wise in the ways of men and ships and the sea, one who has trained numerous young seamen, thus propagating his own type, up-holder of the traditions of the sea:

> "Haven't I turned out youngsters enough in my time, for the service of the Red Rag, to the craft whose whole secret could be expressed in one short sentence, and yet must be driven afresh every day into young heads till it becomes the component part of every waking thought—till it is present in every dream of their young sleep! The sea has been good to me . . . I don't think I have done badly by it either." (p. 44)

Marlow's philosophy includes the recognition that there are other kinds of seamen—the Captain and the other officers of the *Patna*, for example—those who fall short: " 'I did not care a rap about the behaviour of the [others]. . . . Their persons somehow fitted the tale that was public property,' " but *his* type, the best, the recognized, *typical* figure does not fall short. Jim disturbs Marlow because he offers a threat to the solidity of Marlow's universe. He is dangerous because he seems to be " 'one of us' " and yet he lacks " 'a faith invulnerable to the strength of facts, to the contagion of example, to the solicitation of ideas,' " ideas which, to Marlow, erode " 'that belief in a few simple notions you must cling to if you want to live decently and would like to die easy!' " (p. 43). This is a further link between

Marlow and Jim's father who for forty years had considered " 'his little thoughts about faith and virtue, about the conduct of life and the only proper manner of dying' " (p. 341).

It is interesting to note here that in relation to Marlow's ideals Jim's problem is in part a physical one. His physiognomy is appropriate to Marlow's ideal type but inappropriate to his own nature. He is " 'clean-limbed, clean-faced, firm on his feet, as promising a boy as the sun ever shone on . . . . He had no business to *look* so sound' " (p. 40; italics mine).[2]

Jim is not clear to Marlow any more than that virtuous and successful seaman Captain Brierly is clear. This is a mark of the limitations of Marlow's type, yet Jim's case is *not* a complicated one; he has simply moved beyond the bounds of Marlow's vision and those bounds are the standards of successful and right action.

Jim embodies in himself two types of recognized heroic figures. He is the type of young seaman of the mercantile marine on whom Marlow depends in the environment of the sea, and he is the type of heroic and benevolent adventurer, like Rajah James Brooke of Sarawak, on whom society depends to set right its colonies abroad and bring peace to the native communities: " 'The conquest of love, honour, men's confidence—the pride of it, the power of it, are fit materials for a heroic tale' " (p. 226). On both of these typical figures writers of romantic fiction hung adventures, both represented heroic ideals in different environments, and both appeared in real life as well as in fiction. Apart from Rajah Brooke there is the original of little Bob Stanton in *Lord Jim* who drowned trying to save a lady's maid from a sinking ship (pp. 149-50), and would seem to be based on the chief officer of the *Douro* who was drowned under the same circumstances and whose story is told by Conrad in his essay on the loss of the *Titanic*.[3] The hero of adventure fiction and the attitudes and successes typical of him are constantly referred to in *Lord Jim*, and the novel can be viewed against a background of Edwardian popular fiction.[4] We notice that Jim, on the training-ship, sees himself carrying out the typical heroic exploits—"saving people from sinking ships, cutting away masts in a hurricane," confronting savages on tropical shores, quelling mutinies (p. 6). Although he fails, at sea, to live up to the heroic myth, he succeeds in Patusan in becoming the fictional hero, settling disputes among the natives, driving out corrupt rulers; he is ingenious, strong, brave, and he uses that special brand of schoolboy language that insulates against reality.[5] He again appears to Marlow, *visually*, as the type of hero: " 'He stood erect, the smouldering brier-wood in his clutch, with a smile on his lips and a sparkle in his boyish eyes' " (p. 264). " 'He was like a figure set up on a pedestal,' " Marlow recalls, " 'to represent in his persistent youth the power, and perhaps the virtues, of races that never grow old, that have emerged from the gloom. I don't know why he should always have appeared to me symbolic. Perhaps this is the real cause of my interest in his fate' " (p. 265).

And Marlow is right here. He, and Jim, are gulled by the heroic ideal and Jim's uncanny physical appropriateness for the position. And it is not simply heroism in fiction that Jim is set against; it is heroism in life, for Jim is carefully surrounded by Conrad with several quite obscure examples of individual heroism. So Jim's failure, his weakness that derives from his sensitive imagination, is in every way ironic. The enigma of Jim is that of the man marked out by fate for heroism in terms of appearance, desires and training and opportunity who is undermined by the most human of failings. It is this that Marlow finds so difficult to comprehend.

Jim, in his manner of death, ultimately lives up to the ideal that has been presented to him. He overcomes the excesses of his imagination, he accepts the terms of his heroism and his failure to be heroic and takes the punishment due to him—a death in itself heroic. He was wedded to his "shadowy ideal of conduct," and for this reason Marlow can finally conclude that he was " 'one of us,' " only the uncertainty of it all sometimes afflicts him, the suspicion of Jim's being "astray among the passions of this earth." The examination of the heroic type in this instance is an extremely subtle one, for the inward torment arising from failure in such a figure is presented to us through the eyes of a type to whom such failure is well-nigh inexplicable.

The conflict in *Lord Jim* is between the accepted and appropriate ideal in a given environment and Jim's personal doubts about that ideal:

> "What would you have done? You are sure of yourself—aren't you? What would you do if you felt now—this minute—the house here move, just move a little under your chair. Leap! By heavens! you would take one spring from where you sit and land in that clump of bushes yonder." (p. 106)

In *Heart of Darkness*, Kurtz is again a type of a particular heroic figure. He carries on from Jim in Patusan in being a colonizer, but he is more than this. He is an idealist, an explorer, a man of many talents, " 'a gifted creature,' " and also a missionary—" 'an emissary of pity, and science, and progress,' " " 'a bearer of the spark from the sacred fire,' " and a man of action, seeing each station on the river as a " 'beacon on the road to better things.' " He is a Henry Morton Stanley, in fact, and again we have the ideal type existing in fact and in fiction in the appropriate environment.[6] Kurtz is equipped as Stanley was to face the darkness and the jungle, but he has, as Jim has, sensitivity to things Stanley was not sensitive to. But Conrad is not finding the same weakness in the ideal figure in Kurtz as he found in Jim. Jim was sensitive to the destructive powers of the imagination; he came to recognize the danger of the impulse that arises from them, the impulse that breaks the mould of the ideal of conduct. But Jim also made two significant choices which derived from that very ideal —to face the court of inquiry and to face Doramin. He accepted the consequences of his actions; he did not fundamentally question the ideals he tried to live up to nor the rightness of his position within a specific environment. Kurtz goes deeper. He goes so deeply into things that he succumbs to the environment he is meant to dominate and he sees that the ideals he represented are worthless in the face of his complete recognition of the nature of things. He becomes a " 'wandering and tormented thing.' "

Marlow tries to break the spell—

> "the heavy, mute spell of the wilderness—that seemed to draw him to its pitiless breast by the awakening of forgotten and brutal instincts, by the memory of gratified and monstrous passions. This alone, I was convinced, had driven him out to the edge of the forest, to the bush, towards the gleam of fires, the throb of drums, the drone of weird incantations; this alone had beguiled his unlawful soul beyond the bounds of permitted aspirations." (p. 144)

But Marlow also recognizes how far Kurtz has moved from the ideal of conduct: " 'And, don't you see, the terror of the positions was . . . in this, that I had to deal with a being to whom I could not appeal in the name of anything high or low. . . . There was nothing either above or below him . . . . He had kicked himself loose of the earth' " (p. 144). The state reached by Kurtz is expressed in two of his exclamations: " 'Exterminate all the brutes!' " and " 'The horror! The horror!' "

Whereas Jim's father, the old parson, is allowed to learn of his son's disgrace through newspaper reports (p. 79) because Jim has not denied the validity of the type he represented, Kurtz' Intended can be told nothing of the truth, for the truth is too terrible to know—the validity of the type has been destroyed in Kurtz. He becomes " 'this grimy fragment of another world, the forerunner of change, of conquest, of trade, of massacres, of blessings.' " Like Jim, Kurtz is placed among other examples of his type—those who exploit its standing for their own enrichment like the pilgrims, the manager, and the manager's uncle, and those who represent its uncontaminated innocence, like the Harlequin. Marlow himself is, in a sense, an example of the type, the explorer who goes out to the dark places in a spirit of enthusiastic curiosity. But whereas the Marlow of *Lord Jim* fails ultimately to understand the nature of Jim's complexities, the Marlow of *Heart of Darkness,* feeling the pull of savage nature in the jungle, fully understands the collapse of Kurtz, and the instincts within the heroic type that might bring about that collapse. Kurtz becomes his choice of nightmares. Marlow in *Lord Jim* stood back, observed, rejoiced when he saw his protégé returning to the ideal; Marlow in *Heart of Darkness* returns to civilization despising those of mankind who did not know what can happen to a " 'shadowy ideal of conduct' " in the face of savagery.

Thus we have moved from the old parson in his protected environment, to Marlow's inability fully to understand from his own firm point of view Jim's dilemma, to Marlow's comprehension of and participation in the failure of Kurtz to live up to his ideals and withstand the pressures of environment. And it is here that Marlow—and perhaps Conrad—turns impatiently on his listeners—the Lawyer, the Director of Companies, the Accountant—to declare that they, like the parson, cannot in their protected environments, understand such failure on the part of the heroic man:

> "You can't understand. How could you?—with solid pavement under your feet, surrounded by kind neighbours ready to cheer you or to fall on you, stepping delicately between the butcher and the policeman, in the holy terror of scandal and gallows and lunatic asylums. . . " (p. 116)

And later he insists again on the protection afforded by a stable society against the damage inflicted by the wilderness:

> Here you all are, each moored with two good addresses, like a hulk with two anchors, a butcher round one corner, a policeman round another, excellent appetites, and temperatures normal . . . from year's end to year's end . . . . (p. 114)

Yet when he came to write *The Secret Agent* six years later, Conrad took up these protestations of Marlow and looked into the kind of environment he describes. Verloc and his wife, in spite of Verloc's occupation, live between the butcher and the policeman, and the fear of scandal, the gallows and the lunatic asylum.

Again concerned with certain moral assumptions, Conrad examines the type of virtuous ideal proper to civilized society—the self-sacrificing and virtuous female, one who fulfils in one way or another the duties of mother, wife, daughter and sister. Winnie Verloc represents the female, maternal and domestic virtues, dominated by her maternal passion for her brother, her life given over to devotion and self-sacrifice. "As a little girl she had often faced with blazing eyes the irascible licensed victualler [her father] in defence of her brother"

(p. 38); she helps to look after her mother's boarding-house—"a crushing memory ... of countless breakfast trays carried up and down innumerable stairs, of endless haggling over pence, of the endless drudgery of sweeping, dusting, cleaning, from basement to attics" (p. 242); she gives up her lover for the sake of her brother—"a fascinating companion for a voyage down the sparkling stream of life; only his boat was very small. There was room in it for a girl-partner at the oar, but no accommodation for passengers" (p. 243); she marries Mr. Verloc, agreeing "to be very nice to his political friends," because he "was ready to take [Stevie] over together with his wife's mother and with the furniture" (p. 10). And Winnie devotes her life to her brother and to ensuring the domestic comfort of Mr. Verloc.

This type of feminine ideal exists, of course, in fiction—in Maggie Tulliver, in Dickens' heroines—and in real life. Conrad may well have regarded his mother's devotion to his father in this light, and Jessie's contribution to his own comfort and peace of mind. But in Winnie Verloc, the basis of virtue is unstable at two points—Stevie is not a normal boy but an innocent whose emotions at the sight of cruelty are likely to lead him into upsetting the smooth running of society, and her self-sacrifice has forced upon her the need not to examine anything in life too closely—emotions must be suppressed and motives must not be questioned.

Winnie, in her virtuous stance, is the appropriate heroic figure for her environment. The life lived in civilized society, between the butcher and the policeman, can be as dangerous as life in the jungle or on the sea. It is the life of the tight-rope walker performing for half a crown a tumble (cf. *Heart of Darkness*, pp. 93-4). Inspector Heat is shaken by the Assistant Commissioner's close questioning, and he "felt at the moment like a tight-rope artist might feel if suddenly, in the middle of the performance, the manager of the Music Hall were to rush out of the proper managerial seclusion and begin to shake the rope" (p. 116). People in such a society are solely concerned to preserve the status quo—between police and anarchists, between Lady Patronesses and anarchists, between Assistant Commissioner and Home Secretary. The anarchists themselves have no wish to do anything to disturb their present security, and ironically the secret agent himself is devoted to the protection of an embattled society. The Greenwich Bomb Outrage is quickly cleared up as "a domestic drama" and Vladimir dismissed; society can continue its tight-rope walking.

Winnie Verloc fails as the ideal type within this environment only when she sees that her self-sacrifice and refusal to look too closely

Symposium speaker Norman Sherry. (Photographed Billie W. M. Wolfe)

into things have been pointless. It is this that tumbles her from *her* tight-rope into the abyss of fear of scandal, the gallows and the lunatic asylum which await the person who loses his balance. For her then there is only madness and despair and suicide.

Winnie's predicament as the ideal is unlike that of Jim or Kurtz in that she is beset from the beginning by the irony that lack of imagination, the requirement for survival, is what she has cultivated and yet it carries the seeds of disaster for her. And her environment is similarly fraught with irony in that it is not imagination, courage, idealism that is required but caution, blindness, the cultivation of a small, secure domesticity. Winnie conforms, and her very conformity turns against her. Unlike Jim, but like Kurtz, Winnie's fall from the ideal required in her society affords no possibility of recovery. Kurtz is a lost, shattered soul; Winnie, a woman rejected by society, betrayed by Ossipon, has no further heroic attitude to strike, nowhere to run to, only suicide to escape what she sees as a worse fate. Again, Winnie has about her those who survive in such a society, but she, as the acknowledged virtuous female type of that society, is undermined by her own virtues.

Conrad did not come full circle and examine in detail the old parson and his environment, and so we do not know what there might have been in that area that might have revealed the breaking point of that virtuous figure. Perhaps like Winnie, he would have refused to look too deeply into things and this would have proved his undoing; perhaps his letters to Jim indicate an unwillingness to accept his son's failures and their causes. We will never know.

NOTES

[1] *The Collected Edition of the Works of Joseph Conrad* (London: J. M. Dent, 1946), p. 342. References throughout are to this edition.

[2] Cf. also, for example, pp. 42-43, 74, 78, 380.

[3] "Some Reflections on the Loss of the *Titanic*," *Notes on Life and Letters* (London: J. M. Dent & Sons, 1949), p. 227.

[4] Cf., for example, Flora Annie Steele, *On the Face of the Waters* (1897); Bithia Mae Croker, *Diana Barrington* (1888); G. A. Henty, *With Clive in India* (1884); *Colonel Thorndyke's Secret* (1898); *On the Irrawaddy* (1897); *Through the Sikh War* (1894), etc. The genre can be traced later in Ethel M. Dell, *The Way of an Eagle* (1912); A. E. W. Mason's novels; even George Orwell's *Burmese Days* (1935) and E. M. Forster's *A Passage to India* (1924).

[5] For a fuller discussion of Jim's language, see my Introduction to *Lord Jim*, Dent's Collected Edition, to be published later this year.

[6] Cf. my discussion of the influence of Stanley on *Heart of Darkness* in *Conrad's Western World* (Cambridge: Cambridge Univ. Press, 1971).

Flaubert and the Structure of *The Secret Agent:* A Study in Spatial Form

Jeffrey R. Smitten

ABSTRACT

The structure of Conrad's novels has often been described by analogies which imply a particular kind of structural unity. For example, painting has been invoked to suggest that the unity of a Conrad narrative lies not in a coherent, linear plot sequence, but in the reader's apprehension of the narrative as a complex whole existing in a moment of time. I wish to examine the structural techniques of *The Secret Agent* in the light of such analogies in order both to define the novel's unity and to offer a concrete illustration of a theory of narrative form. The theory of narrative form implied by these descriptive analogies has been outlined in Joseph Frank's famous essay, "Spatial Form in Modern Literature" (1945). Frank points to the agricultural fair scene in *Madame Bovary* as a paradigm of the novelistic form he describes. Analysis of this scene discloses two general structural techniques applicable to *The Secret Agent*. They are: (1) fragmentation of the narrative sequence and juxtaposition of those fragments, and (2) unification of the juxtaposed fragments in the reader's mind through his perception of the analogy and contrast among them. Similarly, in *The Secret Agent* Conrad uses the time-shift technique and suppression of transitions to fragment his narrative into parts which are then juxtaposed for ironic effect. The unity of the novel as a whole lies in the reader's apprehension of a configuration of causes and effects and in his apprehension of multiple analogies and contrasts within that configuration. (JRS)

The structure of Conrad's novels has often been described through comparisons which emphasize a particular kind of unity. The comparisons are frequently drawn from painting, and they stress a lack of linear chronological development together with the fact that the narratives must be perceived as wholes rather than as processes. For example, Carl Grabo tells us:

> First [Conrad] sketches roughly a chief figure, then perhaps a bit of background and a second figure, only to return to his first and delineate it in

151

sharper outline. Back and forth he goes touching here and there, often putting in a bit of color whose relation to the rest of the picture is not for some time apparent. A relationship, however, it subsequently reveals. It is not the product of chance, nor of a sudden inspiration. Conrad's stories give always the impression of being wholly imagined before he begins to write.[1]

While Grabo's emphasis falls on juxtaposition within the narrative sequence, he also implies that because of this juxtaposition the reader must try to grasp the narrative as a whole. This concept of narrative totality is manifest in a similar comparison used by A. A. Mendilow to describe the effect of distributed exposition—the technique of Ford and Conrad:

The effect of reading [distributed exposition] is similar to that of watching a picture being painted. The artist need not proceed regularly from one corner of the canvas to another; he is under no obligation to finish one section before beginning on another, but is at liberty to distribute the strokes of his brush wherever he thinks fit. The order and precedence of his work is determined by him and him alone, just as the order and precedence of the act of seeing the picture, the movements of the eye of the viewer, follow no fixed rule. The effect of the whole picture is felt when the whole is seen, not in a fixed order of succession but in what psychologists call "a specious present"—a present that has a narrow temporal spread. Something of the same effect is created by distributed exposition, if the term "exposition" can any longer apply at all. The ultimate synthesis and the organization of the parts into a satisfying whole are left to the reader.[2]

The implication of such a statement is that the unity of a Conrad narrative lies not in the linear development of a plot sequence but in the reader's synthesis of discrete fragments of narrative into a coherent pattern. The various portions of the narrative are apprehended as coexisting facets of a single whole. The reader perceives the novel as though it were a painting all of whose parts exist together in a moment of time.

Both of these comparisons call attention to the possibility that Conrad's narratives have spatial form. The most famous definition of this concept is that given by Joseph Frank.[3] A work is organized spatially when the reader is asked to perceive it as a whole in a moment of time, not as a sequence. The techniques a writer can use to bring about such a perception Frank called juxtaposition and reflexive reference. Juxtaposition refers to the breakup of the narrative line so that words, images, or scenes are set side by side irrespective of their causal-temporal relations. An extreme example of juxtaposition is stream of consciousness, in which memories and present impressions are jumbled together and logical transitions between one idea and another are absent. Reflexive reference indicates the techniques by which the writer impels the reader to connect one juxtaposed fragment with another so a unified whole emerges. Causal-temporal relationships are replaced by other relationships to create unity. It is on this point—the technique of reflexive reference—that Frank is vague. He cites two key examples of spatial form: *Ulysses* and the country fair scene in *Madame Bovary*. However, what he neglects to point out is that each work raises different problems in the technique of reflexive reference. Thus, if we wish to argue that *The Secret Agent* employs spatial form, we must first carefully define the techniques available to Conrad.

Ulysses is unified primarily by its verbal surface, by, that is, its complex system of leitmotifs. Frank tells us that "Joyce composed his novel of a vast number of references and cross references that relate to each other independently of the time sequence of the narrative."[4] The narrative sequence of *Ulysses* is jumbled and arbitrary, but the novel is unified through this system of leitmotifs. The task of the reader is to synthesize all these references and cross references in a moment of time, for, as Frank says, a "knowledge of the whole is essential to an understanding of any part . . . ."[5] Previous critics of *The Secret Agent* have also recognized its disrupted chronological sequence and its arbitrary jumps from scene to scene. And, most have argued that this fragmented narrative is unified by the verbal surface of the novel.[6] They point to many intricate skeins of verbal repetition which, they assume, function as leitmotifs. Clearly, then, if these critics are correct, we ought to locate the spatial form of the novel in the verbal and imagistic repetitions which are so typical of it. I would like, therefore, to confront this problem at the outset and show how verbal repetition is inadequate as a unifying device in the novel.

We need first to distinguish between verbal repetition which serves merely a stitching function and genuine leitmotif. As Clive Hart has said: "Reiteration alone is not enough to convert a phrase into a *leitmotiv* . . . Real *leitmotiv* entails a use of statement and restatement in such a way as to impel the reader to relate part to part; each recurrence of such a motif derives in some necessary way from all its previous appearances and leads on to future resurgences, pointing to correspondences and relationships far beyond those that hold between the individual motif and its immediate context."[7] James Curtis has described vividly the perceptual demands of a leitmotif, clarifying what Hart means by "correspondences and relationships." He uses an analogy from linguistics. Structural linguists distinguish between the rules governing the use of a language and the specific sentences which embody those rules. To understand any specific sentence in a language one must know the set of rules governing all possible usages.

In the same way, in a narrative using leitmotifs one must be aware of the entire system of leitmotifs in order to understand any particular occurrence of that motif.[8] Thus, a leitmotif is not merely repetition; it is repetition pointing toward a coherent system of ideas which governs the entire narrative.

The verbal and imagistic repetitions of *The Secret Agent* looked at in this way do not constitute a system of leitmotifs. Consider, for instance, the repetition of the word "secret." According to Avrom Fleischman, the word appears more than fifty times.[9] But the effect of these repetitions is atmospheric in the sense that the reader is not expected to recall all other specific usages of the word or all other situations in which the word appears. Rather, he responds simply to the sheer intensity produced by such extensive repetition. The reader is not asked to relate particular part to particular part, nor must he interpret each appearance of the word in the light of all the other appearances. Similar arguments could be made for imagistic repetitions such as those involving cannibalism. These images underscore the theme of human selfishness and exploitation. They "contribute to [the novel's] painful tone, enrich its ironic structure, and sum up the terrible failure in human relationships that is the novel's central theme."[10] But, as this statement implies, the repetition gains its effect through emphasis. The meaning of the series of images is largely complete on its first appearance. Each successive appearance only reiterates that initial meaning.

More complex are imagistic repetitions which involve irony or explicit augmentations of meaning. In Chapter I of the novel we are told that Stevie lost his first and only job because he "touched off in quick succession a set of fierce rockets, angry catherine wheels, loudly exploding squibs" on the staircase of his office building after being told "tales of injustice and oppression."[11] This early encounter with fireworks is echoed ironically in his death, in Winnie's comments to her husband such as " [Stevie] would go through fire for you" (p. 155), and in her vision just before she kills Verloc of "smashed branches, torn leaves, gravel, bits of brotherly flesh and bone, all sprouting up together in the manner of a firework" (p. 214). But where do these repetitions themselves lead? They certainly call attention to an irony in Stevie's fate, but they do not point toward "correspondences and relationships far beyond those that hold between the individual motif and its immediate context." If the latter were true, one would expect this fireworks imagery to link explicitly with other strands of imagery, but it does not. Similar limitations may be found, for example, in the persistent references to light, semi-darkness, night, and fog. Elliott

Gose has argued that in these images "we have a central symbolism articulating the moral vision which enabled Conrad to unify his subject."[12] If this were true, we would have to say that the novel is unified by leitmotif. But Gose is forced to assume that the structure of the novel is merely incoherent and therefore negligible (which it is not), and he is often compelled to interpret the meaning of this imagery arbitrarily. And, even so, significant portions of the novel are unaccounted for.[13] One feels that this strand of imagery is simply too slight a vehicle to unify the entire work. Instead, it serves, like the other verbal and imagistic repetitions, to unify only a portion of the narrative, not the entire narrative through allusion to an all-embracing system of ideas. Repetition in *The Secret Agent* is stitching, not leitmotif. It seems logical, then, to look at the structural arrangement of the book to find a set of relationships which unifies the entire work.[14] And, in order to determine what this set of relationships might be, we need to return to our other model of spatial form—the country fair scene in *Madame Bovary*.

Since Frank's discussion of the technique of this scene is somewhat vague, let us reexamine it in some detail. The whole scene actually occupies most of Chapter VIII in Part II, but the section we are interested in begins when Emma and Rodolphe seat themselves in the room overlooking the square and ends with the award to Catherine Leroux. Within this section, Flaubert cuts back and forth between three levels of simultaneous action: the seduction of Emma by Rodolphe, the description of the bourgeois and the speeches of their windy politicians, and the sound of the fair animals. As Flaubert said: "one should hear the bellowing of the cattle, the whispering of the lovers and the rhetoric of the officials all at the same time."[15] Flaubert has thus juxtaposed fragments of narrative which do not have any causal or sequential connections. As a result of this juxtaposition, the significance of the scene is not communicated through progression or unfolding of action but through reflexive reference among the juxtaposed fragments. The reader's interest is not in the moment-by-moment process of the seduction of Emma but in the meaning of that seduction as disclosed by its context. Flaubert's scene can be properly understood only when its units of meaning "are apprehended reflexively, in an instant of time."[16] The structural technique of this scene, however, needs further definition before it can be applied to *The Secret Agent*.

We need to keep in mind that the scene is unified primarily by the reader's perception of analogy and contrast among the three levels of simultaneous action, and Flaubert's use of juxtaposition is here a means of forcing such perception from the reader. Rodolphe's seduction speech and, in part, Emma's response are nothing more than the empty clichés of the politicians; Emma is exploited (to an extent) just as Catherine Leroux is exploited; and, the presence of the animals suggests the intellectual stature of the smiling bourgeois, the fate of Catherine Leroux, and the rural oppressiveness of Emma's life. At the same time, though, Flaubert sets Emma in contrast to this background of bourgeois, animals, and crass seducers by introducing in the midst of this scene her sudden recollections of Léon and the ball at Vaubyessard. Insofar as Emma's dreams have value and dignity transcending her environment, their brief suggestion here sets her apart from her oppressive milieu. Ideally the reader perceives these analogical and contrastive relationships at once, in a moment of time.

It is important to stress the role of analogy here since juxtaposition in spatial form need not always involve analogy. The country fair scene, for instance, derives a measure of unity just from the fact that all of the events are happening at the same time and in the same place. A work might therefore juxtapose units which have no analogical relationship in order to emphasize the complex, elusive nature of experience. This poem by Guillaume Apollinaire merely suggests a tension among its images:

> Trois becs de gaz allumés
> La patronne est poitrinaire
> Quand tu auras fini nous jouerons une partie de jacquet
> Un chef d'orchestre qui a mal à la gorge
> Quand tu viendras à Tunis je te ferai fumer du kief
>
> Ça a l'air de rimer[17]

This is a random series of experiences deriving suggestive power from simultaneity in time and contiguity in space. The experiences are all facets of a single moment, but there is no further connection between them. Spatial form, then, depends upon the reader's associational capacity. That capacity can be stimulated by devices such as simultaneity as well as analogy and contrast. We shall see that *The Secret Agent* makes some use of both these devices.

The problem of applying Flaubert's techniques to an entire narrative also needs further discussion. While it is possible to construct an entire narrative in which all the actions occur simultaneously, that technique is obviously limited to certain rather special novels.[18] An entire narrative could also be unified by analogy so that one scene will echo others and thus be unified simultaneously with distant portions of the narrative in the reader's imagination.[19] But this technique, though it is important for *The Secret Agent*, does not exclusively govern the form of that novel. Ford Madox Ford called attention to a third possibility—one which is particularly appropriate to Conrad—when he discussed chronological looping. The famous passage in which he describes what is wrong with the English novel sketches this technique:

> ... it became very early evident to us that what was the matter with the Novel, and the British novel in particular, was that it went straight forward, whereas in your gradual making acquaintanceship with your fellows you never do go straight forward. You meet an English gentleman at your golf club. He is beefy, full of health, the moral of the boy from an English Public School of the finest type. You discover, gradually, that he is hopelessly neurasthenic, dishonest in matters of small change, but unexpectedly self-sacrificing, a dreadful liar but a most painfully careful student of lepidoptera and, finally, from the public prints, a bigamist who was once, under another name, hammered on the Stock Exchange. . . . Still, there he is, the beefy, full-fed fellow, moral of an English Public School product. To get such a man in fiction you could not begin at his beginning and work his life chronologically to the end. You must first get him in with a strong impression, and then work backwards and forwards over his past.[20]

One may well ask why chronological looping is necessary to "get such a man in fiction." Ford offers two answers. One is merely the specious notion that a novel should reflect in its structure the way men become acquainted with one another. The other is more substantial. The English gentleman's character is a mass of contradictions all existing at once. Ford emphasizes this fact by coming back, after his description of the gentleman's various qualities, to rest on his image as the model product of the public schools: "Still, there he is, the beefy, full-fed fellow." One has to see the gentleman's whole life bearing upon this single moment in order properly to appreciate what he is. Such a mode of perception clearly parallels that required in the country fair scene, but it is induced here by time-shifts, not by analogies or literal simultaneity of events. By working backwards and forwards over the gentleman's past, Ford forces the reader to unify the juxtaposed scenes of the novel not according to chronological sequence but in relation to the gentleman's image as coexisting facets of his character. Very similar remarks have been made about Conrad's novels. One early critic remarked of *Lord Jim* that "at the close, the man Jim stands complete in the reader's mind. From the various weavings and cross-weavings of the narrative one constructs a character sympathetically amplified by a thousand connotations and associations, just as in real life one gradually builds up the character of a friend from numerous loosely associated and non-coherent incidents that merge into a harmonious conception."[21] A point to be emphasized, however, is that in chronological looping all the material of the narrative can be organized not only around a character but also around an event. As

Ford once said, "any piece of Impressionism . . . is the record of the impression of a moment. . . ."[22] Thus, in the same way that the novelist can explore the complexity of character by juxtaposing different aspects of it, so also he can explore the complexity of causes and effects implicit in a single moment or event. This possibility is particularly relevant to *The Secret Agent*.

We can apply these concepts of structure to Conrad's novel by considering two points: in *The Secret Agent* (1) all the events relate back to the moment of the bombing either as a cause or an effect; and (2) juxtapositions within the causal sequence brought about by time-shifts and the suppression of expressed transitions from chapter to chapter force the reader to apprehend any given scene in terms of the entire causal pattern surrounding the bombing. That is, each scene in the novel is to be understood as a coexisting facet of a complete system of causes and effects which rests upon a single moment in time. Although it is never directly rendered, the bombing—or more specifically the actual explosion—is the central event of *The Secret Agent* in a very literal sense. The scenes portraying causes include the interview with Vladimir (Chapter II) and the removal of the mother-in-law together with Winnie's efforts to bring Verloc and Stevie closer together to compensate for that (Chapters VIII and IX). Less direct than these as causes are Chapters I and III. Chapter I hints at the domestic circumstances which help make the bombing possible, particularly the moral indolence which pervades the Verloc household. Chapter III further portrays that indolence in the bedroom scene and dramatizes, in the meeting of the anarchists, the hopelessness of Verloc's finding anyone but Stevie to carry the bomb. Given that lethargic and stupid group, Verloc is extremely hard-pressed to carry out Vladimir's scheme. There are yet more distant causes touched upon in Chapters V, VI, VII, and X. The system of police supervision (based on secrecy) is an ultimate cause of the bombing, while the suggestions of apathy and ignorance evoked in the interviews between Sir Ethelred and the Assistant Commissioner may also be seen as ultimate social causes for the act. Even the Professor's theories of violent revolution (the consequences of personal failure) which are discussed in Chapter IV figure as a cause. The effects of the bombing are witnessed most immediately in Chapters IX, XI and XII, where Winnie learns of the bombing, kills Verloc, and attempts her escape with Ossipon. But, of course, the effects of the bombing range far beyond the Verloc household, so we see in Chapter IV the effect on the Professor and Ossipon, in Chapters V-VII the effect on the police and Sir Ethelred, in Chapter X further exploration of the effects on civil government, and in Chapter XIII the effects of Winnie's suicide (itself an effect of the bombing) on Ossipon and the Professor. Any scene, then, can be integrated into the novel as a whole by viewing it as part of a cause-effect pattern centered around the bombing. And the means by which this pattern is unified can be seen if we examine the relations among causes and among effects more closely.

It should be obvious even from the superficial summary above that Conrad is dealing with a wide variety of causes for the bombing, near and remote, specific and general. They range from tangible facets of the situation, such as Vladimir's threats and schemes, to the most general questions of the moral tone of the society. But the order of the scenes in which this variety of causes is revealed is not temporal. The time-shift occurring between Chapters III and IV displaces material which, chronologically, should appear there into Chapters VIII and IX. Thus, the novel moves from cause to effect, then back to cause and again to effect. Causes and effects are not presented sequentially in the narrative line of the novel; rather, they are juxtaposed for ironic purposes. Indeed, since the reader is forced to view causes in terms of effects, both types of events may be said to coexist in his imagination. The central irony of Chapters VIII and IX exists because the efforts of Winnie and her mother to protect Stevie are juxtaposed with his dismembered corpse shown in Chapter V. Winnie's mother moves out of the house in Chapter VIII to strengthen Stevie's claim in the Verloc family, while Winnie herself, toward the end of Chapter VIII and the beginning of IX, pushes Stevie and her husband together to prevent the former from missing his mother and to instill a sense of obligation in the latter. Both efforts at protection lead only to destruction. The middle of Chapter VIII is devoted to Stevie's display of "humanity" in a moral sense which Verloc will play upon, but irony emerges when the reader recalls Stevie's "humanity" in the physical sense, as shown in Chapter V where the boy is reduced to "an accumulation of raw material for a cannibal feast" (p. 81). The reader's response to these causes is conditioned and controlled by effects; the two coexist in the reader's mind. More subtle examples of such coexistence include Chapter IV which discloses the Professor's reaction to the bombing as well as his role as cause, and Chapters V to VII which show both the effects of the bombing on the authorities and their role as causes. In both instances, the reader is painfully aware of the ironic discrepancy between the characters' roles and their responses to what they have brought about. Such ironic juxtaposition of causes and effects, then, creates a narrative in which, to cite Mendilow, "past is felt not as distinct from the present but included in it and permeating it. Every moment is conceived as the condensation of earlier history, and the past is not separate and completed but an ever-lasting part of a changing present."[23]

In addition to the time-shift, Conrad also avoids expressed transitions between the opening scenes in which the causes are developed. The first three chapters come in chronological sequence, but the narrative movement from scene to scene is abrupt and arbitrary. Chapter I consists of a series of fragmented scenes suggesting Winnie's, Stevie's, and the mother's past. But the movement from one fragment to another within that chapter is so abrupt that time seems, in the words of one critic, "frozen, cut up, and broken."[24] The significance of these scenes and their relationship to the narrative do not become completely clear until Chapter XI when Winnie recalls, just before she murders Verloc, the history of her devotion to Stevie. Chapter II follows chronologically from Chapter I, but its real significance lies in its ironic juxtaposition with the domestic situation in the previous chapter. Vladimir represents a public cause which ultimately must work in cooperation with private, domestic causes to bring about the bombing. Thus, not until Chapters VIII and IX does the reader perceive the true relationship of Chapters I and II. Finally, Chapter III also follows Chapter II chronologically, though an unspecified amount of time passes between them. The chapter as a whole plays variations on the theme of indolence, first displaying it among the anarchists, then in the bedroom scene. But again we have an ironic juxtaposition of private, domestic causes and public ones which only becomes clear when we learn how Stevie comes to be used as the carrier of the bomb. Thus, instead of introducing each new cause by means of an explicit transition so that our hopes and fears for the characters are consecutively developed, Conrad suppresses transitions and forces the reader to understand each new cause as a coexisting facet of a complete system. Put another way, we can say that the chronological sequence of Chapters I-III is trivial. The reader can grasp the true relationship of those chapters only if he is able to connect them with the entire system of causes and effects which unifies the novel.

We have so far dicussed causes and how they are juxtaposed with effects; however, Conrad's arrangement of the effects of the event is also quite significant. First of all, we need to recognize that, in tracing the multiple effects of the bombing, Conrad's narrative appears perhaps even more "obscure and seemingly quixotic in direction"[25] than it did when he traced the causes. For one thing, the focus of attention seems to roam haphazardly from one character to another between Chapters IV and VII which are primarily devoted to observing the effects of the bombing on the authorities and anarchists. The bombing is disclosed in the course of a meandering conversation between Ossipon and the Professor. Thereafter, we follow the Professor on his way home until he meets Heat. We are then given a lengthy flashback concerning Heat's examination of Stevie's body, and, returning to time present, we follow him into his interview with the Assistant Commissioner. Attention then shifts to the Assistant Commissioner, and we follow him first into his interview with Sir Ethelred and finally out to dinner and to Verloc's shop. The presentation of effects is disrupted later in the novel as well. Chapter IX ends with Winnie having just discovered what Verloc had done, but Chapter X breaks away from these domestic effects to follow the Assistant Commissioner into another interview with Sir Ethelred and then to a party where he confronts Vladimir with hints of his case against him. In addition, after following the domestic events to their conclusion in Chapter XII, Conrad adds the conversation between Ossipon and the Professor in Chapter XIII which, while it is related causally to the domestic plot since it shows the effects of Winnie's suicide, does not follow in any necessary way from the events of the domestic plot. Although these various effects can be integrated into the cause-effect patterns of the novel as a whole, such integration is not completely satisfying. It would seem that Conrad is following any effect he wishes without regard to close structural unity. However, these effects are, in fact, very carefully arranged. Their arrangement stems from the associational devices of simultaneity and analogy which we discussed in Flaubert's country fair scene.

The simultaneity among the effects is only approximate, but there is sufficient overlapping so that the reader is led to unify them on that basis. Whereas the multiple causal sequences, although united in that they all come to bear upon a single moment, stretch back varying distances in time, the effects of the bombing, for the most part, are quite circumscribed in time. The explosion takes place between 10:30 and 11:00 in the morning, and Winnie leaves alone on the train for Dover at 10:30 exactly that night. These chronological limits force the reader to be aware of the often ironic overlapping among events. As Ossipon and the Professor speculate about the bombing in the Silenus, Verloc, at that moment in early afternoon, is also sitting gloomily in a bar. About the same time that Heat meets the Professor in a dusky alley, Verloc returns to his shop in a state of panic and desperation. Also overlapping with Verloc's return are the interviews between the Assistant Commissioner and Heat and between the Assistant Commissioner and Sir Ethelred. These simultaneous strands of action culminate at the end of Chapter VII with the Assistant Commissioner standing poised across from the shop ready to apprehend Verloc who is inside muttering about going abroad. Moreover, at approximately this same time, Ossipon begins skulking about the neighborhood, and Heat is about to make his appearance in the shop. Overlapping of action continues with the conversation between Heat and Verloc (which Winnie overhears) occurring at the same time as the Assistant Commissioner's last interview with Sir Ethelred. Perhaps the most striking instance of irony in these overlapping actions occurs when the Assistant Commissioner confronts Vladimir with his case (shortly before 10:30). Almost simultaneously with this confrontation Verloc is killed (8:50) and Winnie sent to her suicide (10:30). The Assistant Commissioner's case is destroyed just when he thinks it secure. The effect on the reader of these overlapping actions is, first of all, to unify what otherwise might seem random and arbitrary. And, secondly, the overlapping actions call attention to complex ironies implicit in varying states of knowledge and perspicacity among the characters. This point leads us to consider analogy.

All the effects of the bombing reflect each other through analogy or contrast. The main effect of the bombing, as Conrad suggested in the novel's Preface (p. 13), is the shattering of Winnie's illusions resulting in the murder of Verloc and her suicide. But Winnie does not so much perceive truth as suffer a dislocation of values. Related analogically to her experience is Ossipon's disintegration portrayed at the end of Chapter XII and in Chapter XIII. He has glimpsed something of the inner significance of his guilt and of Winnie's experience, and that knowledge is destroying him and his illusions. He fears the onset of madness. The effects of the bombing on the other characters are variations upon Winnie's and Ossipon's experience. Verloc and Stevie were both killed as more or less direct results of the bombing, but, unlike Winnie and Ossipon, they die in the fullness of their respective illusions. Moving away from these participants, the effects become less momentous. Inspector Heat just glimpses the destructive absurdity of life, only to retreat back into a protective shell of illusions. Sir Ethelred remains in lofty ignorance of the inner meaning of the events, putting them rather below the nationalization of the fisheries in importance. Michaelis's patroness and her circle are likewise only slightly disturbed. Ironically, at the other end of the social-political scale, the Professor is also unmoved by the events, looking upon them simply as steps toward the destruction of the social edifice. Finally, the Assistant Commissioner has some knowledge of the inner value of events, though he is not shaken by it. Yet he is a butt of irony since his complacency in wrapping up his case is exposed and undercut by the death of the Verlocs. Fate plays tricks on all the characters and discloses their illusions. The analogical connections among these scenes help order them on a level transcending chronological sequence, thus adding to the reader's feeling that the effects coexist.

This having been said, however, we need to pay attention to the conclusion of the novel because it appears to lie outside any unified causal pattern no matter how manipulated. Conrad could have ended his novel with Winnie's suicide, either rendered or implied, but he chose to add the scene in which Ossipon walks the city streets as well as Chapter XIII in which Ossipon and the Professor discuss the events of ten days earlier first in the Professor's shabby lodgings and then at the Silenus. To the working out of the domestic effects of the bombing presented so dramatically in Chapters XI and XII, Conrad has added a static, retrospective conclusion which is not at all necessary to those chapters. Scholes and Kellogg have remarked that readers of modern fiction often have "to look for resolution in the completion of an artistic pattern rather than in a stasis achieved in the lives of the characters."[26] A kind of stasis is achieved in Winnie's suicide, but Chapter XIII throws the emphasis of the novel on the resolution of an artistic pattern. We have seen how Ossipon's disintegration here echoes in various ways the effect of the bombing on the other characters. But there is much more to this closing chapter. It primary significance is that we move away from the bombing as the central focus of the novel toward an emphasis on the related themes of illusion and anarchy which subsume the bombing. We just discussed the theme of illusion in connection with the analogical correspondences among the various effects of the bombing. In this final chapter, those analogical correspondences assume an importance as great as the causal patterns surrounding the bombing. The spatial form of the novel is by this means complicated and enriched. The conclusion echoes, analogically, the other effects in the novel but on a high level of generality. On the one hand, Ossipon, throughout the novel, has been associated with scientific materialism. Yet here the apostle of rationalism is shown sinking into madness as a result of knowledge he cannot accept. On the other hand, the Professor maintains his illusions concerning power and freedom with what looks like rational precision. However, those illusions are, the reader knows, only another form of madness and despair. The significance of Ossipon's and the Professor's states of mind extends far beyond the merely personal. In a form relevant to Conrad's whole society, Ossipon typifies the illusion which dominates so many lives in the novel: that human experience is subject to rational control.

The Professor, especially since he is characterized as "a pest in the street full of men" in the last lines of the novel, suggests an abiding force for anarchy based on madness. Together they define the extremes of the destructive power of illusions. Either to relinquish or to maintain illusions means defeat and destruction. And, as representatives of such extremes, they echo and imply all the other characters' experiences. They thus have broad associational connections with all the other events in the novel, and they serve thereby to unify the novel spatially. The entire narrative comes to bear upon these two closing scenes. However, we should note that this thematic patterning is less specific, less structurally precise than the causal patterns we discussed earlier. Instead, it complements and fulfills the causal patterns by extending their significance beyond the bombing as an isolated incident to the society as a whole.

Critics hostile to the theory of spatial form often argue that since all narratives are sequential it must be that the whole finally achieved has been "built up and controlled by a temporal sequence, however much broken."[27] I hope that this discussion of *The Secret Agent* has suggested such an argument is only partly true. While all narratives are indeed sequential, the important fact is how that sequence is manipulated and what effects the manipulation produces. On the one hand, a narrative can capitalize upon its sequential flow to develop suspense which resolves itself in a final stasis of concluded action. On the other, a narrative can work against that flow to develop an artistic pattern which resolves itself in a final stasis of illumination embracing at once all portions of the narrative.[28] In a novel which works with narrative flow, the reader is immersed in the process of the action. His primary pleasure comes from inferring effects from causes and matching his inferences against the developing action. However, in a novel which works against narrative flow, the reader's pleasure stems from his ability to make various types of associational connections among more or less discrete fragments. It is true that the reader moves toward increasing clarity of vision as he is able to make more and more complex associations, but the goal of this movement is a comprehensive grasp of the novel as though all its parts existed simultaneously. Although it is true that any narrative can be seen as both process and stasis, it is also true that some narratives emphasize the process of action and others the stasis of illumination. Thus, when Conrad, speaking of *The End of the Tether*, emphasized the significance and value emerging from the reader's apprehension of the whole, we know what kind of narrative he had in mind: "in the light of the final incident, the whole story in all its descriptive detail shall fall into its place

—acquire its value and its significance. This is my method based on deliberate conviction. I've never departed from it."[29]

NOTES

[1] *The Technique of the Novel* (1928; rpt. New York: Gordian Press, 1964), p. 176.

[2] *Time and the Novel* (1952; rpt. New York: Humanities Press, 1965), p. 106. See also Ford Madox Ford's comparison of the country fair scene in *Madame Bovary* to a Futurist painting, in his *Critical Writings*, ed. Frank MacShane (Lincoln: University of Nebraska Press, 1964), p. 42.

[3] "Spatial Form in Modern Literature," *Sewanee Review*, 53 (1945), 221-40, 443-56, 643-53. The essay has been expanded and revised somewhat for inclusion in Frank's *The Widening Gyre: Crisis and Mastery in Modern Literature* (New Brunswick: Rutgers Univ. Press, 1963), pp. 3-62. This later version has been cited throughout.

[4] Ibid., p. 16.

[5] Ibid., p. 19.

[6] In addition to the studies cited below, see the following: Wilfred S. Dowden, *Joseph Conrad: The Imaged Style* (Nashville: Vanderbilt Univ. Press, 1970), pp. 112-23; Joseph I. Fradin and Jean W. Creighton, "The Language of *The Secret Agent*: The Art of Non-Life," *Conradiana*, 1 (Fall 1968), 23-35; David L. Kubal, "*The Secret Agent* and the Mechanical Chaos," *Bucknell Review*, 15 (December 1967), 65-77; Sister Jane Marie Leucke, O.S.B., "Conrad's Secret and Its Agent," *Modern Fiction Studies*, 10 (1964), 37-48. Hereafter cited as *MFS*. My purpose is not to discredit these studies but to suggest the limitation of the verbal surface of the novel as a unifying factor.

[7] *Structure and Motif in Finnegans Wake* (Evanston: Northwestern Univ. Press, 1962), pp. 164-65. The term "stitching" has been borrowed from Frank Baldanza, "The Structure of *Huckleberry Finn*," *American Literature*, 27 (1955), 247-55. Of course, many definitions of motif do not make the distinction I am insisting upon here. For such a broader view, see William Freedman, "The Literary Motif: A Definition and Evaluation," *Novel*, 4 (1971), 123-31.

[8] James Curtis, "Spatial Form as the Intrinsic Genre of Dostoevsky's Novels," *MFS*, 18 (1972), 139-40.

[9] "The Symbolic World of *The Secret Agent*," *Journal of English Literary History*, 32 (1965), 197-201. Hereafter cited as *ELH*. See also Fleischman's "The Criticism of Quality: Notes for a Theory of Style," *University Review*, 33 (1966), 3-10.

[10] Jerome Zuckerman, "The Motif of Cannibalism in *The Secret Agent*," *Texas Studies in Literature and Language*, 10 (1968), 299. Hereafter cited as *TSLL*.

[11] *The Secret Agent* (Garden City: Anchor Books, 1953), p. 22. Hereafter cited in the text.

[12] "'Cruel Devourer of the World's Light': *The Secret Agent*," *Nineteenth-Century Fiction*, 15 (1960), 44.

[13] For Gose's dismissal of structure, see pp. 42 and 45. The whole discussion of the symbolic value of natural versus artificial lighting (pp. 43-49) appears forced and arbitrary. Finally, so important a figure as Inspector Heat seems to remain untouched by light imagery.

[14]Previous studies of structural patterns in *The Secret Agent* include Lynne Cheney, "Joseph Conrad's *The Secret Agent* and Graham Greene's *It's a Battlefield*: A Study in Structural Meaning," *MFS*, 16 (1970), 117-31; John Hagan, Jr., "The Design of Conrad's *The Secret Agent*," *ELH*, 22 (1955), 148-64; Robin Lee, "*The Secret Agent*: Structure, Theme, Mode," *English Studies in Africa*, 11 (1968), 185-93; R. W. Stallman, "Time and *The Secret Agent*," *TSLL*, 1 (1959), 101-22; Joseph Wiesenfarth, F.S.C., "Stevie and the Structure of *The Secret Agent*," *MFS*, 13 (1967), 513-17. All of these studies deal usefully with dramatic repetition, time-shifts, and causal patterns. However, none of them has pursued these matters as thoroughly as I believe they should be.

[15]Quoted by Frank, *The Widening Gyre*, p. 15.

[16]Ibid., p. 16.

[17]Quoted from Roger Shattuck, *The Banquet Years: The Arts in France, 1885-1918* (New York: Harcourt, Brace and Co., 1958), p. 257. I am also indebted to Shattuck's entire discussion of what he calls the "arts of juxtaposition" (pp. 251-71).

[18]See Dayton Kohler, "Time in the Modern Novel," *College English*, 10 (1948-49), 18-19, and Sharon Spencer, *Space, Time and Structure in the Modern Novel* (New York: New York Univ. Press, 1971), pp. 155-59.

[19]Novels which fall in this category use what E. M. Forster and E. K. Brown have called "rhythm." See *Aspects of the Novel* (New York: Harcourt, Brace and World, 1927), pp. 149-69, and *Rhythm in the Novel* (Toronto: University of Toronto Press, 1950). The ability of rhythm to unify an entire narrative so that the reader perceives it as a whole in a moment of time is questionable. Rhythm alone can bring together significant portions of narrative, but it would seem to require the aid of other structural devices to create spatial form.

[20]*Joseph Conrad: A Personal Remembrance* (London: Duckworth, 1924), pp. 129-30.

[21]Donald Davidson, "Joseph Conrad's Directed Indirections," *Sewanee Review*, 33 (1925), 171.

[22]*Critical Writings*, p. 41.

[23]*Time and the Novel*, p. 104.

[24]U. C. Knoepflmacher, *Laughter & Despair: Readings in Ten Novels of the Victorian Era* (Berkeley: University of California Press, 1971), p. 246. Knoepflmacher's whole discussion of fragmentation and resulting perceptual demands in *The Secret Agent* (pp. 240-73) is helpful.

[25]Hagan, "The Design of Conrad's *The Secret Agent*," p. 150.

[26]*The Nature of Narrative* (New York: Oxford Univ. Press, 1966), p. 237.

[27]G. Giovannini, "Method in the Study of Literature in its Relation to the Other Fine Arts," *Journal of Aesthetics and Art Criticism*, 8 (1950), 191. Hereafter cited as *JAAC*. See also Walter Sutton, "The Literary Image and the Reader: A Consideration of the Theory of Spatial Form," *JAAC*, 16 (1957), 112-23.

[28]The terminology and general distinction between action and illumination have been borrowed from Scholes and Kellogg, *The Nature of Narrative*, p. 235.

[29]*Letters to William Blackwood and David S. Meldrum*, ed. William Blackburn (Durham: Duke Univ. Press, 1958), p. 154.

Conrad's Legacy: The Concern with Authenticity in Modern Fiction

Ivo Vidan

ABSTRACT

Conrad is the only major novelist who was also a master of a craft outside the liberal professions and who embodied his relationship to that craft, explicitly or implicitly, in all his important writing. His characters are constantly confronted with their "original project" [Sartre], and seamanship becomes an appropriate metaphor of it. The novelistic tradition established by Conrad is apparent in the manner in which an awareness of vocation makes men define themselves through their various assumed codes of ethics. The authenticity of the Conradian personality is tested in terms of its adequacy to its fundamental choice, in a manner unique to Conrad but foreshadowed in the Puritan inheritance of Henry James and the Protestant conscience of George Eliot's heroines. In a peculiar sense Stephen Crane also anticipates the problem of *Lord Jim*. Fitzgerald's drunkard doctor in *Tender is the Night* is closer to Conrad's main concern than the adopted Marlovian technique of *The Great Gatsby*. Hemingway, Malraux, and Saint-Exupéry, on the level of physical, often politically induced adventureship. Graham Greene continued the tradition on the level of religion. Faulkner and Warren, examining the relationships created within a historically articulated community, contributed to this line, which ends in the magnificently orchestrated nihilistic vision of Lowry's *Under the Volcano*. The assertion of freedom in Saul Bellow's generation is under the impact of a formulated body of existentialist ideas. It is no more related to the ordeal undergone through one's avowed calling, which is the distinguishing mark of the Conradian concern for authenticity. (IV)

The title and abstract of this discussion were written early in August 1973, and require a short introductory comment. This is because only three months later, exactly on November 5, was I able to lay hands on Lionel Trilling's *Sincerity and Authenticity*. How surprised I was to read the beginning of Chapter V: "What I take to be the paradigmatic literary expression of the modern concern with authenticity is Joseph Conrad's great short novel *Heart of Darkness* . . . ."[1]

167

I therefore have to begin by disclaiming any inspiration from that book (though like so many of us here I have always felt productive stimulus from Professor Trilling's writings), and I also wish to draw a distinction between Trilling's notion of authenticity and that which will be traced in the present paper.

Trilling points out that by "his regression to savagery Kurtz had reached as far down beneath the constructs of civilization as it was possible to go, to the irreducible truth of man, the innermost core of his nature, his heart of darkness. From that Stygian authenticity comes illumination. . . ."[2] Elsewhere in the book we are told that as the nineteenth century advances "the sentiment of being, of being strong, is increasingly subsumed under the conception of personal authenticity."[3] And also that nowadays "our sense of what authenticity means involves a degree of rough concreteness or of extremity"[4] and that it suggests "a more exigent conception of the self and of what being true to it consists in, a wider reference to the universe and man's place in it, and a less acceptant and genial view of the social circumstances of life."[5]

Trilling's use of the term has its antecedents in Sartrean existentialism, and I do not wish to deny that I feel my source to be the same. The *locus classicus* of its use appears in the *Reflections on the Jewish Question*: "Authenticity, it is obvious, consists in having a lucid and truthful awareness of the situation, in bearing the responsibilities and risks which the situation demands, in taking it upon oneself with pride or humility, sometimes with horror and hatred. There is no doubt that authenticity requires much courage and more than courage."[6]

I give a different shade or stress to my interpretation in that I see this extremity related to the individual's (or character's) awareness of his existence among men, in society, but pertaining to his sense of his own self, not to a role played within the functioning of society's machinery. A composite description from the relevant definitions in the *OED* and Webster is: "as being true in substance, genuine, real, actual, entitled to acceptance or belief, belonging to himself, acting of itself, self-originated." This does not make any explicit reference to the strenuous concept of existentialist authenticity, but it implies all of its constituent parts. There is thus a difference between Kurtz's radical severance from a framework of socially controlled behavior and the assertion of authenticity which we are going to pursue in Conrad's more direct legacy to later fiction.

In the sense in which I wish to use it, the term "authenticity" may be associated with the Protestant idea of "calling" in its post-Lutheran sense of *per vocationem*. R. H. Tawney defined it in the following way: "The calling is not a condition in which the individual is born, but a strenuous and exacting enterprise, to be undertaken, indeed, under the guidance of Providence, but to be chosen by each man for himself, with a deep sense of his solemn responsibilities."[7] Conrad's, of course, is not a universe guided and controlled by Providence, or dependent on it. For that very reason the principle of one's actions and choice lies in the individual. His projections are not primarily towards others, and the norms to which he assents have to be in tune with his own authentic self. The drama here, like that in existentialist writing, is produced by this very autonomy from external powers; the sanctions are imposed entirely by one's own consciousness.

Conrad's explicit pronouncements, however, speak of a diametrically opposite position. In a tribute to the Merchant Marine in 1918 for instance, he affirms "that the main characteristic of the British men spread all over the world, is not the spirit of adventure so much as the spirit of service."[8] And he later says that "what is needed is a sense of immediate duty, and a feeling of impalpable constraint."[9] The tradition-hallowed doctrine of duty and hard work as a redeeming action seems to have been accepted by Conrad throughout his career. We read in *The Mirror of the Sea* that "the moral side of industry, productive or unproductive, the redeeming and ideal aspect of this bread-winning, is the attainment and preservation of the highest possible skill on the part of the craftsmen. Such skill, the skill of technique, is more than honesty; it is something wider, embracing honesty and grace and rule in an elevated and clear sentiment, not altogether utilitarian, which may be called the honour of labour. It is made up of accumulated tradition, kept alive by individual pride, rendered exact by professional opinion, and, like the higher arts, it is spurred on and sustained by the discriminating praise."[10]

This is, undoubtedly, also the intended message of *The Nigger of the "Narcissus."* But if the meaning of Conrad's fiction were so conventionally Victorian, would we still read him? In fact, throughout Conrad's fiction there is a productive tension at work. The positive, constructive principle of dedication to one's chosen walk in life is embodied with the sharpest clarity in the profession of seamen. It is not only affirmed and believed in, but displayed as a basic motive of human action. Yet it is pervaded by anxiety, doubt, and questioning as to one's adequacy—by the lotus-eaters' temptation to give up and to yield to one's complacency and comfort. The tendencies involved in this tension are polarized in the *Nigger*. In the works that follow they are united and develop internally, rather than as an external opposition. The dramatic feeling of existence is uncommonly close to what we know of Puritan consciousness, though a Protestant awareness of responsibility was not Conrad's natural inheritance. One wishes to distinguish it from his aristocratic sense of honor, and attribute it to his peculiar position among the great writers. He is the only major novelist who was also the master of a craft outside the liberal professions, one in which one is constantly aware of the precariousness of one's existence, and his calling—what he once referred to as to his "mysterious vocation"[11]—has to be reaffirmed throughout his writing career. It was that earlier, fundamental choice which later gave its meaning to his skill and art as a writer. This can be seen in the following sentence from *The Mirror of the Sea*, though the accent is on the other end of the analogy: "Like all true art, the general conduct of a ship and her handling in particular cases had a technique which could be discussed with delight and pleasure by men who found in their work, not bread alone, but an outlet for the peculiarities of their temperament."[12] And when we affirm the continuing modernity of Conrad's art, it has to be stressed that this art does not reside in the denial of the positive, accepted principle of work well done, but in the creation, within the consciousness, of an assumed responsibility and of the existential awareness that one requires to make choices.

In an early story, "Youth," this is excellently presented in an atmosphere of unconcerned freedom; it can be found more fully realized in a mature work that sums up earlier crises, *The Shadow-line*:

> I had a general sense of my preparedness which only a man pursuing a calling he loves can know. That feeling seemed to me the most natural thing in the world. As natural as breathing. I imagine I could not have lived without it.
> I don't know what I expected. Perhaps nothing else than that special intensity of existence which is the quintessence of youthful aspirations.[13]

The Shadow-line's symbolic companion piece of a few years before, "The Secret Sharer," externalizes this same drama in a memorable interpersonal relationship. What is at stake, however, is really the "communion of a seaman with his first command."[14] The young captain's "feeling of identity"[15] is tested as he finds himself thrown into a situation requiring a series of risky decisions.

This dramatic substance achieves its culmination in Conrad's major novels centering in what Karl Jaspers has named "extreme" or "boundary situations," in which, as Marjorie Greene puts it, "the ultimate motives and values that govern an individual's life are brought dramatically into focus by the necessity for making a fundamental choice."[16] The choice is tragic: man tries to come to terms with the widest issues that concern him. Yet the concrete circumstances under which this takes place are structured in a way which make man ultimately founder in his attempt. Conrad's vision of that inevitability can be most closely related to the work of Henry James, who is his most interesting predecessor in the exploration of authenticity as we understand it.

Basically there is little difference between the attitude of a Conradian seaman following a code of professional ethics and the explicitly professed amateurishness of an Isabel Archer. They are both open to experience, to what life may bring their way. This, however, does not indicate anything substantially new in the history of literature. James's great innovation was to create a character whose circumstances and status in life do not impose any limitations or directions upon her, and who can therefore ask herself, in essence, what she should do with her freedom. Isabel's freedom becomes the instrument of her vocation. It is a vocation in that she assumes all the responsibility for the consequences of her choice: "One must accept one's deeds. . . . I was perfectly free."[17] The object of Isabel's choice, we know, proves to be unfortunate, but this does not invalidate the authenticity of her original project. This term, project, one should add, is described in the glossary to *Being and Nothingness* as "the For-itself's choice of its way of being" and is "expressed by action in the light of a future end."[18]

In his essay on *The Portrait of a Lady*, Richard Poirier helpfully observes that the *Portrait* is "a novel of ideas more than of psychology, an imitation of moral action more than a drama of motive."[19] It remains an open question, however, whether this makes it a lesser accomplishment, as Poirier judges. Anyhow, it brings James's novel surprisingly close to the type of fiction written by André Gide, which displays *disponibilité* as a concept of being; as we shall see, the context of such thinking attracted Gide to *Lord Jim* and *Under Western Eyes*. Isabel Archer, Jim, and Razumov determine a basically consistent way of living, a response to a calling which, they feel, makes them what they are. It is not their "fine consciences"[20] that we are interpreting, but their engagement in particular types of action; not the logic of their consciousness, but the mode of their existence. None of them is conditioned by the quotidian, and yet each finds himself concretely *en situation*. It is from this angle that we are trying to define the common concern of Conrad's novels and show that a whole group of authors center on Conrad.

Palpable Jamesian traces can be discerned in *The Secret Agent*, and they come, unsurprisingly, from *The Princess Casamassima*.[21] But this particular case of influence is uncharacteristic; the more interesting relationship is one connecting Hyacinth Robinson with

Lord Jim. It is true that James, when he decided to get to grips with the theme of social conflict, *conditioned* his protagonist in the manner of Zola, but in terms of a more schematic symbolism. Hyacinth has an early phase of revolutionary fervor along the lines of his French mother. Later he feels his English father's aristocratic streak assume control over that basic aesthetical conservatism which, as becomes clear, is the authentic mark of his deepest self. Fully conscious of this clash between recently acquired persuasion and earlier assumed commitment, he chose self-destruction. An analogy can be discerned here with Isabel Archer's fate, less violent of course, in terms of plot, and with Jim's and Razumov's realization of having earlier misread their own vocation.

Another, and more direct, antecedent of *Lord Jim* approaches the problem of authenticity by a different method. It is incorrect to associate Stephen Crane with Conrad only through their so-called impressionism, i.e., their technique of presentation. Conrad himself was nettled by this kind of critical judgment.[22] On the other hand, he himself admitted that the *Nigger* and *The Red Badge of Courage* basically shared the theme of testing, i.e., "the moral problem of conduct,"[23] specifically in the case of the *Nigger* testing the men's "faithfulness to the conditions of their own calling."[24] What is significant, however, is the way in which Crane's work foreshadows *Lord Jim* and perhaps influences it.[25] In both novels the young protagonist imagines himself as a hero, and is later brought into a position which forces him to decide whether he can stand up to the requirements of his situation. Later, Henry Fleming justifies his own inadequacy with several alibis that in fact amount to mystification;[26] Jim too tries to tone down his responsibility, though he has a more "acute consciousness of lost honour."[27] They both achieve a victory over their weakness, however precarious. It permits Henry Fleming satisfaction with himself at the end of the novel, which may or may not be disproved later. Jim, not having been able to disavow his own feelings of identity with another culprit against human solidarity, accepts the consequences of his weakness.

One does not wish at this point to involve oneself in the moral antinomies of Jim's behavior, just as one does not pretend to examine from the outside each possible line of action at the disposal of Hyacinth or Isabel. Yet like the stories of these Jamesian heroes and of Crane's brave soldier of incomplete integrity, Jim's story dramatizes the question of realizing one's genuine vocation, of acting in accordance with one's original project: is one's conscious decision in tune with one's substantial character? To see human life in these terms is only part of Dostoevsky's achievement; none of the great nineteenth-century French novelists seem to be aware of it, and only two English-speaking ones anticipate James: Hawthorne, wrestling with his Puritan inheritance, and George Eliot in her scrupulous analyses of her finest heroines. Wilbur Cross significantly wrote that Jim's journey was a rare one—upwards—and that his story was the only notable instance of such a direction since *The Pilgrim's Progress* with the exceptions of *Silas Marner* and *Gwendolyn Harleth*. He adds that George Eliot had taken her design and imagery from Bunyan.[28]

There is no direct connection between George Eliot and Conrad, as there is between either of them and James, or James and Hawthorne. It is our contention that Conrad's experience of the problem of vocation belongs to the existential sphere of authenticity, not to the psychological one of sincerity and conviction. In his treatment there is less need to build up a justification by an account of development, or for a description of the conditioning circumstances: it approaches the freedom of the Gidean "inconsequence," which the author of *The Vatican Cellars*[29] and of *The Immoralist* sensed in *Lord Jim* and *Under Western Eyes*.[30] As Stein explains, Jim's problem is ultimately "How to be?"[31] In a world in which we do not feel our actions sanctioned by a Divinity, our being will be colored with whatever authentic calling we may surmise or grope towards. It may have been too early for George Eliot to see this in the abstract terms of an entirely unconditioned choice of a Jamesian aesthetic morality, let alone to discern the way out in the paradox of immersing into the destructive element. Yet in our post-Nietzschean world we are all fascinated by the perilous integrity which this catching phrase suggests of heroes before and after Conrad's.

Still, we maintain, to accept Kurtz mainly because of his ambiguously limited, ultimate "horror" exclamation is a modern interpretation, and not Conrad's. He was fascinated by Kurtz, but also horrified by him at least as much as Marlow professes to be. Conrad's nineteenth-century consciousness, in spite of all its profound adumbration of an almost Blakean awareness of nihilistic boundlessness, accepted all the Victorian values that his scepticism would still allow room for. His ambiguous attitude towards Kurtz is to some extent opposite to the one towards Decoud, whom he condemned without actually making the reader feel the destructive emptiness attributed to the *boulevardier*.

Conrad seems to have condemned some of his own non-constructive inclinations in Decoud, and yet made him into a person of action, responsibility, and commitment![32] We may grant that Decoud is a *dilettante*—but then, who in *Nostromo* is authentic? The problem of integrity as a quality of being rather than of moral conviction is developed in numerous subtle variations in Conrad's vastest fictional composition. This is so, even though the presentation is more single-minded and the suggestive ambiguities more concentrated in *Lord Jim*, and though in *Heart of Darkness* the readers who have been reared on Lawrence or Genet can discern earlier unsuspected possibilities of demonic dialectics.

It is time for us to trace this concern with authenticity in authors who have undoubtedly experienced Conrad's impact in handling this particular theme. It does not seem that Conrad's greatest works produced an immediate creative response. Leaving aside the still unresolved question of Conrad's possible impact upon Virginia Woolf, the first direct effect of *Lord Jim* upon modern letters seems to be in *The Great Gatsby*.

Throughout his writing career Fitzgerald gladly acknowledged his debt to Conrad, and yet his statements in conversation and letters do not seem to point to any essential link between them. What he got out of the Preface to *The Nigger of the "Narcissus"* must have been a very general injunction to write accurately;[33] in one of his letters to Hemingway there is a remark about the dangers of too easily appropriating Conradian rhythms and his use of quoting his characters' phrases in a reported speech.[34] On several occasions he acknowledges that they both acquired Conrad's "dying fall" device to end a story.[35] To the early Fitzgerald, *Nostromo* was the finest English novel since *Vanity Fair*.[36] An interesting and puzzling remark occurs in a letter written to his daughter in July 1939, long after *The Great Gatsby* and five years after *Tender Is the Night:* "*Lord Jim* is a great book—the first third at least and the conception, though it got lost a little bit in the lawcourts of Calcutta or wherever it was. I wonder if you know why it is good?"[37]

The heroes of Fitzgerald's two most important novels are both idealists, highly single-minded in their ambitions—like Nostromo or Jim. In terms of narrative procedure *The Great Gatsby* is closer to Conrad, because it is made up of Nick Carraway's account of his acquaintance with Gatsby and of crucial moments in Gatsby's history. This is comparable to Marlow's role in relation to Kurtz and to Jim. The technical parallels have been studied by several critics, most systematically by R. E. Long,[38] who also examines the analogies between the various characters. What remains to be pointed out is the dynamics of structure, i.e., the relationship between narrator, hero, and the world in which the "Icarian"[39] pattern of the hero's career takes place.

Marlow has a well-defined set of values, of which one is constantly aware as one follows his efforts to assess Jim's intentions and the deeper motives underlying his behavior. The shifting background to their contact is that of people living according to or against a standard code of behavior, not—as in Nick's New York suburbs—that of a fixed if many-faced social environment defined by a plethora of revealing details. Nick does not reveal a Marlovian moral assurance and is himself part of that dense world of flux, paradox, the grotesque, incongruousness, and confusion that make up the novel. Of such a world Gatsby is an extreme expression; and yet, because of the stability of his dream, he is at the same time a symbol of opposition to it. In that, surprisingly, he is closer to Kurtz than to Jim—in spite of appearing well meaningly disingenuous, and therefore likeable. His symbolic function makes him a static, passive character, whereas Jim lives in a fictional world that permits constructive action both at sea and on land. Jim's tragedy is the inevitable outcome of well-intentioned involvement, which repeatedly proves to have been mistaken, and for motives that remain a secret to Jim, and direct the reader to look for patterns outside the text. In *The Great Gatsby* no genuine vocation is at issue, as it is in Conrad. In each case, however, the ruling ambition proves to be a mistaken choice. It is contradicted by the character's limited potentialities for what the choice would actually exact from him.

The Great Gatsby is a concentrated drama, a spatial book dominated throughout by a major symbolic figure; *Tender Is the Night* is the unfolding of a history, a process[40] of gradual perception for the reader—and for the hero that of self-realization. There does not seem to be a technical similarity between it and Conrad's novels; nevertheless we find an essential parallel with Conrad. *Tender Is the Night* is a drama of vocation.

Dick Drover, a scientifically gifted young doctor, gives in to glamour and to frivolity that accompanies irresponsible wealth. And, as a critic suggests with reference to the theories of George Herbert Mead, "the full poignancy of Dick's decline . . . is to be seen in the other way in which the individual internalizes the attitudes of others—by becoming what he is thought to be."[41] His drama as a drunkard is only an expression of his insubstantiality, his inauthenticity. This betrayal of vocation must have been the reason why, in his General Plan of the novel, Fitzgerald called Dick "a spoiled priest."[42] Again, unlike Conrad's isolated protagonists, Dick is part of the social world circumstantially presented, but often full of irrelevance and of inexplicable links in terms of plot and of character behavior. Fitzgerald's heroes are images of Fitzgerald himself trapped in his own charm and his earlier weakness for splendor and triviality, and his later miseries with his own sick wife and his dependence on drink. Dick is no cover-up for the author's self-portrait; he is, as Malcolm Cowley says,[43] a synechdoche for the world—that world which, through Dick and as a playground for Dick's personal drama, Fitzgerald so soberly sees in its crisis of dissolution. None of Conrad's individualized characters have the same kind of function: the symbolic suggestiveness of Kurtz lacks the particularities of Dick Drover's history.

There is an important difference between Fitzgerald and other writers in the context of our theme. He never grapples with the problem of expressing authentic existence and seems to be aware of potential authenticity only by implication: through showing the resilience of Gatsby's dream within the inauthentic, the socially conforming, moulded by the conventional. The choices of James's and Conrad's characters, though dramatized *en situation* enact the freedom of the active autonomous personality like that "lonely impulse of delight" which Yeats attributed to Major Robert Gregory leading to his death as an airman.[44] Equally so, the code of Ernest Hemingway—not sceptical, nor fatalistic in its tragic vision—allows for an autonomy of human determination. As Earl Rovit puts it, "the Hemingway code is the ethic, or philosophic perspective, through which Hemingway tries to impart *meaning* and *value* to the seeming futility of man's headlong rush toward death. . . . It also provides for a significant measure of *freedom* for human actions within which morality can operate and human responsibility can be judged in terms of *active* rather than *passive* responses."[45]

It is very probable that Hemingway's literary articulation of his code would not have been the same if he had not had Conrad and Crane's example before him. His own highly appreciative utterances[46] about these two authors are not revealing; the compliments paid to Conrad in the *Transatlantic Review* obituary issue are backhanded to say the least.

"Abstract words such as glory, honour, courage or hallow were obscene beside the concrete names of villages, the numbers of roads, the names of rivers, the numbers of regiments and the dates."[47] The first half of this famous sentence from Hemingway's war novel *A Farewell to Arms* could also apply to Stephen Crane, though the second half appears to suggest mere reporting which in fact we do not find even in Hemingway's seemingly matter-of-fact writing. In Crane the pretended socially imposed values are suppressed by a faithful description of the field of perception. In both cases a moral attitude is linked with an appropriate literary style. The point of the moral is its reticence and that unformulated understanding between men brought together under conditions of precarious existence. This is the way in which the four shipwrecked in Crane's "The Open Boat" and the soldiers in *A Farewell to Arms* experience a manly solidarity of a kind which brings to mind Conrad's Prefaces to the *Nigger* and *A Personal Record*, and Malraux's term "fraternité virile."

Another and more selective form is the unspoken recognition of members of that never-established club of accurate, devoted sportsmen who recognize each other in some undefined way: Henry and Count Greffi in *Farewell* or Jake and the strange Count in *The Sun Also Rises*, to whom Lady Brett twice refers by the Conradian phrase "one of us." Hemingway's appreciation of a clean job, of professionalism, is reminiscent of Marlow's clinging to honest work against the unsubstantial atmosphere in *Heart of Darkness*. It amounts to something close to, but not quite identical with, authentic vocation. The greatest of Conrad's explorations into the nature of human struggle for an adequate stand in a world of contingency are all tragic. The attempts to live authentically in Hemingway's novels are also tragic failures. They seem to be symbolized by Jake Barnes's impotence in *The Sun Also Rises*: he is open to the possibilities of societally unstructured living and all the time feels the impossibility of genuine achievement. The only moments of satisfaction which he finds are in the arcadian fishing scenes outside the main drift of his crowd's pseudoactivity. In Hemingway's best novels the impossibilities of building a lasting workable meaning in one's personal life are expressed on the very edge of sentimental self-dramatization. In the late works he admires Robert Jordan, the professor turned imported guerrilla specialist for explosives, and the fisherman Santiago. Both are the author's willed wishful self-projections, rather than figures of lived experience like Lord Jim or Decoud, in which the author enacts his own dilemmas. Hemingway's correlatives of Conrad's basically successful sailors are the Spanish matadors and dignified plebeians like the waiter in "A Clean, Well-Lighted Place." These are symbolic enactments of a ritualistic view of human self-satisfaction in terms of a clean, sportsman-like professionalism, as against the willed self-projections like those in the longer works after 1935.

It would seem that "readiness is all," if one is to be potentially authentic. If we are not back at that initial figure of the European novel, the *picaro*, we have relegated the possibilities of realizing the unconditioned to such people, whose walks in life are those of adventurers—not incompatible with pure adventure as vocation.

In a passage quoted earlier, we found Conrad the Victorian refusing adventure as a reliable principle of living; the whole notion of values embedded in responsible craftsmanship seems to protest against it.

And yet, adventure as vocation means, just like the exercise of seamanship, a constant reaffirmation of one's authentic choice of a particular way of living. It is, as a character reflects in Malraux's *Royal Way*, a quest, and thus it is "the outcome of a man's resolve to turn life into account."[48] Or as is said by another character, Perken, whose existence is marked by his repeatedly facing death: " 'Life is so much raw material; what is one making of it?—that's the question. It's true one never can make anything of it, really; still there are several methods of making nothing of it. And in order to live one's life *according to plan*, one must have a short way with life's threats, the threat of growing old, of wearing out, and so forth. So a revolver is an excellent life-insurance, for it's easy enough to kill oneself when death is a means . . . .' "[49]

In spite of its apparent nihilism, this comes close to the solemnly ritualized pattern of behavior of Hemingway's most attractive figures; in glimpses it can be discerned in the *Red Badge of Courage* and several shorter stories by Stephen Crane. Outside American literature its most impressive proponent is undoubtedly André Malraux, who is also Conrad's closest literary disciple outside the English-speaking world.

As late as 1939 Malraux revealed his interest in Conrad by referring to different aspects of his technique in a short essay on the novel and the film.[50] In all of his first three novels, written between 1928 and 1933, one may detect the impact of Conrad, though only in the second one, *The Royal Way*, is the influence of Conrad obvious. The novel ascribes to fictional characters a genuine episode from the author's life: a dangerous journey deep into the jungle of Indochina with the purpose of bringing home valuable material—sculptures from the ruins of Khmeric temples. The parallel with *Heart of Darkness* is evident, though Malraux, in order to be able to extract the metaphysical significance of perilous existence divides the role of Kurtz between two different characters, Perken and Brabot. Perhaps it is the often repeated yearning for loyalty and human dignity, "longing for communion in the face of death,"[51] as Joseph Frank puts it, that accounts for Malraux's emotional involvement in the Chinese revolution, the wider subject of the two other novels. In *The Conquerors* the personality of a single-minded and individualistic revolutionary, of mixed European origin, Garine, is gradually revealed by a friend: first from hearsay on a journey to Canton where he is to join Garine and through reflexions over documents concerning Garine, and later through an eye-witness account. The Marlow technique from both *Heart of Darkness* and *Lord Jim* is applied to a character admittedly different from

Jim, but not entirely unlike him in the ambiguous effects of his actions. Malraux's third and best novel, *Man's Fate*, on the other hand, has something of the pattern of *Nostromo*. Though not a moral fable, it is a political drama like Conrad's, and its many strands are perfectly integrated in a way which makes the private and public action of its heterogeneous characters depend on each other. Unlike *Nostromo*, it tries to present involvement in a way which is tragic yet authentic, and therefore ultimately satisfactory.

Another French author of Malraux's generation is also close to Conrad in several ways. Antoine de Saint-Exupéry was not a sailor by profession, nor did he experience adventure as a purpose in itself. But he was an airman, who read Conrad well—he refers to Conrad in his semi-autobiographical writing about his own craft.[52] His accent is not so much on vocation as is on responsibility. Yet he too sees the practice of his profession—under extremely precarious circumstances, over desert and mountain chains, in tempest and war—as a choice which implies the acceptance of duty at a time when aeroplanes were as different from those of today as Conrad's sailing ships from present-day liners. Man makes himself through his own acts[53]—this is the message that can be detected in this drama of authenticity. Like Conrad's fiction it finds its embodiment in the tenuous human relations that develop under extreme pressure and, often, psychological and physical isolation.

Saint-Exupéry is often considered more as a brave humanist than as an artist of strong originality, and he certainly is not a thinker who through his moving books would convey excitingly new insights. In French literature authentic living finds its most authentic interpretation as a subject of Jean-Paul Sartre. But Sartre's works, like those of Camus, are too conscious of the problems which authentic novelists create in the very process of shaping their fictions. Instead, these two write theirs as companion pieces to their own philosophy. Adam Gillon and other Conrad critics after him have found fascinating analogies with Sartre.[54] Yet it would be a mistake, factually and methodologically, to view Sartre's more radical, more developed, more articulated thinking about this subject as in any way dependent on Conrad. It is in fact questionable whether Sartre has ever been aware of Conrad —he has certainly never shown it in the way he has about Faulkner; though his interest in *Sartoris* and *The Sound and the Fury*[55] does not coincide with what in Faulkner's work primarily concerns us here.

Critics, on the other hand, have indicated certain points in common between Sartre and Faulkner's most intriguing study of authenticity as a problem, namely *Light in August*. T. H. Adamowski speaks of Christmas's life style in terms of Sartre's existential psychoanalysis of Baudelaire, namely, in Sartre's words, of "that irrevocable choice by which each of us decided in a particular situation what he will be and what he is."[56]

Christmas, indeed, is a Negro because he choses to be Negro, irrespectively of whether this corresponds to biological facts or not. On one level he really assumes full responsibility by accepting the consequences of his free decision, and becomes authentic like Hyacinth Robinson or as Jim becomes after having realized his repeated failure. Faulkner's frequent reading of Conrad may not have produced a direct literary influence, but was itself undoubtedly caused by a deeply felt affinity. Faulkner's experiments in composition and his grandiloquence may partly at least be an inheritance from Conrad, developed further, up to the point of deliberate distortions of verisimilitude, temporal unity, and grammar. And yet, on a different level, are Faulkner's monomaniacs[57]—people like Christmas or Quentin Compson—capable of freedom, or are they original, even idiosyncratic and extreme re-creations of Naturalistic characterization in the wake of Zola—and possibly Frank Norris?

An awareness of the problem of authenticity occurs frequently in Faulkner. His main contribution to the prevailing literary mood of the Thirties, otherwise a comparatively minor achievement, *The Wild Palms*, may interest us here because Harry Wilbourne and Catherine abandon the unanxiety of a steady job and secure food because they wish to maintain the pristine feeling of their love in the teeth of socially regulated living, the "vice" of respectability.[58] On the other hand, the famous self-abnegating choice of Isaac McCaslin in "The Bear," relaxed self-possession of Faulkner's black hero, Lucas Beauchamp in *Go Down, Moses*, are conciliatory gestures by the author, satisfactory to an academic criticism wishing to integrate modernistic imagination into a positive, socially constructive and morally acceptable framework. But are they more authentic as literature than Hemingway's late heroes are?

It seems that an exposure to the historical tensions of the American South makes novelists sensitive to the phenomena of identity, self-awareness, and existential choice. An author of considerable standing, if not of Faulkner's stature, but free from Faulkner's exaggerated idiosyncracies, offers unique opportunities for a study of this theme, Robert Penn Warren. We are even closer to Conrad here, because in Faulkner's work the problem of authenticity does not seem to be filtered through a feeling of vocation, except perhaps when Isaac McCaslin foregoes his patrimony (a case opposite from that of Gould in

Nostromo). The basic pattern of Warren's works may be defined as a transformation of bad faith into self-realization. This holds true also when characters do not actually achieve "redemption," as in *Night Rider* and *World Enough and Time* as well as when they do, as in *All the King's Men*. The narrative structure of the latter is analogous to that of *The Great Gatsby* and *Heart of Darkness*. The narrator, however, has a much more important role to play than he does in these earlier novels. He is not a refractory mirror and commentator like Nick and Marlow. It is in him that the process of change, the affirmation of authenticity struggles through. The narrator, Jack Burden, and the protagonist, Willie Stark, both act in bad faith. Willie, the demagogue politician acts as if he were fulfilling a calling, but, in his ambitious drive for popularity and power, he suppresses his sense of responsibility to his original intentions. Jack's cynical tone indicates detachment, yet also dependence on Willie, and he pragmatically misuses his original vocation for history. On the one hand, Jack obediently digs up and interconnects facts "useful" to his master; on the other he conveniently suppresses his memory, accepting at the same time a mechanistic and fatalistic view of the world ("The Great Twitch") and recurs to the escapist position which he calls "The Great Sleep."

Warren's distinctive contribution to the Conrad tradition in this and, to a lesser extent, in other novels, appears to be a blending of the gradual, analytic procedure of *Lord Jim* with the philosophical explication of a *Nostromo*-like pattern, namely of society in process; no wonder that Warren's is perhaps the best single essay on the world of *Nostromo*.[59] Jack Burden is aware of history as conditioning the present and the future, of history as destiny. But, as a historian by profession, he also knows that history is a complex effect of forces at work, including the activity of the historian's mind—through the interpretation of facts, of a total situation, of a developing structure. The choice of such a pursuit calls not only for moral responsibility within its own terms but for more. Since Conrad no one—apart from Warren —seems to have connected an awareness of the general problem of authenticity with the actual practice of a narrator as historian. Perhaps Warren is the last serious novelist in America with a sense of the larger movements of history in his pulses.

To explore Conrad's impact upon Graham Greene is a job which would go far beyond the limits of our present subject. Greene has himself affirmed that he stopped reading Conrad because of the influence that Conrad had upon his writings.[60] In Greene's early fiction, indeed, more Conradian motifs and external features of his technique can be found than in the work of any other novelists one remembers. An at-mosphere of betrayal, manhunt, isolation, hope-and-fear, pervades all the first three books, whether the particular borrowing is most re-mindful of *The Arrow of Gold, Victory, Under Western Eyes*, or that Stevensonian masterpiece by Conrad and Ford, *Romance*. *It's a Battlefield*, the last of the early novels, is to an important extent a pastiche of *The Secret Agent*.

"Conrad's *Heart of Darkness* impressed Africa as an imaginative symbol on the European mind,"[61] wrote Greene at a time when that story had not left any unmistakeable traces on his own works, apart perhaps from the way in which an ominous atmosphere is created through description. After almost thirty years Greene rereads *Heart of Darkness*, which he now finds faulty.[62] He is in the Congo, in search of material for what becomes *A Burnt-Out Case*. The atmos-phere is no longer ominous and except for a few details reminiscent of *Heart of Darkness*, the Conrad borrowings are all from *Lord Jim*. This is the more significant since Greene's diary testifies that his hero's motives are at first unclear to the author himself. Querry, the great Catholic architect who has lost his sense of vocation, withdraws to the remotest station on the big river deep in Africa, to a leper colony run by priests. As the reader is shown, in an effortlessly achieved series of points of view, Querry is accepted on his own terms and given a sense of social integration. But the world finds him out through the meddling offices of a minor rascal, with whom Querry discovers a faint analogy—a parody of Lord Jim's relationship to Gentleman Brown.

The relevant theme for our purpose, however, is that of vocation. It is explicitly discussed on several occasions in the novel in an incon-clusive way and, though in a Catholic context, it implies the engage-ment of the individual's self in the Conradian sense. As in *Lord Jim*, Querry's feeling of vocation might have been restored if it were not prevented by the interference from the world outside his present en-vironment. Greene once wrote: "How little in truth are we changed by events, how romantic and false . . . is a book such as Conrad's *Lord Jim*."[63] Nevertheless, the crisis of authenticity is much subtler in Jim's case than in Querry's; Jim is guilty and Querry is not. Circum-stances put Jim's involvement to trial, out of which a satisfactory issue is impossible. Querry's death is brought about by a contrived plot, irrelevant to the problem of vocation that gives the book its serious dimension.

Warren and Greene, both in their late sixties, are possibly the last living authors whose work is under Conrad's direct influence. Yet it is a novel by an author dead since 1957 that functions as a magnificently orchestrated finale to the tracing of the Conradian preoccupation that we have here tried to rehearse. The intricate symbolism of Malcolm Lowry's *Under the Volcano* brings that novel's texture into the orbit of *Ulysses*, and there may be other literary influences at work which may seem to qualify the importance of Conrad's impact. The very framework of the novel, however, is indicative. Not only does the story concern a few foreigners in an exotic setting dominated by huge mountains (reminiscent of *Nostromo* and *Victory*), but the interplay between the characters also seems to be overshadowed by a fatality which can be felt in terms of actual historical conflicts. The story could be summed up as the consul's unsuccessful attempt to overcome his inertia in relation to individuals and to avoid involvement in the political incidents of the moment; yet drink has made him incapable of acting according to whatever sense of personal vocation he may once have had. His position recalls Heyst's and Jim's, but these two are, by comparison, romantic activists. *Lord Jim* is probably most present in the novel, and not only because it is explicitly mentioned by Lowry.[64] The consul's crime against human solidarity committed in the past aboard a ship and the pariah dog, symbolizing isolation and inadequacy, recall Conrad's novel. So does the sense of guilt in the Consul's brother Hugh. His avoidance of engagement in the Spanish civil war brings to mind the behavior of Jim and of Dr. Monygham.

Lowry's admiration for Fitzgerald[65] and in particular his interest in *Tender Is the Night*,[66] one surmises, may have come from his feeling of comparable failure and imperfect capacity due to drink. The disintegration of the consul and the author's need, subjective, rather than actual, for an esoteric system of references[67] to maintain unity and underline significance in his work, both express an awareness that the last important follower of Joseph Conrad felt it impossible to exercise an authentic vocation.

The problem of authenticity reappears, of course, in a series of brilliant authors, notably in America, such as Bellow, Ellison, Mailer. It is central to the awareness of freedom in much of their work, but it does not concern us here within the framework of our title. Their work differs from that we have examined here in two respects. They consciously develop the implications of a modern anxiety in the context of a formulated body of existentialist ideas by French and German thinkers. Furthermore, unlike these later writers, the group which is under the direct impact of Conrad sees boundary situations as ordeals undergone in terms of their characters' calling. Although most of them have been agnostics, they would all agree with Dietrich Bonhoeffer that "vocation is responsibility and responsibility is a total response of the whole man to the whole of reality."[68]

NOTES

[1]Lionel Trilling, *Sincerity and Authenticity* (Cambridge: Harvard Univ. Press, 1972), p. 106.

[2]Ibid., p. 108.

[3]Ibid., p. 99.

[4]Ibid., p. 94.

[5]Ibid., p. 11.

[6]Jean-Paul Sartre, *Réflexions sur la question juive* (Paris: Paul Morihien, 1946), pp. 116-17. The translation of one part of the passage comes from Anthony Riehards Manser's *Sartre* (London: Athlone Press, 1966), p. 155.

[7]R. H. Tawney, *Religion and the Rise of Capitalism* (Harmondsworth: Penguin Books Ltd., 1938), p. 217.

[8]Joseph Conrad, " 'Well Done,' " in *Notes on Life and Letters* (London: J.M. Dent & Sons, 1949), p. 189.

[9]Ibid., p. 191.

[10]Joseph Conrad, *The Mirror of the Sea* (bound with *A Personal Record*; London: J. M. Dent & Sons, 1950), p. 24.

[11]*A Personal Record* (bound with *The Mirror of the Sea*; London: J. M. Dent & Sons, 1950), p. 119.

[12]*The Mirror of the Sea*, p. 31.

[13]Joseph Conrad, *The Shadow-Line* (bound with *Within the Tides*; London: J. M. Dent & Sons, 1950), p. 83.

[14]Joseph Conrad, "The Secret Sharer," *'Twixt Land and Sea* (London: J. M. Dent & Sons, 1947), p. 143.

[15]Ibid., p. 120.

[16]Marjorie Greene, "The German Existentialists," *Chicago Review*, 13 (Summer 1959), 50.

[17]Henry James, *The Portrait of a Lady* (Harmondsworth: Penguin Books, 1971), pp. 488-89.

[18]Jean-Paul Sartre, *Being and Nothingness*, trans. Hazel E. Barnes (New York: Washington Square Press, 1968), p. 806.

[19]Richard Poirier, "Drama in *The Portrait of a Lady*," in *Twentieth-Century Interpretations of The Portrait of a Lady*, ed. P. Buitenhuis (Englewood Cliffs: Prentice-Hall, 1968), p. 35.

[20]Joseph Conrad, "Henry James," *Notes on Life and Letters* (London: J. M. Dent & Sons, 1949), p. 17.

[21]Cf. Ivo Vidan, "*The Princess Casamassima*: Between Balzac and Conrad," *Studia Romanica et Anglica Zagrabiensia*, 21-22 (1966), 259-76, esp. 272-76.

[22]Cf. Ivo Vidan, "*The Red Badge of Courage*: A Study in Bad Faith," *Studia Romanica et Anglica Zagrabiensia*, 33-36 (1972-1973), 93-112, esp. 93-94, 98-99, and 109-12.

[23]Joseph Conrad, "Stephen Crane," *Last Essays* (bound with *Tales of Hearsay*; London: J. M. Dent & Sons, 1955), p. 95.

[24]Ibid., p. 94.

[25]Vidan, "*The Red Badge of Courage*: A Study in Bad Faith," p. 112. Carl Nelson, in "The Ironic Allusive Texture of *Lord Jim*: Coleridge, Crane, Milton, and Melville," *Conradiana*, 4, No. 2 (1972), 47-59.

[26]Cf. Vidan, "*The Red Badge of Courage*: A Study in Bad Faith," passim.

[27]Joseph Conrad, *Lord Jim* (London: J. M. Dent & Sons, 1948), p. ix.

[28]Wilbur L. Cross, *Four Contemporary Novelists* (London: Macmillan, 1930), p. 55.

[29]The title of the American translation is *Lafcadio's Adventures*.

[30]André Gide, *Journal 1889-1939* (Paris: Gallimard, 1948), entries for 23 February and 2 August 1930 (pp. 971, 1002); cf. Ivo Vidan, "Thirteen Letters of André Gide to Joseph Conrad," *Studia Romanica et Anglica Zagrabiensia*, 24 (1967), 145-68, esp. 147-48.

[31]*Lord Jim*, p. 213.

[32]Cf. Albert J. Guerard, *Conrad the Novelist* (Cambridge: Harvard Univ. Press, 1958), pp. 200-01.

[33]F. Scott Fitzgerald, "Introduction," *The Great Gatsby* (New York: Random House, 1934), pp. vii-ix.

[34]*The Letters of F. Scott Fitzgerald*, ed. Andrew Turnbull (New York: Dell Publishing Co., 1966), p. 326.

[35]Ibid., pp. 336-37, 389, 530.

[36]*Fitzgerald Newsletter*, No. 40 (Winter 1968), 14.

[37]*The Letters of F. Scott Fitzgerald*, p. 75.

[38]Robert Emmet Long, "*The Great Gatsby* and the Tradition of Joseph Conrad," *Texas Studies in Language and Literature*, 8, No. 2 (1966), 257-76, and No. 3, 407-22.

[39]Ibid., p. 276.

[40]Cf. Alan Trachtenberg, "The Journey Back: Myth and History in *Tender Is the Night*," in *Experience in the Novel*, ed. Roy Harvey Pearce (New York: Columbia Univ. Press, 1968), p. 146.

[41]Lee M. Whitehead, "*Tender Is the Night* and George Herbert Mead," in *Tender Is the Night, Essays in Criticism*, ed. Marvin J. La Hood (Bloomington: Indiana Univ. Press, 1969), p. 170.

[42]*Francis Scott Fitzgerald*, ed. B. Poli, A. Le Vot, G. and M. Fabre (Paris: Librairie Armand Collin, 1969), p. 345.

[43]Malcom Cowley, Fitzgerald's *Tender Is the Night*—The Story of a Novel," *New Republic*, 20 August 1951, p. 19.

[44]W. B. Yeats, "An Irish Airman Foresees His Death," *Collected Poems* (London: Macmillan & Co., 1955), p. 152.

[45]Earl Rovit, *Ernest Hemingway* (New Haven: College & Univ. Press, 1963), pp. 109-10.

[46]On Crane, see *The Green Hills of Africa* (New York: Scribner's, 1953), p. 22, and *Men of War*, ed. E. H. (New York: Crown, 1942), pp. xvii-xviii, xxix; on Conrad, *Transatlantic Review*, October 1924, reprinted "Conrad, Optimist and Moralist," in *By-line: Ernest Hemingway*, ed. W. White (New York: Scribner's, 1970), pp. 114-15.

[47]Ernest Hemingway, *A Farewell to Arms* (London: The Albatross, 1947), p. 152.

[48]André Malraux, *The Royal Way*, trans. Stuart Gilbert (New York: Vintage Books, 1961), p. 44.

[49]Ibid., p. 143.

186

[50]"The Novel and the Film" (Part V of Malraux's *Esquisse d'une psychologie du cinema*), in *The Creative Vision, Modern European Writers on Their Art*, ed. Haskell M. Block and Herman Salinger (Gloucester, Mass.: Peter Smith, 1968), pp. 162, 163.

[51]Joseph Frank, "André Malraux: the Image of Man," *Malraux: A Collection of Critical Essays*, ed. R. W. B. Lewis (Englewood Cliffs: Prentice Hall, 1964), p. 72.

[52]Antoine de Saint-Exupéry, *Airman's Odyssey*, trans. Lewis Galantière and Stuart Gilbert (New York: Reynal and Hitchcock, 1942), p. 44.

[53]Jean-Louis Major, *Saint-Exupéry, l'écriture et la pensée* (Ottawa: Editions de l'Université d'Ottawa, 1968), p. 140.

[54]Adam Gillon, *The Eternal Solitary: A Study of Joseph Conrad* (New York: Bookman Associates, Twayne Publishers, 1960); Ira Sadoff, "Sartre and Conrad: Lord Jim as Existential Hero," *The Dalhousie Review*, 49, No. 4 (1969-1970), 518-25; R. K. Raval, "Lord Jim: an Existential Analysis," *Journal of the Maharaja Sayjirao University of Baroda*, 17, No. 1 (April 1968), 57-70; et al. See also Bruce Johnson, *Conrad's Models of Mind* (Minneapolis: University of Minnesota Press, 1971), pp. 89-105.

[55]Jean-Paul Sartre, *Literary and Philosophical Essays*, trans. Annette Michelson (London: Rider and Company, 1955).

[56]T. H. Adamowski, "Joe Christmas: The Tyranny of Childhood," *Novel*, 4 (Spring 1971), 242.

[57]The expression is used in Jean Weisberger's title "Faulkner's Monomaniacs: Their Indebtedness to Raskolnikov," *Comparative Literature Studies*, 5 (1968), 181-93.

[58]William Faulkner, *The Wild Palms and The Old Man* (New York: The New American Library, 1954), p. 76.

[59]Robert Penn Warren, " 'The Great Mirage': Conrad and Nostromo," in *Selected Essays* (New York: Random House, 1958), pp. 31-58.

[60]Graham Greene, *A Sort of Life* (London: The Bodley Head, 1971), p. 208.

[61]Graham Greene, "Fiction," *The Spectator*, 10 February 1933, p. 194.

[62]Graham Greene, *In Search of a Character* (London: The Bodley Head, 1961), p. 51.

[63]Quoted in "Graham Greene: The Man Within," *The Times Literary Supplement*, 17 September 1971, p. 1102.

[64]Malcolm Lowry, *Under the Volcano* (New York: The New American Library, 1966), p. 60.

[65]In "Through the Panama" Lowry's character thinks of Fitzgerald as of "The Last Laocoön." See Lowry's *Hear Us O Lord from Heaven Thy Dwelling Place* (New York: Capricorn Books, 1969), p. 31. The phrase was taken by Robert Sklar for the title of his book on Fitzgerald.

[66]Malcolm Lowry, *Selected Letters* (New York: Capricorn Books, 1969), pp. 180, 203, 309, 390, 442.

[67]Cf. Perle Epstein, *The Private Labyrinth of Malcolm Lowry: "Under the Volcano" and the Cabbala* (New York: Holt, Rinehart and Winston, 1969).

[68]Dietrich Bonhoeffer, "The Structure of Responsible Life," in *On Being Responsible*, ed. James M. Gustafson and James T. Laney, Issues in Personal Ethics (New York: Harper and Row, 1968), p. 70.

Luncheon Presentation

Conrad as Editor: The Preparation of *The Shorter Tales*

Donald W. Rude

ABSTRACT

Critics and biographers of Joseph Conrad have long overlooked the posthumous anthology *The Shorter Tales of Joseph Conrad* (Garden City, New York: Doubleday, Page and Co., 1924). This fact is unfortunate, for unpublished letters from Joseph Conrad to F. N. Doubleday reveal that Conrad was deeply involved in planning the volume. A study of the letters also adds to our understanding of the author's view of his own short fiction and enhances our knowledge of his relationship with F. N. Doubleday. (DWR)

In December of 1924, Doubleday, Page and Company issued a thick volume entitled *The Shorter Tales of Joseph Conrad*. Priced at the then exorbitant figure of $5.00, the volume had as its special feature a "Preface," contributed by the author, which must be counted among the final pieces of expository prose, if not the last such piece, completed by Joseph Conrad prior to his death. While the "Preface" was later incorporated in the *Last Essays*, the collection itself, perhaps because it contained no new works of fiction, has been largely ignored by Conrad's biographers.

This fact, I think, is unfortunate, for the history of the volume reveals that Conrad himself was deeply involved in its preparation, the full extent of this involvement being revealed in a group of six letters written to his American publisher F. N. Doubleday, only two of which have been published, and none of which has been discussed. The letters cast new light on Conrad's views of his own short fiction, offer insight into his working relationships with the Doubleday firm, and attest to the faith in Doubleday's judgment which Conrad had acquired in the final years of his career.[1]

Conrad's association with Doubleday and the firm which he headed had been a long and profitable association which flourished after the publication of *Chance*, when Doubleday began to acquire the American rights to Conrad's earlier works and laid plans for the Sun-Dial Edition of the author's collected works. The relationship deepened as the commercial success of each new Conrad novel worked to the mutual benefit of both men, and it turned to real friendship after Conrad met Doubleday in England in early 1919. Indeed, by 1923, when Conrad finally visited America, the promotion of the author's works had become as much of a personal goal as a commercial one for the American. During this visit, the two men working together finalized the details for the publication of the deluxe Concord edition of the author's works. In an unpublished letter, written July 10, 1923, following a summer visit from the Doubledays in England, the author recalled that meeting. He wrote:

> I have been much cheered by your good letter and the sight of the Concord edition advertisement. It is an excellent conception and brings the reality of the new edition vividly before my eyes. I can see a mile-long row of volumes in cases vanishing at one end and growing at the other for years and years.
>
> My belief in the Concord Edition is absolute and indestructible. There is an atmosphere of good luck and good will about it which no other scheme seems to have had in the same degree.... My thoughts go back to that morning when, in the soft light filtered through young foliage into the room beyond the billiard room, we agreed upon the name, and you explained to me the form and get up of that edition—you and I alone, with the protecting personality of Florence hovering in the near background— I grow tenderly (and cheerfully) sentimental. I beg you both to believe that I am speaking seriously.[2]

The letter, which suggests something of the intimacy that had grown up between the two men, discusses the details of the publication of *The Rover*; then, Conrad turns his attention to a recent Dent publication: the school edition of "Youth" and "Gaspar Ruiz," a volume for which he had provided an "Author's Introduction." Conrad suggests the publication of comparable volumes in America, and offers to provide Doubleday "with explanatory notes . . . ."[3] This must be one of the few instances in which the author expressed a willingness to see his stories wrenched out of their original contexts and published separately.

Perhaps this suggestion prompted Doubleday to propose the publication of a larger volume of tales a few months later. Conrad first mentions a proposed volume of stories in a letter dated February 7, 1924:

I expect to hear soon from Eric [Pinker] about the scheme for a book of collected short stories. I assure you, my dear Effendi, that even if I were not certain that in all your schemes you think of my welfare (more than I deserve to be thought of) I would still be reluctant to negative [sic] any scheme of yours. . . .[4]

He goes on in the letter, published in G. Jean-Aubry's *Life and Letters*, to express some scepticism at the proposal, noting the essential unity of each of his volumes of stories. Commenting on *Youth*, he observes, "I can't somehow imagine any of those stories taken out of it and bound cheek and jowl with a story from another volume. It is in fact unthinkable."[5]

Such thoughts must have been uppermost in Conrad's mind a few days later when he rejected the Doubleday proposal. The scheme for the volume proposed by Doubleday has not survived, but we can glean its essential features by examining Conrad's memo responding to it. To be called *Stories of the Sea*, the proposed anthology would have contained 16 or 17 stories selected on the basis of a common length, 22,000 words. Conrad's friend, Muirhead Bone, was to have been asked to contribute an introduction.[6]

Conrad's response seems almost short-tempered. He begins by taking exception with Doubleday, Page's proposal to model the volume after its successful collections of stories by Robert L. Stevenson. Writing of himself in the third person, he notes, "Conrad is much less of a literary man and, in any case, is a very different person." He objects to the length of the list of stories proposed for inclusion, and suggests that *Heart of Darkness* is far too long for a collection of works of 20,000 words, before taking exception with length as a valid principle of selection, writing "I definitely negative that sort of classification." He rejects the notion of enlisting Muirhead Bone's services, commenting that "He has got his own work to do," and adding that he "frankly" doesn't "think that J. C.'s work wants any sort of introduction, as literature."[7]

However, Conrad suggests that such an enterprise might benefit from an author's preface which explains "the principle of collection." Amazingly, after these harsh words, Conrad concludes by volunteering to provide such a preface for a collection of stories, a proposal which he himself has devised.

In offering a "Scheme" of his own, which accompanies the memorandum, Conrad noted that his proposal was predicated on four assumptions:

a. That a volume of 500 pages of Short Stories written at different times, in different moods, in different styles, will look and feel unreadable, and like a jumble of things in a box—from a literary and artistic point of view.

b. That to tear such a mass of matter out of the solid body of work having its own character and purpose may not turn out a good commercial proposition; for by its very bulk it may destroy the curiosity as to the rest of his whole production, instead of whetting the curiosity and creating a desire for a better acquaintance.

c. That a certain (if not very obvious) unity of purpose while associated with variety of treatment and subject is likely to appeal to the taste and even the feelings of the readers better than a mere heap of sixteen or seventeen stories, (each fairly long) and liable to tire out an ordinary person by the change of mood and the point of view.

d. That a book meant, I take it, for a Christmas trade and for purposes of being giv[en] as a present to various kinds of people, can be made to look worth the money by a larger margin and general get-up in all its other details without containing upwards of 200,000 words.[8]

It is interesting, I think, to note the concern with the commercial value of the work proposed. Though Conrad's distaste with an omnibus volume lacking a unified character of its own remains visible, he is also eager to provide his public with an attractive volume, possessed of an appealing quality of its own. He goes on to suggest the publication of a volume containing "about 124,000 words, with the Preface of say 4000 more." The stories he has selected, he writes, "all deal with seamen in their various relations: professional and with people ashore."[9]

Conrad proposed a volume in two sections: Part I containing "Youth," "The Secret Sharer," "The Brute," and "To-Morrow"; and Part II, containing "Typhoon," "Because of the Dollars," "The Partner," and "The Inn of the Two Witches." He explains the unifying principles guiding his selections:

Part First deals with young men: the triumphant feeling in the struggle with the sea (Youth): the sense of comradeship of the sea between two young seamen (S. Sharer); the above strictly professional. The other two involve women and shore relations: a young seaman losing the girl to whom he is engaged (Brute); and "To-Morrow" giving the strength of appeal of a roving life.[10]

"Of course those stories," he continues, "have more than that in them, but certainly they may be looked upon in the above light." Part Two of the anthology will deal "with mature men of the sea: Capt. McWhirr wrestling with the Typhoon . . . The Dollars, character study of a humane seaman; The Partner presents a seaman victim of a plot concocted by people ashore; and finally, the Inn is based subtly on the fidelity of the old seaman Tom to his young officer, which seems even to endure after death."[11] After assuring Doubleday that these ideas will be developed in his Preface, Conrad rejects the title for the volume proposed by Doubleday, Page. It "should not be called STORIES OF THE SEA," he writes, "for in truth these are stories of seamen."[12]

Conrad twice discussed the volume in later letters to Doubleday. On March 27, he wrote that the matter of the "scheme" for the volume had been settled during Doubleday's absence from Garden City. The letter also provides us with the author's insight into the value of having a special author's preface:

> I think that in republishing any of my former work it cannot but do good to have some fresh matter included; if only for the reason that it would force every collector of Conrad items to buy the book, or his collection would not be complete. And of course, it may, I suppose, have some effect also with the general public.[13]

Conrad here displays an unusual concern with making the book attractive to bibliophiles as well as to the general reader. Other unpublished correspondence with the publisher indicates that Conrad thought it important that each of the new collected editions in America have some distinguishing feature that would attract the Conrad collector. As the prefaces had enhanced the Sun-Dial Edition, frontespieces would make the Concord Edition attractive. In any case, we see Conrad possessed of considerable commercial acumen.

The final unpublished reference to the volume occurs in a letter dated May 8, 1924. Conrad writes:

> The preface for the "Shorter Tales" was posted in time to catch the "Majestic" on Wednesday last. I did not think it advisable to make it very long. I just said what I felt I had to say and that is all. I hope you will approve. There is a reference to you in it which does not express all my feelings, but in matters of sentiment a man ought to be reserved.[14]

The "Preface" submitted to Doubleday is curious. Fully one-third of it restates Conrad's hesitation concerning the compilation of the volume. This apology provides interesting glimpses into the author's views of his earlier volumes of short stories and his view of this volume for which he served as editor. Of the stories chosen for inclusion, Conrad writes, "not one . . . was . . . achieved without much conscious thought bearing not only on the problems of style but upon their relation to life as I have known it, and on the nature of my reactions to the particular instances as well as to the general tenor of my personal experience." "This," he continues, "gave to each of the successive sets of tales . . . a characteristic unity of its own." Preparing his earlier prefaces had, Conrad writes, "confirmed . . . [his] impression that each of [his] volumes had a consistent unity of outlook covering the mingled subjects of civilization and wilderness, of land life and life on the sea."[15] As examples, he cites *Tales of Unrest* and *A Set of Six*. Although the reader hopes for some descriptive statement of the unifying principle of these volumes, Conrad wrote in the most general terms, mentioning the diverse scenes found in *Tales* and the "consistent mood of clear and detached presentation" found in *A Set of Six*, a volume he describes as his "least atmospheric."[16] The unity of all the volumes was, he insists, the more dear to him "because their grouping was never the result of a preconceived plan. It 'just happened.' " "And," he goes on, "things that just happen in one's work seem impressive and valuable because they spring from sources profounder than logic."[17]

Conrad's desire that the volume have a comparable kind of unity expresses itself repeatedly in the "Preface." Such a work should, he writes, possess "a character of its own" and not be a "thing of shreds and patches," adding that "the characteristic trait of the stories" is that each focuses on "a seaman presented either in the relations of his professional life . . . or in contact with landsmen and women, and embroiled in the affairs of mankind which dwells on solid earth."[18] Here and elsewhere the author's phrasing illustrates the dependence of the "Preface" on the earlier prospectus sent to Doubleday. When Conrad points out a second theme in the volume, the contrast between youth and maturity inherent in the volume, his comments echo the pattern which he ascribed to *Youth*, a volume dealing with "three ages of man" in his letter of 7 February to Doubleday. This fact suggests that Conrad's schemata for the volume may have been generated even before he read and rejected the Doubleday proposal.

Conrad also seizes on the opportunity the "Preface" provides to refute again the public's popular conception that he was an author of sea stories. In a characteristic mood, he declares that to have called the volume *Stories of the Sea* would have been misleading. His stories

> deal with feelings of universal import, such as the sustaining and inspiring sense of youth, or the support given by a stolid courage which confronts an unmeasurable force of an elemental fury simply as a thing that has got to be met and lived through with professional constancy . . . . I modestly hope that there are human beings in them, and also the articulate appeal of their humanity so strangely constructed from inertia and restlessness, from weakness and from strength and many other interesting contradictions which affect their conduct . . . .[19]

Conrad's words on the relationship of his work to the sea may have been partly intended for his American publishers, who had, with their Deep Sea Edition of his works, capitalized upon the public's image of him as a sea writer. Much earlier Conrad rejected the firm's proposal to designate its first collected edition of his complete works as the "Otago edition," telling Doubleday that "in the particular design of the edition my inclination is to avoid all reference to the sea. . . . I am something else . . . than a writer of the sea—or even of the tropics. . . .

I am acknowledged to be something if not bigger, then at any rate as something larger."[20]

The volume itself is one of those "interesting contradictions" in the author's career, and judged by its "Preface," his feelings toward it remained ambiguous. His distrust with the conception—even when altered to reflect his own taste—and his suspicion that the volume would further the public view of him as a sea writer—remain in evidence to such an extent that one wonders why he allowed the volume's publication.

Conrad provides an answer to such speculations. While his inclination seems to have been to accept the "general mystery" of those things which "just happened" in his earlier collections of stories, Doubleday's desire for the volume justified its creation. The publisher, he wrote, is an "idealist" whose "business . . . consists mainly in being the intermediary between certain men's reveries and the wide awake brain of the rest of the world. I have learned to trust his conclusions implicitly on that ground. Also for reasons of a deeper personal kind, his words have great weight with me."[21]

Doubleday's arguments, unfortunately lost to us, must have been convincing to have persuaded the author in favor of the volume's publication. Whatever the case, they resulted in giving us an opportunity to see Conrad in the role of editor, and they prompted his final printed reflections on his art, an art which, he tells us, "aimed at an element as restless, as changeable as the sea, and even more vast;—the unappeasable ocean of human life."[22]

NOTES

[1] I am deeply indebted to the Trustees of the Joseph Conrad Estate for granting me permission to quote from Conrad's unpublished correspondence with F. N. Doubleday, and to John Sundell of J. M. Dent & Sons Ltd. for his generous assistance. I should also like to thank the Trustees of the Princeton University Library for making a microfilm of the Conrad letters in the library's Doubleday Collection available to me.

[2] TLS (Typed letter, signed), Princeton University Doubleday Collection (hereafter called Princeton).

[3] Ibid.

[4] G. Jean-Aubry, ed., *Joseph Conrad: Life and Letters* II (Garden City, New York: Doubleday, Page & Co., 1927), 338; hereafter cited as *Life and Letters*.

[5] Ibid.

[6] TLS, dated 12 February 1924, Princeton.

[7] Ibid.

[8] Ibid.

[9] Ibid.

[10] Ibid.

[11] Ibid.

[12] Ibid.

[13] TLS, Princeton.

[14] TLS, Princeton; F. N. Doubleday agreed to let the warm encomium stand in the "Preface" to *The Shorter Tales*; Conrad expressed his pleasure that Doubleday has recognized the "spirit" of the passage "which is that of affection" in a letter dated 2 June 1924. See *Life and Letters* II, 344.

[15] Joseph Conrad, "Preface," *The Shorter Tales of Joseph Conrad* (Garden City, New York: Doubleday, Page & Company, 1924), p. vi; hereafter cited as *Shorter Tales*.

[16] *Shorter Tales*, pp. vi-vii.

[17] *Shorter Tales*, p. vii.

[18] *Shorter Tales*, p. x.

[19] *Shorter Tales*, pp. x-xi.

[20] TL (Typed letter), dated 19 May 1916, Quinn Collection, Manuscript Division, New York Public Library. The letter from which I here quote is labelled "Copy" and is unsigned. Its presence in the Quinn Collection, no doubt, reflects Quinn's involvement in the preparation of the Sun-Dial Edition. I should like to thank the staff of the Manuscript Division, New York Public Library, for their assistance, and for making the Conrad items in the Quinn Collection available to me.

[21] *Shorter Tales*, p. viii.

[22] *Shorter Tales*, p. ix.

NOTES ON THE AUTHORS

Dr. Alan W. Friedman, a native of Brooklyn, earned the B.A. at Queens College, the M.A. at New York University, and the Ph.D. at the University of Rochester. He studied a year in Scotland (at the University of Edinburgh) and a year in England (on an NEH Fellowship). His grants included State and University Fellowships at Rochester and a National Endowment for the Humanities Fellowship. He is currently Associate Professor of English at The University of Texas at Austin and Director of Plan II, the University's multidisciplinary Honors Program. Recently he has coordinated a symposium on Modern British Fiction and edited the conference papers. He has also served as an editor for *Texas Studies in Literature and Language* and *Abstracts of English Studies.* He has published *Lawrence Durrell and "The Alexandria Quartet": Art for Love's Sake* and articles in such journals as *Modern Fiction Studies, Victorian Poetry, The Southern Review,* and *Contemporary Literature.*

Dr. Adam Gillon, a native of Poland, is Professor of English and Comparative Literature at the State University of New York at New Paltz. He received the M.A. at the Hebrew University of Jerusalem and the Ph.D. at Columbia University. He has taught at the University of Kansas, and was Head of the English Department at Acadia University in Canada. He is the author of a number of books, including *The Eternal Solitary: A Study of Joseph Conrad, Cup of Fury* (a novel), *Introduction to Modern Polish Literature* (with L. Krzyżanowski), and *Contemporary Israeli Literature.* Dr. Gillon has written numerous articles, reviews, short stories and several plays. He received the 1967 Alfred Jurzykowski Foundation Award for his translation of Polish literature; he has also received grants from the Joseph Fels Foundation, the New York State University Research Foundation, the Fulbright Foundation, the British Council, and the Canada Council. He has presented papers at several national and international conferences (MLA, ICLA) and has lectured at major universities. Professor Gillon is currently preparing two books concerning Conrad, a novel, and two critical studies of Julian Tuwim and Vladimir Mayakovsky.

Dr. Bruce Harkness is Dean of Arts and Sciences at Kent State University. He earned the M.A. and Ph.D. in English at the University of Chicago. Beginning as an Instructor in English at the University of Illinois (Urbana), he rose to Professor and Assistant Chairman of the Department and Director of Graduate Students. In 1963 he assumed the Chairmanship in English at Southern Illinois University (Carbondale), and in 1964 he became the Associate Dean of Liberal Arts and Sciences at the University of Illinois. In 1966 he became the Dean at Kent State University. Professor Harkness has published college textbooks concerning literature and a number of articles on modern British fiction and textual analysis. His special interests are Joseph Conrad, literary criticism, and textual criticism (bibliography). His articles concerning Conrad have appeared in such journals as *Nineteenth-Century Fiction, Modern Fiction Studies,* and *College English.*

Dr. David Leon Higdon, who received the M.A. and Ph.D. from the University of Kansas, is the General Editor of *Conradiana* and an Associate Professor at Texas Tech University. A recipient of several University and American Philosophical Society grants, he has published essays on theory of fiction,

Chaucer, Defoe, George Eliot, Thackeray, Conrad, and Woolf. Currently he is completing a study of "time shapes" in English fiction and, with his co-editor, Dr. Floyd Eugene Eddlemen, is preparing a critical edition of *Almayer's Folly*.

Dr. Marion C. Michael is Chairman of the Department of English at Texas Tech University. He earned the A.B. in English at the University of Georgia and the M.A. in English at the University of Virginia. Before completing the Ph.D. at the University of Georgia, he spent two years as a Research Fellow at the University of London, where he was primarily concerned with the works of Conrad. Professor Michael has taught at the University of Georgia, Southeastern Louisiana College, and Auburn University. Among his publications are studies of Faulkner, Augusta Jane Evans Wilson, Madison Jones, and Conrad. He served as a panelist on the Conrad Seminar at MLA in 1971 and as chairman of the Conrad Seminar at MLA in 1972. He also served for three years as editor of "News, Notes, and Queries" for *Conradiana*. With O. B. Emerson, under the auspices of the Society for Study of Southern Literature, he is currently preparing a revised edition of *Southern Literary Culture: A Bibliography of Masters' and Doctors' Theses*. He is also General Editor of the Textual Studies Institute at Texas Tech; the Institute was created to produce definitive editions of Conrad's works.

Dr. Zdzisław Najder, literary critic and philosopher, was born in Warsaw and received the M. Phil. at the University of Warsaw, the B. Litt. (oxon.) at Oxford University, and the D. Phil. at the University of Warsaw. He has taught at the University of Warsaw, Columbia University, the University of California, Berkeley, the University of California, Davis, Northern Illinois, and Yale. In addition to a number of articles concerning American, English, German, and Polish literature, he is the author of *Conrad's Polish Background, Nad Konradem* (critical essays), and of a book on values and evaluative judgments which appeared in Polish in 1971 (the English edition will be published in 1974). Currently he is preparing an edition of Conrad's Collected Works in Polish and is working on Conrad's biography to be published in 1974. Along with F. R. Karl, he is compiling an edition of Conrad's letters. Dr. Najder is a member of the Polish Writers' Union, the Polish Philosophical Society, and the Polish Semiotic Society; he is coeditor of the journal *Twórczość*, published in Warsaw.

Dr. Irmina P. Pulc, born in Poland, received the Ph.D. in Comparative Literature from Harvard University. She has taught in the English Departments of Purdue University (Fort Wayne Campus) and Mount Holyoke College, and most recently in the Comparative Literature Program at the University of Massachusetts. She held an Andrew Mellon Post-doctoral Fellowship at the University of Pittsburgh. Her publications include articles on Conrad and Shakespeare, and translations of Polish poetry (the latter forthcoming in *The Polish Review*). At present she is preparing a book on Conrad, to be entitled " 'The Visible World': A Study of Conrad's Descriptive Style." She regularly contributes notes and reviews to *Conradiana*.

Dr. Donald W. Rude, Assistant Professor of English at Texas Tech University, earned the B.A. and M.A. degrees from Wichita State University and the Ph.D. from the University of Illinois. He is the General Editor of *Conradiana*. With Dr. Kenneth Davis, he is currently preparing a critical edition of Joseph Conrad's *The Nigger of the "Narcissus."* His publications include a study of the history of the London Stationers' Company as well as an anthology, *Allienation: Minority Groups* (1972).

Dr. Norman Sherry holds the second chair of English at the University of Lancaster, U.K. Born in Newcastle-upon-Tyne, he graduated from Durham University. To further his research on the sources of Joseph Conrad's eastern novels, he assumed a post of lecturer in English at the University of Singapore. The results of this research were submitted for the Ph.D. degree at the University of Singapore. Professor Sherry returned to England first as a lecturer and then as senior lecturer in the English Department of the University of Liverpool. In 1970 he was appointed Professor of English at Lancaster. He is chairman of the International Conrad Conference to be held in July 1974 in Canterbury. He has published many articles, including some in the *Manchester Guardian* (he was a correspondent in Singapore for this paper), and books on the Brontes and Jane Austen. His work on Conrad includes *Conrad's Eastern World*, *Conrad's Western World* (the latter chosen as a book of the year by Graham Greene in *The Observer*, 1970), *Conrad: The Critical Heritage*, and *Conrad and His World*. Professor Sherry is at present working on a book on Thomas Hardy and another on a cluster of writers in the Edwardian period. He is special literary adviser to the publishers Dent and has lectured extensively in England, the Far East, and Poland.

Dr. Jeffrey R. Smitten is Assistant Professor of English at Texas Tech University. He received the B.A. and M.A. degrees from the University of California at Berkeley and the Ph.D. degree from the University of Wisconsin. Before coming to Texas Tech, he spent a year at Linacre College, Oxford, on a University of Wisconsin Research Studentship. He is currently at work on a study of patterns of aesthetic perception in the novels of Laurence Sterne.

Dr. Ivo Vidan is Professor of English and American Literature at the University of Zagreb, Yugoslavia. He graduated from Zagreb University and received the Ph.D. at the University of Nottingham, England. He has taught in several Yugoslav universities and, during a summer session, at the University of Massachusetts at Amherst. Recently he spent a year at Yale University on an ACLS research fellowship. Professor Vidan is an editor of a Yugoslav critical journal, and his books in the Serbo-Croatian language include *The Unreliable Narrator: Procedure and Vision in Works by Three Modern Generations* and *The Stream of Consciousness Novel*. He is now preparing for publication a collection of his essays, "Reading in a Context," and is working on a long study of freedom and responsibility in the modern novel. In English he has published articles on Conrad, James, and Crane. Professor Vidan is National Editor of *Conradiana* for Yugoslavia.